SIDETRACKED IN WISCONSIN

Sidetracked in Wisconsin

A Guide for Thoughtful Travelers

Mary Bergin

The Painted Forest, *Ernest Hupeden, Valton, Sauk County*

First edition, first printing

Designed and produced by Flying Fish Graphics
Printed in Korea

Library of Congress Control Number
2006924789

ISBN 978-0-9761450-4-2

Itchy Cat Press
An Imprint of Flying Fish Graphics
Blue Mounds, Wisconsin 53517
ffg@mhtc.net

(below) A little of this, a little of that at Tenuta's, Kenosha.

Dedicated, with gratitude,

To Caroline and Frank—for your positive energy and good humor in guiding this project to its completion. This book is a product of your faith and inspiration.

To the photographers at The Capital Times—for patiently teaching me about cameras and photography. It is an honor to see your work in this book.

To Aunt Calla—for breaking the rules and instilling a sense of adventure. Your independent spirit has always made a favorable difference.

To Dick—for being a steady source of support, honesty and logic. I need and appreciate the balance that you add to my life. (He is kind, too, having learned to give insulin to Abby, our endearing flabby tabby, so I could continue this work without regret. Having a cat with diabetes can quickly complicate the life of a travel writer.)

INTRODUCTION

Let's start with confessions, Wisconsin . . .

—I often take you for granted.

—You don't get enough credit for your depth of character and natural beauty.

—After a half-century of study, I know that I still have a lot to learn about you.

Wisconsin is more than a pretty face. It's is a state of incredible diversity, tradition and dynamic accomplishment as well as great modesty. Contrary to popular mythology, we are about far more than great beer, brats, cheeseheads and polka parties.

You can stay close to home and think you're in another country, find stunning and unusual getaways on a tankful of gas, feel among kindred spirits in the most remote areas, eat the finest of foods in the smallest of towns. The line between city and country is blurring, as creative thinkers gladly relinquish urban trappings for rural tranquility.

Much of what you see every day is worth cherishing, but sometimes an outsider's perspective can be the most convincing.

Consider this: A couple of Louisiana women came into Wisconsin to talk up Highway 51, which runs 1,286 miles from our Hurley and Lake Superior to their Lake Pontchartrain and Laplace, not far from New Orleans.

According to the Louisianans, the road is full of Americana and it could become as well-known and respected as the famed Route 66 across the American west. We just have to let people know about it.

The work has begun to do just that. If we take the southerners' advice, we won't ignore our carhops, drive-in theaters, restored indoor theaters, statues of cows and lumberjacks, Northwoods carvings of eagles and bears. And, yes, our squeaky cheese curds.

I have lived in Wisconsin for all but two of my 50 years and have no intention of calling anywhere else home. "Will you have enough to write about?" a friend asked when I began "Roads Traveled," a weekly travel column that typically is about Wisconsin or a border state. Uh-huh. It's years later, and the heap of rich topics hasn't diminished much. This could go on for quite a while, without gross repetition.

I bristle when I see the booths of Midwest destinations idle during travel writer trade shows. The lines form for Spain, Hawaii, or for luxury resorts with big marketing budgets.

Wisconsin's portfolio tends to go unnoticed—even among the natives.

We so hate to toot our own horns in Wisconsin. This reticence sometimes makes me wince: For example, I might be in your town asking, "What is there to do?" Too often the answer is "Nothing." Sometimes you qualify that by saying you "don't live around here." You're from the next town, 10 miles down the road.

I can't help but think that we'd want to do better, if we knew more about—and believed in—the variety of historic, human and natural beauty that surrounds us. I ponder this, with a glass of wine, after an exhausting and fascinating day on the road. During the past 24 hours, I have learned:

—How to make great soup from scratch. The teacher was Marcel Biró, one of the nation's rising-star chefs, who calls Sheboygan home.

—What Houdini and Joe McCarthy had in common. The explanation comes from Terry Bergen, an Appleton museum director whose work generates controversy and inquiries from around the world.

—Where the nation's oldest continuously operating bowling alley is located. It is in the basement of the nicely preserved Fond du Lac Elks Club No. 57.

I am easily amused and fortified, from the Biró beef consommé with exquisite quenelles, to the chili dog and tap of Capital Amber that become my supper at The Magnet in Oshkosh. That was yesterday. Tonight it was fine lake perch at a VFW fish fry, 50 miles away. And tomorrow it will be something new . . . different . . . unexpected.

All of it makes a tremendous cornucopia of culture, richly flavored by our diverse traditions and fascinating past.

What you have in this book are discriminating glimpses of who and what make Wisconsin worth knowing. It is not meant to be a comprehensive travel guide that tries to please everyone or include every shop or stop with an "open" sign in the window.

It's pretty easy to peg my soft spots: food, Frank Lloyd Wright, Sheboygan County, underdogs and mavericks, relatively unknown but pretty landscapes. But that's just for starters.

Thanks very much to *The Capital Times* of Madison, Wisconsin's feisty and progressive news source, for allowing reprints of staff photography and feature stories that I wrote for the newspaper. It is a nice complement to what I've found on my own time, on all the wonderful roads traveled, gravel to multi-lane, Port Wing to Pleasant Prairie.

—Mary Bergin
Madison, Wisconsin

•

About the Author

Mary Bergin is a longtime newspaper journalist whose weekly "Roads Traveled" column appears in daily newspapers from Wausau to Kenosha, Eau Claire to Green Bay. She also is a freelance magazine writer and staff feature writer for *The Capital Times*, Madison, and is the newspaper's former features editor. Her newspaper work began in 1976, as a reporter at the *Oshkosh Northwestern*.

A graduate of the University of Wisconsin-Oshkosh, she remains devoted to her alma mater as a member of its Journalism Advisory Board.

She also is proud to be a member of First Unitarian Society, whose Madison home is a national landmark. The building was designed by Frank Lloyd Wright, who was a member of the congregation.

Raised on a rumpled dairy farm in Sheboygan County, a Sunday drive to Horicon Marsh was the closest her family got to a family vacation. Mary can count on one hand the number of times she went to a beach before getting a driver's license.

She didn't see Chicago until her 4-H club took a field trip there in the late 1960s: It included a bus ride to the Museum of Science and Industry, a windshield tour of Skid Row, disparaging remarks from chaperones, then burgers at an expressway Oasis restaurant.

It all perplexed her for a while.

While working at the former Schwartz Hotel in Elkhart Lake, and meeting other resort waitresses from as far away as England, Mary got her first favorable taste of the diversity that the world could offer. Waitressing was how she paid for her college education.

She moved to Tulsa, Oklahoma, and Owensboro, Kentucky, in the 1980s, working for newspapers and seeing Cincinnati, Memphis, Nashville, the Ozark and Smoky mountains during spare time. She wrote about a little bit of everything: bluegrass and burgoo, the Ku Klux Klan and the miners of Muhlenberg County, life along the Ohio River's quirky, sleepy and charming burgs.

"I couldn't wait to get out of Wisconsin, and I eventually was glad to return," she says. "This is home, and I appreciate it more because I left for a while."

Although Wisconsin is her favorite place, Mary increasingly travels the world. She was a 2003 Women of Wings delegate to Chiba, Japan (a Wisconsin sister-state), and co-led a delegation of Midwest Travel Writers Association members to Korea in 2006. She has earned membership into the Society of American Travel Writers, the continent's premiere organization for travel journalists.

She routinely seeks global connections to Wisconsin, considering it one small way to build bridges of cultural awareness and appreciation in this increasingly complex, misunderstood and troubled world.

Contents

Northwest Quadrant

Southwest Quadrant

Southeast Quadrant

Northeast Quadrant

Attractions, hours and prices are subject to change without notice. Confirm these things before starting your trip.

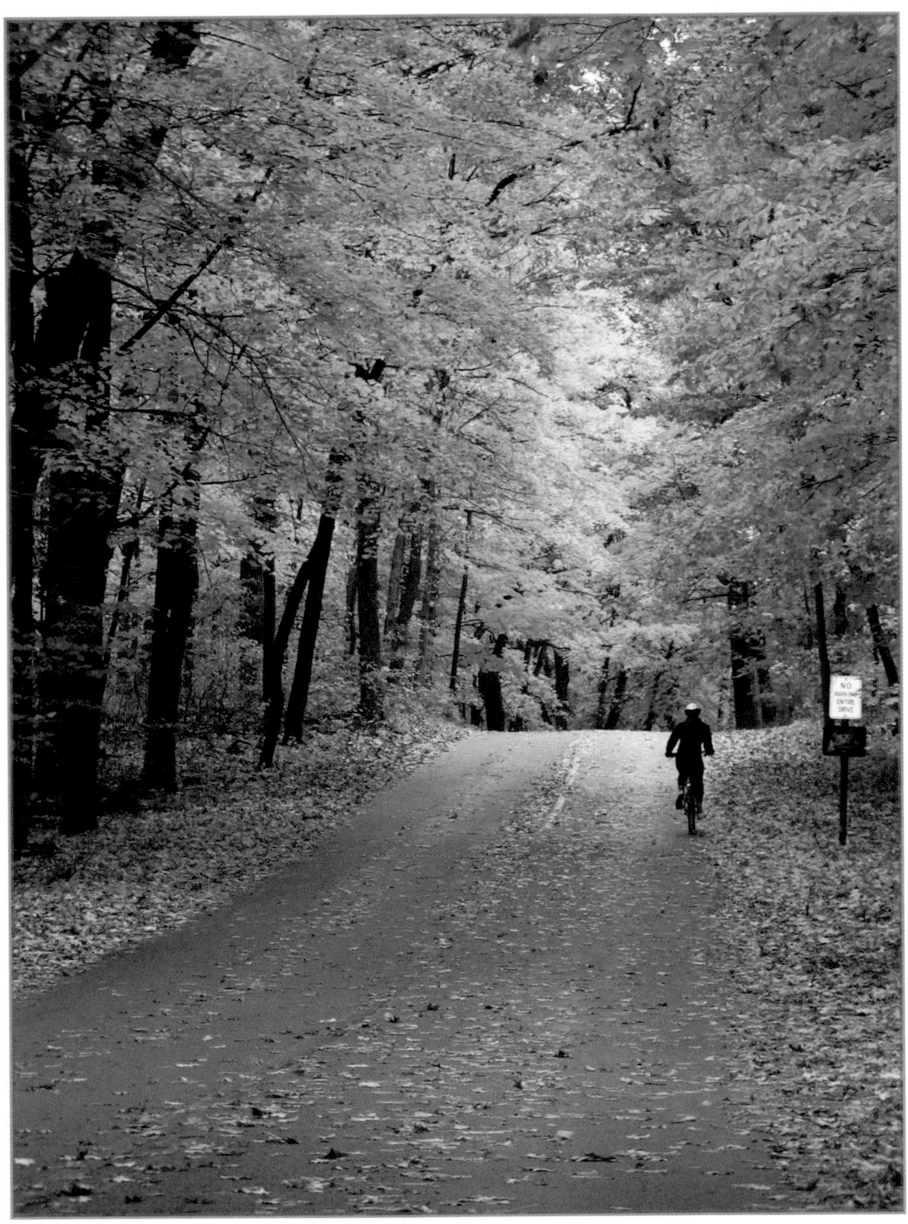

The University of Wisconsin Arboretum, Madison, at the peak of autumn.

N
Northeast
Northwest
Southwest
Southeast
Wisconsin
Superior
Bayfield
Ashland
Delta
Hayward
Couderay
Phillips
Lac du Flambeau
Rhinelander
Laona
Washington Island
Chetek
Hudson
Chippewa Falls
Menomonie
Eau Claire
Wausau
Door County
Green Bay
Wisconsin Rapids
Babcock
Appleton
Warrens
Two Rivers
Manitowoc
Oshkosh
Princeton
Sheboygan
La Crosse
Markesan
Wisconsin Dells
Kohler
Elkhart Lake
Sauk County
Baraboo
Cedarburg
Plymouth
Sun Prairie
Watertown
Fond du Lac
Oconomowoc
Spring Green
Madison
Milwaukee
Mount Horeb
Dodgeville
Greendale
Mineral Point
Monroe
Browntown
Green County
Racine
Potosi
Kenosha
2
53
63
13
51
8
141
29
94
90
43
151
41
12

Activity on Madison's Capitol Square slows in winter.

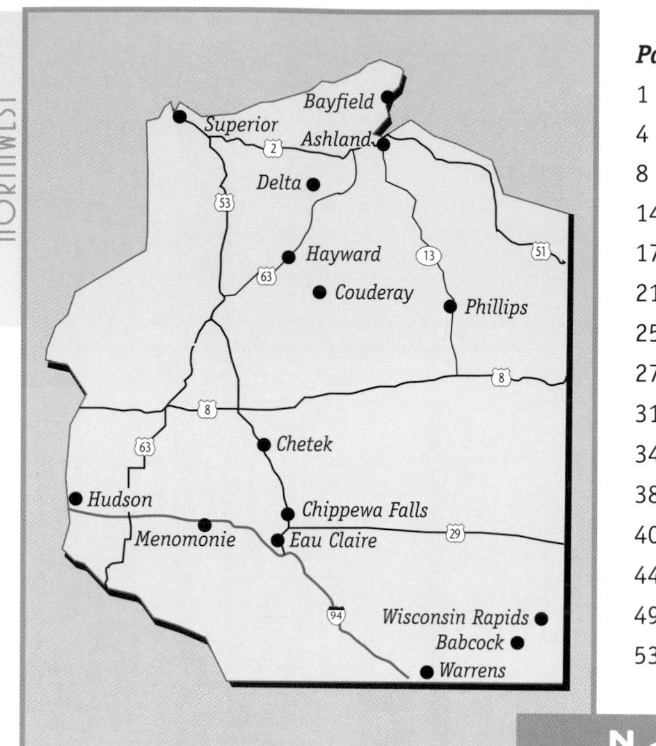

NORTHWEST

Observation: "Small town" need not mean "small minded."

A diner in a town that's not on most maps serves delectable gourmet fare. One of the nation's most romantic getaways thrives in a remote part of Wisconsin. A world-class music museum has a Superior location. A man with a dream opens a Hayward barbecue joint en route to making his first million.

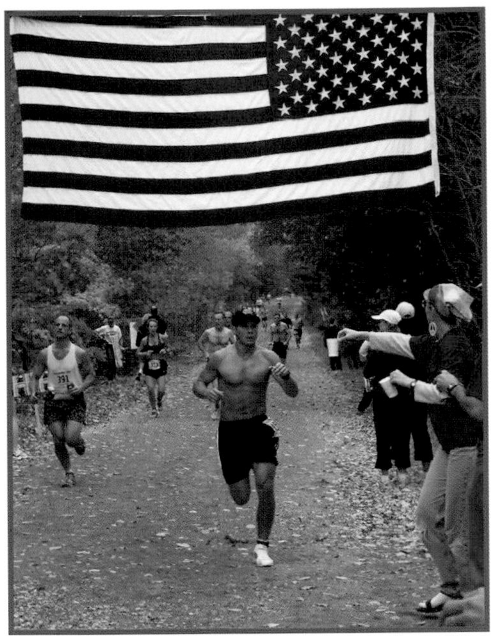

WhistleStop Marathon in Ashland.

Ashland & Beyond: Pounding Pavement

Picture a slick—as in damp—October morning on the top of Wisconsin. At sunrise my companion and I enter an edge of forest. Trees are brilliant with color. The air is brisk. A side road off of Highway 2 guides us past isolated lakes, scurrying critters.

It is a trail of seclusion, but just for a short while. We park the car as we reach a clearing, where hundreds of others are gathering.

I zip my jacket, tug at my hood, find and caress a cup of coffee. The temperature is somewhere in the 40s. My partner guzzles from a water bottle, stretches his limbs, strips to a T-shirt and shorts. He'll remember this day as "a little cool." I shiver and dare not whine.

It is almost race time, and I am grateful for my status as a spectator. In minutes, I will be back inside the car, heater cranked, and on my way to breakfast. Dick will methodically trot away, into wind and a steady, stubborn drizzle.

Before the morning ends, he will have followed railroad trestles, crossed part of **Chequamegon National Forest**, passed dairy farms and trout streams. Exactly 26.2 miles later, he'll be wrapped in a thin blanket of shiny mylar, eating a bowl of chili and feeling pretty relieved.

That's my memory of the annual **WhistleStop Marathon**, whose route is from Iron River to Ashland.

It's also one of the state's smaller marathons (587 finishers in 2005). That can be a draw—particularly compared to the herding of runners through the chute at the end of Chicago's marathon, which registers 40,000. The two tests of endurance have been on the same weekend, one day apart.

Dick has run both, although certainly not in the same year. For me, the events are opportunities to explore. In Ashland, that meant ducking into shops along Main Street, including the old-time JCPenney. That was one kind of nostalgia; another was in the architecture, like the 1884 building that contains **New England Store**, a gift/jewelry shop and one of the city's oldest businesses.

Outside of town is the **Northern Great Lakes Visitor Center** and its observation tower, for viewing Lake Superior and the Apostle Islands. Inside are exhibits about the culture and natural forces that shaped this part of Wisconsin. One of the more unusual souvenirs comes from **Timeless Timber**, items (canes to wine racks) made from virgin timber recovered from the bottom of Superior.

I don't always play tourist while Dick runs himself ragged. During **Milwaukee's Lakefront Marathon**, also in October, I positioned myself along the scenic route, which begins in Grafton, hugs Lake Michigan's shoreline and ends at Veterans Park.

That's a game of guessing where your marathoner will be along the course, yelling words of encouragement, then moving the car a few miles to do it again, and again. (Tip: A shout of "looking good" around Mile 20 fools no one, even the oblivious runner.)

My own track goals remain modest, and my eye is on the late October **Road America Walk/Run** that takes people, strollers and wagons with kids around the hilly, four-mile racetrack near **Elkhart Lake**. It's a far more gentle way to acknowledge the arrival of autumn.

•

When Dick turned 50 a couple of years ago, he decided to spend about eight hours of his birthday in front of the Kohl Center in downtown **Madison**. Yes, he's a bit eccentric. We were among the hundreds of volunteers who helped pull off the city's first **Ironman Wisconsin triathlon**, the super-human event which squeezes a 2.4-mile swim, 112-mile bike ride and 26.2-mile run out of its participants.

The fastest man would take eight hours, 46 minutes, 30 seconds to complete this grueling agenda. The last official finisher arrived about seven hours later.

We chose to work along the marathon route. The athletes passed us twice, near the start and near the end of the run, a wicked double-loop that also was the last leg of the triathlon. It was a fascinating day and a great study in human perseverance, vulnerability, stubbornness, endurance. We handed out cups of water for a while, then chunks of fruit. We'd tote around cases of energy drinks, round up trash, hoot and holler.

After dusk, there was warm broth out as well as ice chips, for the aching men and women who by now shuffled more than jogged. Most of these 1,800 athletes, even if they were in a trance while competing, seemed to appreciate our simple actions, gestures and chants. It was enough to bring us back for more, one year later.

For information about Ironman Wisconsin, go to **www.ironmanwisconsin.org** or call **608-226-4780** to learn about volunteer opportunities; some have nifty titles like "body marker" and "finish line catcher."

•

Few things are certain in life, and that includes the marathon races that I've seen. Courses will vary in flatness, scenic nature, climate, the potential to lure spectators and fans. What's typical? Expect a race-sponsored pasta dinner on the eve of a marathon, for convenient carb-loading, plus a marketplace with loads of running merchandise and event material. And if you're a non-runner, it'll likely be a challenge to find your marathoner after the race ends. The bigger the number of registrants, the more likely that fences will separate you from the post-race gathering area. That's a drag, and that's a real good reason to be a post-race volunteer.

An extensive resource for running events is at **www.runnersworld.com**, the website for *Runner's World* magazine. A good supplement to that, for Wisconsin, is **www.badgerland-striders.org**, named after the running club that organizes the annual Lakefront Marathon in Milwaukee. The state's earliest fall marathon—the **Fox Cities Marathon** in late September—takes runners from Neenah to Kaukauna, before ending in Appleton. The same weekend is the **Octoberfest** ethnic food and music celebration in downtown Appleton.

If you're along for the ride and not volunteering on race day, take a hike while your companion pounds the pavement. The **Outagamie Historical Society** and **Fox Cities Convention and Visitors Bureau** have free maps for self-guided tours of Appleton. It's a lesson in local history and includes information on two prominent former residents, magician **Harry Houdini** and novelist **Edna Ferber**.

Wisconsin marathons include:

Trailbreaker Marathon (April), Waukesha, www.trailbreakermarathon.com
Waukesha tourism, www.waukeshacountywi.com

•

Journeys Marathon (May), Eagle River, www.journeysmarathon.org
Eagle River tourism, www.eagleriver.org

•

Green Bay Marathon (May), Green Bay, www.cellcomgreenbaymarathon.com
Green Bay tourism, www.packercountry.com

•

Mad City Marathon (May), Madison, www.madcitymarathon.com
Madison tourism, www.visitmadison.com

•

Paavo Nurmi Marathon (August), Hurley, 715-561-4334
Hurley tourism, www.hurleywi.com

•

Fox Cities Marathon (September), www.foxcitiesmarathon.org
Fox Cities tourism, www.foxcities.org

•

Lakefront Marathon (October), www.badgerlandstriders.org
Milwaukee tourism, www.visitmilwaukee.org

•

WhistleStop Marathon (October), www.whistlestopmarathon.com
Ashland tourism, www.visitashland.com.

The Karner blue butterfly makes its home in only seven states.

BABCOCK: WHERE BUTTERFLIES & BOMBERS CO-EXIST

Just outside of Babcock, population 218 and near the Wood-Juneau county line, are two spectacular aerial displays that co-exist amicably despite their huge differences.

You can't see one, and you can't miss the other. Both are reminders of the frailty and interdependence of life.

In **Sandhill Wildlife Area**, the tiny and endangered Karner blue butterfly thrives. It is a weak flier, with a wingspan of only an inch. A brilliant blue-violet in color, it is found in only seven states.

The U.S. Fish and Wildlife Service's Karner recovery plan is 293 pages long.

On the nearby **Hardwood Bombing Range**, a half-dozen high-performance F-16 Fighting Falcons may be soaring at once. The combat plane can exceed Mach 2 in airspeed and has a wingspan of 32 feet, 8 inches. Known for its accuracy more than its looks, the aircraft has been used to destroy targets large and small.

There are hundreds of these fighters in operation worldwide.

The butterflies and the bombers fly less than five miles from each other, and sometimes their paths intersect. "This is the tension zone," says **Neal Paisley**, Sandhill's wildlife manager, referring not to what is airborne but to where "north meets south and the plant/wildlife inventory is immense."

This is the part of Wisconsin where the state's northern forests and southern prairie grasses merge, which means a rich mix of vegetation and creatures because of the unusual environment.

The Karner blues thrive on wild lupine, and that plant grows well in this area. Some of the other less common species that live on or visit Sandhill's 9,460 acres include Blanding's turtles, trumpeter swans, prairie chickens and—especially in October—thousands of sandhill cranes.

Lt. Col. Brendan Smith has an above-ground view of the bombing range.

Neal calls his work "active habitat management.... The area is much more diverse in habitat than it would be if the area was left to its own devices." He calls the Hardwood range a good neighbor that is conscientious about its work and sensitive to the impact it could have on protected and other species.

Although this is an inert range, meaning that it doesn't drop live bombs, it is a noisy area in which visitors are advised to wear earplugs. One of 13 Air National Guard ranges in the nation, and affiliated with Camp Douglas, it covers about 7,000 acres. About 95 percent of the aircraft flown here are F-16s.

Hardwood is both a working military site and an attraction, says **Lt. Col. Brendan Smith**, who acknowledges that "this is something you don't get to see in many places." These are fully trained fighter pilots, many of whom also fly full time for commercial airlines.

"Targets are set out—like a helicopter at the intersection of two runways—and these flying units will pick them out, tell us (by radio) how they'll deliver their ordnance, then drop their bombs," says **Master Sgt. Greg Royce**. "Then we score them."

Speed and accuracy are measured, both in scenarios like this and other electronic simulations that involve the planes coming under attack. "We also will move targets around and ask the pilots to find them," Greg says. "Some are pretty challenging to find."

A goal, Brendan says, is to do dive bombs and other maneuvers so often that, if

DETOUR

Babcock is a one-restaurant town, and the **Country Café** has a weathered look that belies its sweet reputation. Cranberry pie (and variations with apples, raspberries and/or nuts) is the specialty; one major customer has been the **Warrens Cranberry Festival**, where hundreds are sold in three days every September. Look for the café on Hwy. 80.

The nearby **Necedah National Wildlife Refuge**, established in 1939, covers 43,000 acres and—among other things—helps protect and restore the whooping crane population. Young cranes, hatched at a wildlife research center, are brought to the refuge each summer to learn how to follow ultralight aircraft that eventually will lead the birds along a migratory route to Florida. Crane training begins early in the morning and sometimes can be witnessed by visitors from an observation tower at the refuge.

•

in a real war situation, "you're so used to doing it that it comes naturally and is almost an internal reaction."

The BDU-33, a 33-pound steel practice bomb, typically is dropped at Hardwood, but the payload can be as large as an MK-84, a practice bomb that weighs a ton. The way a plane handles will differ, depending on its cargo.

Since the 9/11 terrorist attacks, "we've not seen as many aircraft or sorties (flight missions) here because some of these pilots are doing their jobs in other places," says Greg, referring to wartime activity.

He holds environmental preservation as a priority, as does his boss. "We have a great environmental record," Brendan says, noting the amount of wild lupine on the acreage and his staff's attempts to protect the endangered Karner through prescribed range burns, firebreaks that protect the butterfly environment.

During seasonal bird migrations, pilots will be told to raise their altitude of flight, so their planes move above the Canada geese, cranes and trumpeter swans.

"We share some of the same concerns as the wildlife refuges and have developed a reasonable method of coexistence," Greg says.

The Hardwood Bombing Range often is open to visitors. Call before visiting, to get information about the bombing schedule for the day. Night missions typically are not open to the public.

Grilled brats at the bombing range? You betcha. Just wear earplugs.

Bring earplugs and, if the weather is warm enough, a picnic lunch. There are grills, picnic tables and a shaded viewing area. Admission is free, and at least one staffer will be around to answer questions.

Sandhill Wildlife Area, operated by the state Department of Natural Resources, has hiking trails, observation towers and a 14-mile auto trail (which is open from April into October). Wildlife and wilderness workshops, particularly for youths, are held year-round.

•

Hardwood Bombing Range
near Hwys. 80 and F, Babcock
608-427-1509

•

Sandhill Wildlife Area
Hwy. X, Babcock
www.dnr.state.wi.us
715-884-2437

Lake views, near sunset, are quiet BT—Before Tourists.

BAYFIELD: SIMPLE, NATURAL ELEGANCE

As we drove in the **Chequamegon National Forest**, near the northernmost part of Wisconsin, we spotted a beak and tuft of white in the ditch. We did a U-turn at the next crossroad, retraced our route, then turned again.

The bird was easy to spot against the quack grass—now that we were intent upon finding it—and the creature certainly was aware of us. As our car slowed to a crawl, huge wings flapped and the raptor gained height quickly. The takeoff occurred barely a car length in front of us. It all happened in little more than a flash.

For the alert bald eagle, this was a strong and graceful flight to the safety of a tree-top perch, dozens of feet above ground. We likely had interrupted its breakfast.

I have seen this magnificent bird at wildlife rehab facilities, and as a soaring speck near water, but never quite like this—close, in motion, focused and determined.

One day earlier, another creature made an impact more subtly. We were preoccupied with our first tandem bike ride, on Madeline Island, and were only beginning to settle into a smooth pedaling pace.

The road was deserted, sun bright, air slightly brisk. While turning my head left, I spotted a solitary doe in a clearing, having a roadside munch, no more than 50 feet away. The animal seemed engaged by our antics, chatter, sometimes wobbly movement.

Seeing a whitetail is not unusual. Having it lack fear while you share its habitat, even for a minute, is. A few miles later, we were at Big Bay Town Park, with its pristine sand, tranquil bay, lack of people and noise.

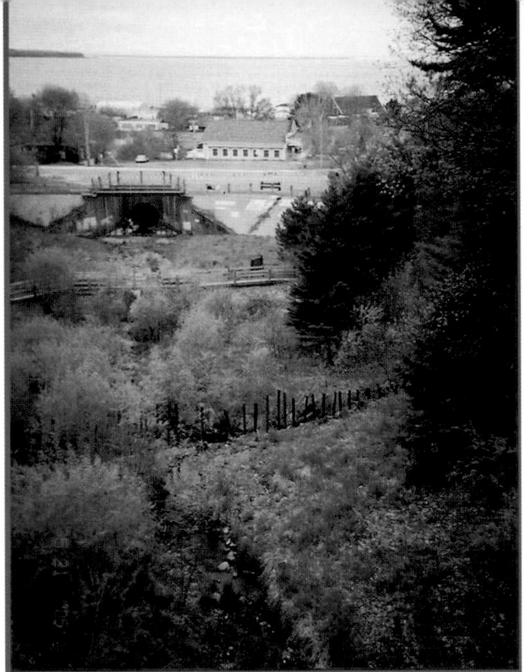

Iron Bridge hiking trail follows a ravine.

These are fleeting moments, and I am trying to savor more of them as they occur. That is one reason why time in the Bayfield area can be more than a simple weekend away.

The area is picturesque and peaceful enough to increase your chance of discovering something precious.

There is much to recommend in and near Bayfield, even before the bustle of summer tourism kicks in. Or maybe we really mean "especially before" the influx of tourists.

We stayed at **Le Chateau Boutin**, which is a part of the grand and acclaimed **Old Rittenhouse Inn**, long owned by **Jerry** and **Mary Phillips**. The inn is a part of the Select Registry (**www.selectregistry.com**), which lists 400 of the best small lodging properties in North America.

Our South Room was more like a suite, with a fine mesh of comfort and class. A fireplace was neatly stacked and ready to light. Nearby was a whirlpool big enough for two. The windows of our two dormers overlooked the moody Great Lake; a cozy leather chair, in front of one, would have made even a rainy day a pleasure.

Downstairs, near the entrance, a plate of freshly baked cookies arrived in late afternoon. Six of us shared champagne, wine and a lake view from the inn's porch, then retreated to one of the finest five-course meals we've ever had.

Rittenhouse dinners have a fixed price, and the choices are both complicated and seductive. A part of the prelude, especially if **Julie Phillips** (Jerry's sister) has your table, is hearing the description of what's available but not on the menu. It's good mini-theater, presented by Julie with passion and a bit of drama.

So to say that I had lake trout stuffed with lobster and shrimp does the entree little justice, knowing what Julie could do with the description.

Brother Jerry is a savvy businessman who realizes that owning pretty and historic Victorian properties isn't enough to stay ahead of the competition. That's why he and Mary have developed an extraordinary menu, too.

The couple also have added special events, especially during the winter. There are festive Wassail dinner concerts in December, cooking demos and liquor-themed weekends (wine, beer, martini, margarita). Costumed murder mystery dinners are available, too, and

Le Chateau Boutin's porch overlooks Lake Superior.

can be booked privately.

In 1973, friends couldn't believe Jerry and Mary were leaving Madison to be innkeepers in remote Bayfield. "Now there are tons of us who want to live in a community and feel we can still make a difference," he says.

Be it kayaking or hiking, antique shopping or gallery hopping, a night at Big Top Chautauqua or a drive to see orchards of apple blossoms, this is a part of the world where progress and entertainment may have atypical definitions that become more special as the world gets more congested.

•

Bayfield County Tourism
www.travelbayfieldcounty.com 800-472-6338

•

Rittenhouse Inn, 301 Rittenhouse Ave., Bayfield
www.rittenhouseinn.com
800-779-2129

The South Room is more like a homey suite.

DETOUR

The Old Rittenhouse Inn's annual Wassail dinner concerts, which began in 1975, are lavish, three-hour affairs with five-course meals. Menu choices are a blend of Tudor favorites such as flaming figgy pudding with regional gourmet specialties, like Lake Superior Chowder and Apple Blackberry Pork Chops. Local residents—attorneys to beekeepers—serenade the diners with Renaissance to contemporary holiday music.

How elaborate and inviting is the Rittenhouse during the holidays? It was good enough to be one of three locations featured on a Japanese telecast about Christmas a few years ago. The TV crew's only other footage was shot in New York City and the Vatican. Thousands of feet of white lights and pine bough roping turn the 1890 mansion into a giant, twinkling cake. Santa visits, and a sleigh filled with packages is parked on the front lawn.

Up to 900 can be seated under the Big Top Chautauqua canopy.

Under the Big Top

Lake Superior Big Top Chautauqua is best known for its quirky and melodic tent shows, but the cast also helps teach state history to children. Their DVD video "30th Star," a musical celebration and study of Wisconsin at the time of statehood, was distributed in 2005 to all public school districts in the state.

It is one part tent show, another part historic images, plus old and new film footage, including some shot aboard the **S/V Denis Sullivan schooner**, a scientific research vessel launched in 2000 and the first tall ship built in Wisconsin in 100 years.

Funded with $100,000 from a U.S. Department of Education grant, the "30th Star" project also includes an online study guide for teachers in multiple disciplines—geography to music, history to social studies—and content is appropriate for fourth-graders to high schoolers.

Teachers have the option of presenting the video in its entirety, or focusing on just one part of it at a time. There are 10 chapters/segments, with themes such as logging,

immigration and mining.

"It's not a linear, sequential, chronological approach," says **Betty Ferris**, co-director of the project with **Warren Nelson** and **Bruce Bowers**. The video "uses images, songs and metaphors to evoke the time that is being represented," and she considers that mix "a powerful way to help people connect with the place they live and the era we're talking about."

"30th Star" began as a musical tribute that Warren and Betty (as Nelson-Ferris Concert Company) were commissioned to create for the sesquicentennial celebration of Wisconsin's statehood. The 1998 performance, or excerpts of it, presently is a part of Big Top Chautauqua's revolving repertoire.

The nonprofit arts group began business in 1986; founder Warren is a Wisconsin Academy Fellow, an award that recognizes distinguished lifetime achievement in the sciences, arts or letters.

Big Top Chautauqua's original, historical musicals are a mixture of wacky, witty and wistful entertainment. Nationally known performers complement the local cast for about 70 nights each summer, under the canopy of a beautiful 160-by-70-foot all-canvas, 2,500-pound tent. Up to 900 can be seated in the tent, which is at the base of Mt. Ashwabay, three miles south of Bayfield.

On big nights, when weather permits, the sidewalls are lifted to create a huge, open-air setting that comfortably holds much larger crowds.

•

Big Top Chautauqua's website has a 360 degree view inside the tent and a time-lapsed movie clip of the annual tent raising. Besides seeing the summer lineup, the website shows where to catch the troupe on the road.

•

Lake Superior Big Top Chautauqua
101 W. Bayfield St., Washburn
www.bigtop.org, 888-244-8368

The state's most plush accommodations also are among its most remote.

CHETEK: INCREDIBLE ISOLATION AT CANOE BAY

First come the rustling stalks of corn, one field after another. There are dots of farmhouses and ripened vegetable gardens, splashes of wildflowers and thickening foliage, as the road loses its center marking and begins to twist.

Then the route becomes desolate, with no sign of human life. You instinctively brace for a darting of deer, as dusk approaches and a mist of rain clouds the windshield.

Eyes squint and search for a sign, any sign. It turns out to be simple, elegant and wooden. There is one more turn to go, a half-mile stretch with a speed limit of 10 mph. Only the slow rhythm of wipers cuts the silence in this remote patch of Wisconsin. Radio chatter turned to static quite a while ago.

Having directions is crucial, and they aren't on the Internet.

I am about 15 minutes east of Chetek, between Eau Claire and Rice Lake. My visit comes on the last evening of an eight-day and 800-mile road trip around the Upper Midwest. So I am tired, the weather is gloomy, and the destination turns out to be incredible.

The plushest and most acclaimed accommodations in Wisconsin also seem to be the hardest to find and the least advertised—unless you happen to catch the unpaid accolades.

"Couple nirvana," writes *USA Today*. "The setting is sublime, the food is fabulous," offers the Food Network. The Zagat Survey calls this the top hotel in the Midwest, and one of the 10 most romantic lodgings in the nation. *Wine Spectator* gives it a "Best of" award, one step beyond its Award of Excellence.

This is **Canoe Bay Resort**, whose spacious cottages and duplexes are isolated but full of amenities. Designer John Rattenbury was a Frank Lloyd Wright protege; the property oozes with the legendary architect's love for clean lines and earthy materials. It was the first Midwest inn to earn a four-star Mobil Travel Guide rating, the only Paris-based Relais & Chateaux lodging in the Midwest.

This is a smooth meeting of art and environment, a far cry from the Seventh Day Adventist camp that had been abandoned here in the 1980s. Today the most modest quarters, at 275 square feet, was $325 per night in 2005. The most astounding, the Edgewood, is 2,083 square feet (plus a gigantic wrap-around deck) and $1,800.

The prices are per couple. Even Edgewood is not meant to accommodate more than that. The resort is for adults only, with 21 lodging options and meeting space for up to 14 people.

Owners **Dan** and **Lisa Dobrowolski** bought these 280 acres in 1992, opened them to guests in 1993. There are sentimental attachments beneath the business investment: Dan, a former Chicago TV weatherman, used to fish around this glacial area as a boy.

"It's morphing and changing," Dan says of the property. "Like a running river, it gets deeper and more complex."

"It suits our own sensibilities," says Lisa, an Ohio native with a journalism background. "We find it relaxing and restorative."

My Heavenly Suite faces one of three lakes, with two decks outside and two gas fireplaces aglow inside. The tinkling of a Scarlatti sonata drifts as the door opens to a warmly lit haven of cedar walls and arched ceilings. Recessed lighting and bouquets of fresh flowers soften my mood. Fresh fruit and chef-made granola quell the appetite.

Unable to arrive for a dinner seating before 7 p.m., what is described as a light supper awaits in a small refrigerator. It is more fruit, wedges of three cheeses, crackers. Under another lid is a chicken breast over wild rice, a salad of greens with paper-thin radish and kohlrabi slices. For dessert: a pumpkin spice muffin with cream cheese filling.

Chef Scott Johnson's cuisine tends to be organic, serving free-range poultry and grass-fed beef. Even flours are made on-site, and a local potter made the breakfast dishes. Eat in the dining room, where jackets are required for gentlemen, or indulge in the Wine Cellar Dinner, which exceeds $200 per couple.

Swimming, fishing and paddling are possible on a 50-acre Canoe Bay lake. There also are hiking and snowshoeing trails. Visitors can feed fish by hand, sweat in an elaborate exercise room, browse the in-house library for a newly released book or DVD, laze by the dock in summer, ride a horse-drawn sleigh in winter.

The Dobrowolskis make it all appear effortless, but everything is a complicated web—from getting *The New York Times* delivered in a timely manner to finding appropriate menu ingredients and fixing back-up generators in stormy weather.

"Whenever people are doing something extraordinary, it doesn't fall in your lap," Dan says. "You have to work and think all the time."

"I've never felt so alone—yet so well cared for," wrote a couple from Williams Bay, in a guest diary.

What I regret is not the rain or fog, but that I chose to accept Lisa's invitation when I knew that I'd be spending a night at Canoe Bay alone. Although a fine place to decompress solo, what an extraordinary setting for a twosome.

•

Canoe Bay Resort, Chetek
www.canoebay.com, 800-568-1995

Fast Facts

Only three Wisconsin sites make the cut in Patricia Schultz's *1,000 Places to See Before You Die* (Workman Publishing, 2003). They are **Canoe Bay Resort**, the **Apostle Islands National Lakeshore** near Bayfield and **The American Club** resort in Kohler.

•

The fixed price, evening meal at Canoe Bay is big on natural ingredients. One menu example: House Smoked Salmon, Salad of Fennel & Kohlrabi with Pine Nut Vinaigrette, Seared Diver-Harvested Scallop with Lobster Risotto and Yellow Tomato Beurre Blanc, Warm Chocolate Cake with Peanut Butter & Banana Ice Cream.

•

Glacier movement created the 50-foot-deep lake at Canoe Bay. It is clear and fed by springs, not a major stream or river. Glacial moraine was used to build huge fireplaces inside the resort's Lodge and Inn.

•

Cooling off on a hot summer day in Chippewa Falls.

CHIPPEWA FALLS: WOOD CHIPS & MICROCHIPS

This is an old lumber town, birthplace of Seymour Cray's supercomputers and home of the nation's seventh oldest working brewery. With a population just shy of 13,000 in 2002 and about 10 miles north of Eau Claire, Chippewa Falls also has earned national recognition for its respect and preservation of the past, particularly downtown.

Time magazine called this one of the nation's top 10 small towns in 1997. "Once home to one of the world's largest sawmills, the town moved from wood chips to microchips," the article said, explaining why Chippewa Falls didn't die. "After hours, computer mavens snowmobile across Lake Wissota and drink Leinenkugel beer."

The National Trust for Historic Preservation chose the city as one of a dozen "distinctive destinations" nationwide in 2000. The oldest building here? It's reportedly the only remaining historic wooden structure (an 1885 ordinance required construction with brick materials).

All of the hubbub began about 1996, when Chippewa Falls earned a Great American Main Street Award. Dozens of business and residential facades had been renovated. That also was about the time The Metropolitan Shops, in an 1889 lumber company building,

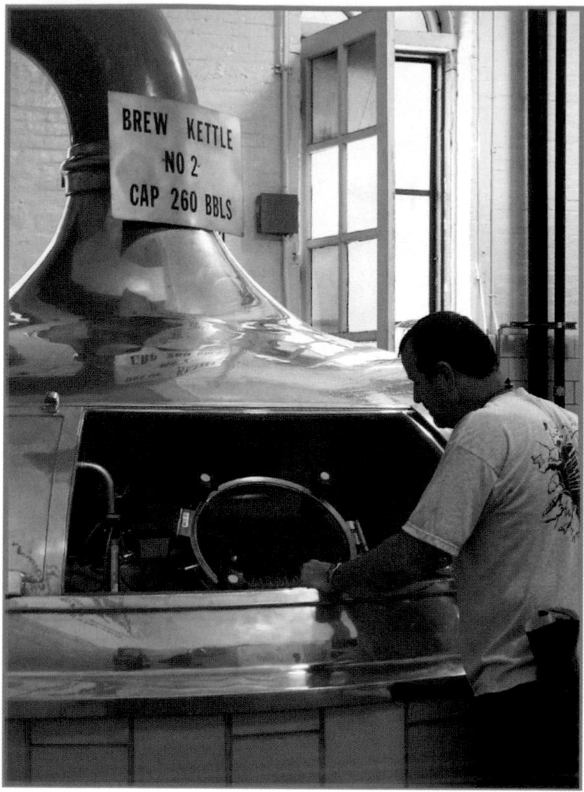

At work at Brew Kettle Number 2.

were introduced. Tenants ranged from Bohemian Ovens to Cow Caviar (a food gift shop with local products) before the shops closed.

Factory outlet space for **XMI**, a local manufacturer that is a national distributor of fine men's fashions, particularly neckwear, is downtown. **Mason Shoe Manufacturing Company**, called "the world's largest shoe catalog sales company," also has an outlet store here.

In the early 1900s, the city had five shoe factories. At its peak, there were almost a dozen; one of them made 1,500 pairs daily and employed 175 people.

The **Chippewa Falls Museum of Industry and Technology** includes "the world's only complete supercomputer collection" and other history lessons about local industry that date back to the 1840s.

Some industrial fingerprints have withstood aging well. Free tours of the **Jacob Leinenkugel Brewing Company**, which opened in 1867, are available. The Leinie's Lodge gift shop is open all year.

On Sunday mornings, **Gordy's IGA** is the busiest shopping hub downtown. Most everything else seems tidy but quiet. Church steeples pop out above hilly treetops. Huge murals are laden with images of wildlife.

There have been tidbits of fame that have little to do with history. This was the hometown of the title character in the Woody Allen movie "Annie Hall." XMI has sold neckties to celebrities, including David Letterman. Nearby **Lake Wissota** was mentioned clearly but inaccurately in the blockbuster movie "Titanic." It is a 6,300-acre man-made lake that wasn't created until a few years after the Titanic sank in 1912.

So nationwide exposure comes and goes, but that's of little consequence to Ruth

Dahms, a former junior high teacher here. She says it is simply community spirit that will help Chippewa Falls and its residents thrive for the long haul.

"We take care of each other," she says. "Early on, a neighbor saw me working late one night and brought over a plate of spaghetti. I didn't even know her then."

A significant part of future city development will use the water as a magnet for tourists, including a riverfront park for outdoor concerts and a bike path that follows Duncan Creek—downtown and to the brewery. A challenge will be the negative impact that the rerouting of Highway 29 will have on businesses. The new highway, designed to improve traffic flow and safety, bypasses the city instead of cutting into the heart of it.

•

Chippewa County Tourism Council, Chippewa Falls
www.chippewacounty.com
866-723-0331

Fast Facts

"Since the start, **XMI** has always tried to convey a lifestyle that allows its customers to have fun, make a statement and show that they are not afraid to evolve," the clothing manufacturer says online. Ralph Lauren gives XMI founder Bert Pulitzer credit for teaching him about neckwear. Each tie is handmade in Chippewa Falls; neckwear choices include bold Civil War and American flag designs.

•

Shoe sizes made and sold by **Mason Shoe Manufacturing** range from 4 to 17, with widths from AAAA to EEEEEE. The company's first product, upon opening in 1904: Leather boots for lumberjacks.

•

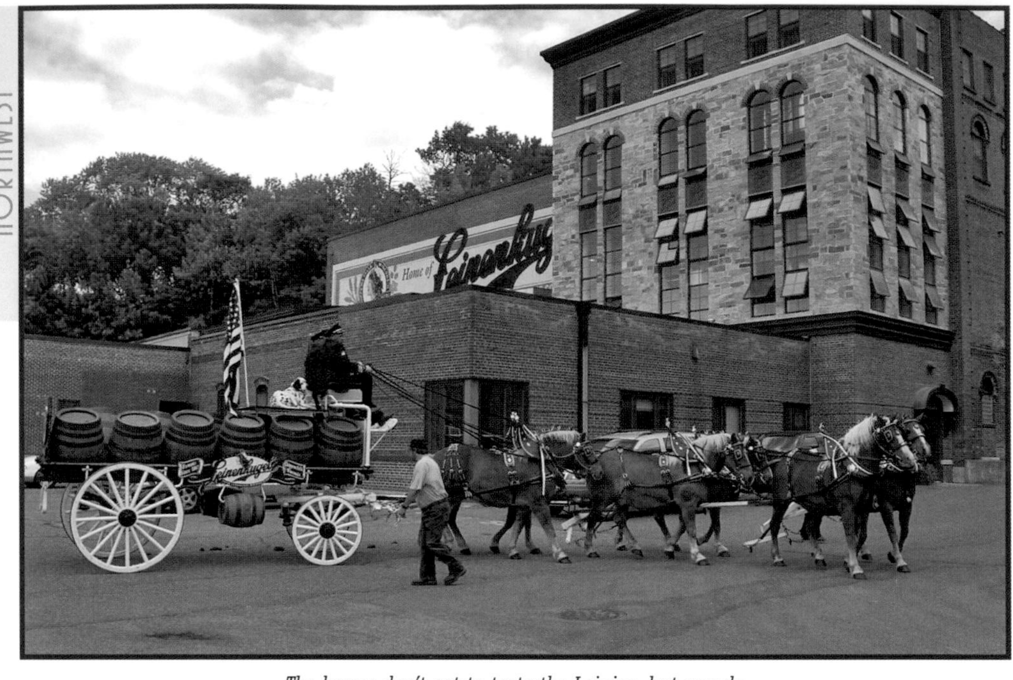

The horses don't get to taste the Leinies, but you do.

Go to **www.leinie.com** for a peek into **Peg's Recipe Box**, a collection of foods and beverages that require at least one bottle of Leinie's. Here is one cool example, submitted by Joel Radke of Menomonie:

Beer Margarita

4-5 shots vodka
4-5 shots tequila
3 cans Leinie's (Original or Honey Weiss)
12-ounce can limeade concentrate

Mix and serve over ice. **Serves 4-6.**

COUDERAY: Tracking 'Moose'

If your tourist enterprise relies on certain weather to succeed, diversify—or you're doomed to failure. That's a bit of advice from **Richard "Moose" Speros**, as outgoing secretary of Wisconsin's Department of Tourism, and it was given on a January day when no part of the state had a snow cover.

Moose was state tourism secretary until 2003, and he knows how to separate what is in and out of his control. The weather's a no-brainer. So is a change of political affiliation in the governor's chair. Speros became state tourism's administrator in 1991, when Governor Tommy Thompson was in office, and was out when Democrat Jim Doyle took over.

Moose left state government work at age 66, but that doesn't mean he retired. The proprietor of the **Tiger Musky Resort**, about 40 acres on the Chippewa Flowage near Hayward, never really took his hands off the business. But he also acknowledges that his family has "gotten so good at running it, they don't really need me."

Moose Speros is still working but doesn't wear a tie much anymore.

So now Moose has the time to fish, boat and hunt a bit more. He latched onto a 37-inch muskie, as he was jigging for walleye. Threw it back, of course.

He spends the deer hunting season around Hayward, and Buffalo County. Doesn't always shoot one himself, but is glad to witness the bounty of his grandsons.

His best business ally and advocate has been **Millie**, his wife since 1955. "If she'd walk in here now, she'd give you a hug," Moose says. "She doesn't know how to say 'hello' any other way."

Her attention to detail and people is one reason why the Tiger Musky Resort sounds atypical. Millie Speros sends more than 3,000 birthday cards per year, collecting birthdates from the fishing licenses that she sells.

Largemouth bass as big as your baby.

"If it's your birthday when you stay with us, she makes you a pizza or a cake, and we make a big deal out of it," her husband says. "Sure it's a trick, a gimmick, but Millie's very sincere about it."

She also finds out the first names of everybody in a family, including the dog. She makes horse-radish pickles, for the Bloody Marys, and they are in high demand. When a repeat customer arrives—and Moose says that's 88 percent of his business per year—"we have somebody looking for their license plate and greeting them by name when they get out of the car."

The personal touch, he says, is what can make a vacation memorable. And it has made the backwoods Tiger Musky a haven for average families as well as federal judges and professional football players. Jury's out on whether that's because of the resort, Moose's connections or Millie.

"My family stayed at Tiger Musky five times, the summers of 1965-70," writes a Raleigh, N.C., man at www.tigermuskyresort.com. "I caught my first (and only) muskie there when I was 13. These were some of my fondest memories."

"The weather is beautiful one day, perfect the next," says another customer, regarding his move to Australia. But "we would much rather be hanging out at the beautiful Tiger Musky."

Moose shrugs and notes that his property is amid "true wilderness." He knows he could make more money if the area were developed but says he'd rather protect the environment.

He stayed at the Tiger Musky for the first time in 1965 and bought it about 10 years later. Still stationed with the U.S. Air Force in Sioux Falls, S.D., "I drove home on weekends, 400 miles one way," until his military retirement.

"This area is me—it's what I'm about," says the guy who earned his nickname

Moose loves Millie's cooking, and she is glad to share this cake recipe, which is described as easy, delicious and Moose's favorite.

Mandarin Orange Cake

Cake:
2 cups sugar
2 cups flour
2 teaspoons baking soda
2 eggs
2 (8-ounce) cans mandarin oranges, drained
1 teaspoon vanilla

Mix all in a large bowl. Pour into a 9 x 13 pan. Bake 25 minutes at 350 degrees.

Topping:
1 1/2 cups brown sugar
6 tablespoons butter
6 tablespoons milk

Bring to a boil. Pour over warm cake.

because of the name of an F-100, single-seat fighter that he flew.

"Wisconsin is the heart of the Heartland," Moose adds, "and I've been selling a product that I believe in."

•

Tiger Musky Resort
11251 W. Tiger Musky Road, Couderay
www.tigermuskyresort.com, 715-945-2555

A merganser gets a running takeoff.

DETOUR

A 1920s getaway for Al Capone and other gangsters is in the same general neighborhood as the Tiger Musky Resort. **The Hideout** is a well-kept and well-hidden museum and restaurant. It's casual as well as fine dining, big on steaks and Chicago Red Hots. Isolated, and open seasonally. Check out **www.alcaponehideout.com** or call **(715) 945-2746**.

•

The **Chequamegon-Nicolet National Forest** is more than 1.5 million acres in 11 Northwoods counties, established in 1933 after intense logging threatened to devastate the area. "We are fortunate in that these forests are resilient," the National Parks Service writes online. "If left alone, we knew they would recover from the destructive logging practices of the late 1800s and early 1900s. . . . Today, the second growth forests are teeming with life and providing us with a variety of natural resources."

•

A part of the **Lake Superior Big Top Chautauqua's** musical repertoire is "Centennial Green: The Over and Understory of the Forest Service in Song," a production commissioned to celebrate the 100th anniversary of the U.S. Forest Service in 2005.

•

The 1940 Silk City diner is from New York.

DELTA: ONE SHINY DINER

A dozen miles south of Iron River, off Hwy. H and inside Chequamegon National Forest, are the best Norwegian pancakes around. They are thin and sweet enough to hold their own, without a drenching of syrup.

"First-time customers have to sample the pancakes," jokes the cook, **Todd Bucher**, who grew up in Fond du Lac. "We lock the door until that happens."

That is how a little pancake arrived after my order of deep-fried mac and cheese (a strange but pleasant snack). The combination of the two items is about all that I would not recommend about **Delta Diner**, which opened in 2003.

Delta isn't on the state map, and that is a part of the charm. The diner creeps up quickly, a shiny and neon-bright sight that surely has earned a lot of double takes amid the acres of tall pines and miles of unmarked roads.

Todd likes being in the middle of nowhere, on this land that had long been vacant. The Delta Store used to thrive here, selling everything from fish bait to hot meatloaf, until the building burned in 1972.

"That left a real void," says Todd, who opened Delta Diner with his wife, **Nina**. "The common perception was that nothing could be built here."

He is the kind of guy who would drive 40 miles out of his way to get to a good

Todd seeks and finds good karma in the Northwoods.

diner, and believes that others would do the same.

"It's a different feel than a restaurant," and he seems to thrive on those dynamics. Crowds are fine, he says, but the trade-off is that there is no time to get to know your customers.

When you belly up to the diner's counter for lunch, it's suburban tourist next to local laborer, Ph.D.s sharing a coffeepot with folks making minimum wage. They're likely to end up talking, and Todd sees great value in that.

"There's some good karma going here," he says of the intimate, 38-seat dining area. During peak business, it can be an hour wait for a seat, then another 40 minutes to get fed.

Todd is a former advertising/marketing guy who worked for outdoor magazines until deciding to seek a simpler life. Nina operates **Taste Budz**, a coffeehouse and deli in Iron River. "We're trying to build this business on word of mouth," he says.

The menu is both diner fare and atypical. Yes, breakfast is a big deal. All the standard choices are there, plus Mexican Eggs Benedict on Thursdays (two eggs over cornbread and covered with a chipotle sausage sauce). The Greek omelet came off the menu ("it takes 26 steps to make"). The Delta Hot Cakes should be taken literally (they have jalapenos).

There are blue plate specials that sometimes include Wild Rice Turkey Casserole or Cajun Red Beans and Rice. Chili is a specialty, but it's a sea of white—no tomatoes.

And the desserts? Among the signature pieces: a dense banana cake with chocolate frosting, and Swedish cream with fruit.

The frame of this 1940 Silk City (the manufacturer) diner was broken down and in New York when the Buchers bought it. Most of the rebuilding was done in Ohio; then the structure was hoisted onto a semitrailer and driven to remote Bayfield County. Todd calls his neighborhood the last undeveloped part of Wisconsin.

"Check out the canoeing on the White River," he tells a couple of honeymooners. "It's not fast water, but there are a lot of curves."

•

Delta Diner, 14385 Hwy. N, Delta
www.deltadiner.net, 715-372-6666

Threshing grain, 1905, by Frank Feiker. *[Wisconsin Historical Society image number 31816]*

EAU CLAIRE: CULTIVATING FARM HISTORY

There is a lot about rural living that I take for granted, having grown up on a 120-acre dairy farm. I assume that everybody has seen a cow being milked, that nobody cares how a manure spreader operates, that there always will be 4-H clubs and small-town poultry parties.

There are places that acknowledge farming history, but **Janet Dykema** says that "unless you had a farm experience, there often is little context" provided for the tools and machinery that typically are on exhibit.

"Most people today are two or three generations removed from this way of life," notes Janet. While director of public programs at the **Chippewa Valley Museum**, Eau Claire, she was involved in an extensive exhibition entitled "Farm Life: A Century of Change for Farm Families and Their Neighbors." The museum completed the project in 2004. It cost about $500,000 to develop and put in place, and nearly half of the cost was provided by the National Endowment for the Humanities. The Endowment also helped finance a condensed version that began a nationwide tour in late 2005, a 16-panel exhibit of photos and text that will make its way from New Mexico to Pennsylvania, Minnesota to Colorado.

Why is all this such a big deal? There has been a dramatic decline in the number of Wisconsin people involved in agriculture, observes **Frank Smoot**, the museum's director of publications. How dramatic? It was almost 50 percent of the population a century

A herd of cows relaxes as their owner harvests their winter meals.

ago, he says, compared to 3 percent in 2005.

"Farm Life" is a way to both acknowledge the past and analyze its impact on rural life in 2005. "It's a way of life that still drives a lot of what we do today," Frank says. "It's fundamental to the way we see ourselves and define our character."

This has been an ambitious undertaking—the largest and most sophisticated that the museum, created in 1975—has undertaken. There are four themes: field work, the rural community, the farmhouse and the barn. Oral histories—86 of them—help keep the focus on people instead of objects.

The exhibit is self-guided, although curriculum-based tours have been developed for student groups.

We learn how technology has changed the way farmers work and interact. Combines replaced threshing crews, tractors replaced horses, electricity lessened the need for hand milking. All changed the rhythm of work. "The change from horse to tractor on the farm was gradual, but it was revolutionary," exhibit organizers write. "A person using a machine could do the work of several people, and several people with machines could do the work of a whole neighborhood."

Greater efficiency obviously didn't eliminate all challenges. Urban and rural worlds have collided in many ways. A second income—made off the farm—has become typical and necessary. One-room rural schools are extinct; traditional crafts like rug braiding may be on the same path.

Who has chores? What is egg money? Why hold a barn raising? Does anybody still play sheepshead, polka at wedding dances or make from-scratch pies for bake sales? The answers are here, a nice mix of nostalgia and substance.

•

Chippewa Valley Museum
Carson Park, Eau Claire
www.cvmuseum.com, 715-834-7871

•

Round barn, near Ontario, 1965, photo by Paul Vanderbilt. [Wisconsin Historical Society image no. 29710]

Barn Beauty

If you consider the farm barn to be an ordinary and ho-hum part of Wisconsin's landscape, you're missing a significant symbol of your historical, economic, ethnic and occupational identity, according to **Ruth Olson**.

She is associate director of the **Center for the Study of Upper Midwestern Cultures**, at the University of Wisconsin-Madison. The center emphasizes languages and everyday culture; barns are a pet project.

"Barns really matter to me," the Burnett County native says. "A part of it is growing up on a family farm. I have seen how important the barn is in this state."

Building techniques may showcase precision, as in the tightly constructed log barns that were a mark of their Finnish creators. Or they may be purely practical—bigger hay mows to acknowledge a growth in dairy production.

We have gabled, gambrel and hip roofs, barns made from logs, boards, fieldstone, wood block masonry. There are barns with square stone silos, house barns for both people and animals, barns with porches, barns built into the side of hills. A tobacco barn is a lot different from one to shelter cows—or a sty for pigs.

Ruth's own family's barn is gone. "My brother wrote an obituary for the barn, about how it served three generations," she says. More than 1,000 barns come down each year in Wisconsin, a situation that Ruth considers a big dismantling of cultural heritage.

One of Ruth's goals is to develop a series of driving tour maps, so people can better understand the diversity of Wisconsin barns still standing.

"Wisconsin is full of really decent people, and a lot of it stems from the intimacy of the family farm," Ruth says. "The barns are full of stories and details that I think are worth keeping.

"It is about decency, honesty, developing a strong work ethic and perseverance. Where do you learn to live with animals, where do you learn to feed animals before yourselves? You take care of those who can't take care of themselves.

"This is all about more than decorating a house in a country theme."

•

Center for the Study of Upper Midwestern Cultures, UW-Madison
http://csumc.wisc.edu, 608-262-8180

•

DETOUR

Vernon County has the most standing round barns in the United States (but the total number is unclear; there are eight in the Hillsboro area). Many were built by Algie Shivers, and the design seemed to work well until the late 1920s, when hay was baled into squares instead of being stored loose.

•

The **Cheyenne Valley Heritage Road Tour** plots out Wisconsin's largest rural African-American settlement in the 19th century. The 40-mile tour loop is a project of the Cheyenne Valley Heritage Committee, Hillsboro.

•

Volunteers in **Rusk County** are the first to do a comprehensive survey of barns in Wisconsin. Documentation includes barn style, location, ownership and whether the building is still standing. A goal is to duplicate this documentation statewide.

Three generations of Sun Prairie's William Renk family, 1947, by Angus B. McVicar.

[Wisconsin Historical Society image number 29710]

Famous Dave's BBQ is an American Indian success story with more than 120 restaurants.

Hayward: What Made Dave Famous

One of the coolest American Indian success stories involving Wisconsin tourism has little to do with gaming casinos and the luck of the dice, and much to do with the will to succeed.

"When you set out to be the best, you want to give the best of yourself," says **Dave Anderson**. That hasn't always been easy.

He knows the meaning of failure, bankruptcy, intimidation and stage fright. So he applied himself, looked for mentors and eventually became one himself. Dave has worked hard to become a person who can effectively promote a business, or an idea. "I'd practice reading in front of a mirror two hours a day, shake hands with myself, wink at myself, count and do the ABCs with a lit candle in front of me—learning how to not put it out," he explains. It was part of learning to successfully promote himself, and his business.

What's Dave's story? In the mid-1990s, he opened a barbecue shack—**Famous Dave's**—about nine miles out of Hayward, near a pretty and wooded part of Round Lake. Today, as the founder of a barbeque restaurant empire, he describes himself as one of the largest lake property owners in Sawyer County, with $12 million in lakefront investments.

Dave has become famous, as has his restaurant. By the end of 2005, there were more than 120 of the barbecue stops in 31 states, with development agreements signed

NORTHWEST

for 205 more franchise locations. The total includes the first site, which is part of **Grand Pines Resort**, a getaway that is rustic in appearance and savvy in its marketing.

"At first I'd cater to Beer Belly Joe Fisherman," Dave told the American Indian Alaska Native Tourism Association in 2004. But as the type of customer changed, so did Dave's place.

He introduced Rocktoberfest, with live music on Saturday nights. Then there were Gourmet Getaway Weekends, $600 per couple for two nights in a lakefront cabin that has a fireplace and Jacuzzi, plus a one-day cooking class, cocktail reception, dinner and Sunday brunch.

As an American Indian, he learned "You stay in the background and don't speak until you're spoken to—that's how I was brought up, and that's got to change." He acknowledges the challenges that American Indians face but says it's a cop-out to simply give up.

"We have no one to blame but ourselves," he says, acknowledging the high suicide, alcoholism, drop-out and unemployment rates. "We have young people growing up without hope."

Dave wants his peers and their children "to have a passion about our rich, colorful history and our traditions." Success, he says, is about being the best and being involved.

"I have a dream to be the best of the best," and that motivated him to hand-select every one of the 3,000-plus blues tunes that are played inside of Famous Dave's restaurants, as well as the recipes for barbecue sauces and desserts that have become award winners.

Famous Dave's BBQ Shack, on Big Round Lake in Hayward, served as many as one thousand people per night when it opened in 1994. One year later, he had a second site, in Minneapolis, and the food critics began to take notice.

The rest, as they say, is history. Business today is more sophisticated, as is the training. Ten weeks at Hog Heaven University are required before a "pitmaster" is allowed to prepare ribs at a Famous Dave's. The original restaurant still stands, too, a tribute to the beginning of one man's dream, and success.

In 2004, Dave was appointed assistant secretary of the U.S. Department of the Interior, working in its Bureau of Indian Affairs. He resigned after one year on the job, saying that he preferred to focus his energy on "developing private sector opportunities for Indian entrepreneurs." Famous Dave's appointed him chairman emeritus in 2005, allowing him more latitude to concentrate on this goal.

•

The Original Famous Dave's at Grand Pines Resort
12355 W Richardson Bay Road, Hayward
www.grandpines.com 888-774-2674, 888-774-3023

DETOUR

What else is remote and noteworthy when you're hungry in northern Wisconsin? Check out **Cottage Cafe** in Port Wing, near the state's northern tip, jutting into Lake Superior. The town is known for its Labor Day weekend fish boil. The cafe is known for its berry pies and for having Jolene Anderson as a former waitress. Jolene, a star guard on the UW women's basketball team, was 2005 Big Ten Freshman of the Year. Look for her picture behind the cash register.

Fast Facts

Which is correct: Native American or American Indian? **Bobbi Webster**, public relations director for the **Oneida Nation**, simply shrugs. She is more concerned that non-Indians recognize the individuality—in native dress, language, history and rituals—that each tribe contains. Bobbie predicts that tribal partnerships will increase during the next decade, as all have a similar goal: responsible tourism development that is sensitive to American Indian cultures and the environment. "It will create a positive learning experience but not be an exploitation," she predicts. "We need to protect both our natural resources and our unique differences."

•

Proceeds from the sales of *Backroads & Sidestreets,* a Famous Dave's cookbook, go to The LifeSkills Center for Leadership, which helps Native American youths "design and live a purpose-driven and regret-free life." Dave Anderson founded the Minneapolis-based organization in 2001.

•

A half-hour northeast of Hayward, on Hwy. 77, is the **Clam Lake Lodge**, known for its fine dining in a rustic setting, deep in Chequamegon National Forest. It's an area where deer are about as likely as people to roam the town streets. The lodge and restaurant are open seasonally; reservations recommended.

See **www.clamlakelodge.com** or call **715-794-2518.**

Tribal gaming revenues pay for health clinics, elderly care and schools.

MENOMONIE: EDUCATED GAMBLES

Visits to four reservations comprise a five-night **Northeast Wisconsin Native American Cultural Tour** that is being marketed to Europeans. Around 70,000 people see everything from lacrosse matches to finger weavings, intertribal dances and drum groups at the annual **Indian Summer Festival**, in September on Milwaukee's lakefront festival grounds.

Despite all these noble efforts, American Indians here and nationwide continue to be best known for their casinos. Tribal gaming revenues more than tripled from the 1990s to the first decade of the new millennium and increased 15 percent nationwide from 2003 to 2004, says the National Indian Gaming Commission. The eight-state region that includes Wisconsin was up 6 percent from 2003.

The quick growth suggests "an incredible pent-up demand for casino-style gaming"

Potawatomi Bingo Casino has one of the state's few four-diamond restaurants, Dream Dance.

in the United States, concluded two University of Maryland researchers who studied 20 years of American Indian casino growth and its effects. Ed Hall of the U.S. Bureau of Indian Affairs refers to a Mobil Travel Guide study that observes "a huge audience for a guide to Indian country casinos."

Why not just go to Las Vegas? "Because these are tribal casinos," Ed responds during an American Indian tourism conference in Wisconsin. "A lot of people are inspired by the idea that your casinos are using their money to build or benefit a community."

A big disappointment, he adds, is that casinos typically don't provide much information about the tribe that owns the enterprise. He calls that a missed opportunity.

Go to Casino City online (**www.casinocity.com**), and you'll find more than two dozen places to gamble on American Indian property in Wisconsin. That includes the 78-slot **E & EE Oneida Casino** near Green Bay, **Ho-Chunk's** 2,500 slot machines and 50-plus table games near Wisconsin Dells, Bayfield's **Isle Vista Casino**, and the **Little Turtle Hertel Express** near Webster.

In 2004, travelers spent $646 million wagering in Wisconsin, says the state Department of Tourism. Although that includes dog track bets, too, the overwhelming percentage is from casino gaming.

The profits have lessened poverty and mortality rates on reservations, but American Indians aren't necessarily getting the best-paying jobs. "In many cases, most of the people employed by casinos are not Native Americans," concluded the Maryland researchers, William Evans and Julie Topoleski.

Sharon Giroux says Wisconsin and Minnesota have more than 40 casinos between them. She is not a gambler, but her professional life is all about playing odds, helping her students beat as well as benefit from them

"There is a need to have educated people in the gaming industry," says Sharon, who has developed the **Gaming Entertainment Management** program at the **University of Wisconsin-Stout**. It is a part of the hospitality and tourism department's curriculum.

Completion of the four-course program—plus classes in marketing/sales, accounting, law/liability and hospitality for the handicapped traveler—will earn the student a college minor. The four courses—in gaming management, casino operations, psychosocial issues and casino tourism—also stand alone as a certificate program, for high school grads who are not pursuing a college degree.

UW-Stout and **Native American Tourism of Wisconsin** began a partnership in 2004; Sharon is one of the few non-Indians on NATOW's council.

Her passion for better-educated American Indians in the gaming industry stems from doctoral thesis work. She studied racism, discrimination and shame among Lac du Flambeau youths. The high school dropout rate for these teens was 53 to 73 percent during one decade.

After 50-plus interviews, the professor's 500-page dissertation concluded "intense fear among young people" existed, in part as an aftermath to spearfishing protests of the 1980s and early 1990s. The teens also felt pressure to be true to cultural traditions as well as to conform to a primarily white student school system.

"A shoe on one foot, a moccasin on the other" is how Sharon summed up the situation. "It wasn't a matter of not wanting to go to school," she says, regarding students' decisions to drop out. The attrition rate continues to be high among teens on the Lac du Flambeau reservation.

Although a high school degree is a prerequisite, the UW-Stout program is an attempt to help the state's American Indian population gain a higher level of identity and employment in the fast-growing gaming industry.

•

UW-Stout Hospitality & Tourism Department, Menomonie
www.uwstout.edu, 715-232-1203

Fast Facts

The five-night Native American Cultural Tour, put together for northeastern Wisconsin, includes visits to the Oneida, Menominee, Stockbridge-Munsee Band of Mohicans and Forest County Potawatomi reservations. On the agenda: historical re-enactments, pow wows, interaction with tribal elders. For more, see **www.native-tourism.org, 888-867-3342.**

•

Readers of *Midwest Gaming & Travel* magazine annually select their favorite Native American casinos. Who gets the most nods in the 34 categories (Best Selection of Slot Machines to Best Concert Venue)? In 2005, Milwaukee's Potawatomi casino edged out Ho-Chunk in Wisconsin Dells. Oneida in Green Bay did well in bingo categories, and poker playing at Keshena's Menominee casino was a hit. For more, see **www.midwest-gamingandtravel.com.**

Fred Smith's unusual companions in Phillips. (See next page.)

One way to recycle bottles.

PHILLIPS: SET IN CONCRETE

The astounding artwork of a retired lumberjack and ginseng farmer who could neither read nor write gained a spot on the National Register of Historic Places in 2005.

Fred Smith's Wisconsin Concrete Park hits you like a ton of, well, *concrete* while driving on Highway 13. The ubiquitous collection of 237 sculptures and other objects on 16 acres is the second concrete art environment in the state to gain national status (**Fox Point artist Mary Nohl's** outdoor collection was the first).

In Phillips, art conservators—usually from the Chicago area—are hired to maintain the self-taught sculptor's work, which without intervention would deteriorate because of weather extremes.

In 1977, one year after his death, more than 70 percent of the collection was damaged because of a severe windstorm. Fundraisers and the diligence of volunteers have

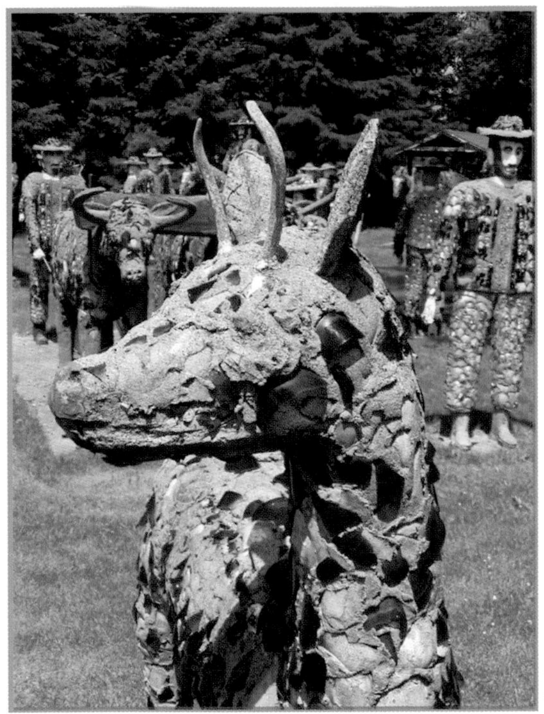

Work began when Fred Smith was 63.

helped stabilize the site, now a public park owned by Price County.

It is a tribute to the ingenuity of a complex man who lived simply and found an effective way to communicate without words. He also was a self-taught fiddler.

Fred Smith didn't begin these sculptures until age 63. A part-time bartender who rarely drank, he shattered a lot of Rhinelander Shorty beer bottles and used the glass shards as embellishments. The same happened to pieces of dishes and other containers, plus wire, stones, antlers, paint and whatever else seemed appropriate.

Some sculptures began as wood skeletons, wrapped in wire and covered with hand-mixed cement. It would not be unusual for the farmer artist to build the big-as-life animals and people in pieces, pouring cement into molds that were dug in the ground. After the cement dried, the forms would be hoisted upright.

"Nobody knows why I made them, not even me," he was quoted as saying. "This work just came to me naturally." It became an obsession, as well as his legacy.

The artist knew but didn't seem to care that some people thought he was crazy and considered his work an eyesore. He wouldn't sell his work or create any on commission.

"I welcome visitors. I like to watch their reactions," he reportedly said. "But I never sell any 'cause it might spoil it for others."

•

Fred Smith's Wisconsin Concrete Park
N8236 S. Hwy. 13, Phillips
www.friendsoffredsmith.org 800-269-4505

Helmi Harrington is a genius on the accordion.

Superior: All About Accordions

Frankie Yankovic and Lawrence Welk would have loved this place, way up in the city of Superior, way down in the basement of a former Presbyterian church.

Here rest about 1,000 accordions, the humble and the complex, the world's most rare models and the more commonplace. There are about 700 more of these instruments upstairs, where the church altar has been converted into a professional concert stage.

A World of Accordions museum opened in 2004, as part of the **Harrington Arts Center**. The facility is unusual because it chronicles the world history of the instrument. Music scholars from as far away as Austria have come to use the museum's archives. Some of the world's finest accordionists have performed in the 1,000-seat concert hall.

It is all the work of **Helmi Harrington**, whose mother made a living by playing, repairing and teaching others how to play the accordion. The two moved to the United States from Germany shortly after World War II and Helmi's birth.

Harrington Arts Center also is the home of the nation's only technical college program for accordion and concertina repair. Helmi came up with the curriculum in 1991 and says a good technician can make as much as a doctor. Her students come from all over the country.

"This is what I've chosen to do with the earnings of my life," she explains, nodding toward the museum's contents. She describes the accordion as both a humble and "exceedingly complex" family of instruments. It also is one that "set forth a dream that took decades to realize, and you're standing in it now."

Helmi, who has a doctorate in musicology and has been a Mensa member, worked her way through school by playing and teaching the accordion, although her intent was to become a concert pianist. She recalls that a gifted classmate at the University of Houston gave her a simple button accordion. It was a mere toy, she thought, especially when placed next to the spotlight of the classmate's grand piano.

The friend's present got Helmi to thinking about how there should be a way to preserve the immense history and cultural connections that the accordion has fostered. "It is the modest, everyday, salt-of-the-earth people who invented the accordion, reinvented it and made it popular," she explains. The instrument was popular because "it could quickly return the ethnic heritage to a culture," providing the tunes and rhythms to dance and celebrate.

The first accordion patent goes back to 1829.

Helmi's collection has been carefully built—"everything is here for a purpose," the curator says. She patiently explains how the instrument evolved from a simple push-pull of bellows to an elaborate collage of scales, keys and pitches. Some accordion makers added bells and horns. Others put the music on rollers, like a player piano, to make the music-making look easy.

Then there is the Pigini Mythos, a $65,000 instrument that wasn't sold to just anyone. "You'd have to prove that you could play before you could buy it," Helmi says.

Accordion ornamentation can be elaborate, with detailed carvings, etchings, rhinestones, abalone. Keyboards became curved, or were moved to the center, as manufacturers became more competitive during the height of vaudeville. Eventually there was mass production and sales through Sears and Roebuck catalogs. Now a mere half-dozen accordion manufacturers remain.

The Superior museum contains examples of all of this, as well as figurines of accordionists and artwork made by the musicians. There also is a small collection of accordion humor. "Yes, we can laugh at ourselves," Helmi says.

She keeps 20 to 25 accordions for herself, "when I want to feed my soul," and gives accordion lessons from her home studio. She is thankful that the instrument has a big following in northern Wisconsin.

"It's a fine place to be," she says, but her work is not finished. Helmi notes that Castlefidardo, Italy, has the world's largest accordion museum. "We're going to fight that," she says matter-of-factly.

•

A World of Accordions, 1401 Belknap St., Superior
www.accordionworld.org 715-395-2787

More than 1,000 of the world's most simple to complex accordions have a Superior home.

Fast Facts

The accordion concert hall is named after Hanni Strahl, "The Accordion Lady of Texas" and Helmi Harrington's mother. "I have often thought about what this woman, my mother, valued in life; there were no 'secrets' of success," she writes. "Hers was an uncomplicated formula: Turn everything into an advantage, conserve resources, waste nothing, save for the future, know who are your friends, and remain true to self."

Mother and daughter in 1949 escaped to Texas from war-destroyed Cologne, Germany. "She had seen her home and homeland destroyed, and watched her family and friends die by starvation, bombs and Nazis," Helmi says. "She expected no golden path in the New World, and was not afforded one, but was grateful to be allowed to work diligently and to achieve an honorable lifestyle" by teaching accordion lessons and doing instrument repairs.

•

Ovations

A World of Accordions earned a **GEMmy Award** from the Midwest Travel Writers Association in 2005. The honor goes to destinations that are lesser-known gems because of their uniqueness and the potential to experience another culture or tradition.

Other MTWA GEMmy Award recipients in Wisconsin are the **EAA AirVenture Museum**, Oshkosh; **Heritage Hill Living History Museum**, Green Bay; **Fox Cities Children's Museum**, Appleton; **Little Norway**, Blue Mounds; **Wisconsin Veterans Museum**, Madison; **The Fireside**, Fort Atkinson; **H.H. Bennett Studio**, Wisconsin Dells; and **Bayfield Heritage Tours**, Bayfield.

•

Wisconsin loves to polka and has a **Polka Hall of Fame** (awards and artifacts are in the Chandelier Ballroom, Hartford).

See **www.wisconsinpolkamusic.com** for more about the bands and festivals that give the state its oommpah!

Cranberry Discovery Center is part museum, part gift shop.

WARRENS: BERRY BUSINESS

The fruit that plays a bit part at Thanksgiving dinner has a bigger role as the star of a highway route, tours and festivals that have become high-profile. Wisconsin, long known as the Dairy State, can boast about cranberries, too.

The modest berry is one of the few that is native to North America, and Wisconsin produces more than any other state—about half of the nation's supply. The cranberry also has given the people of Warrens, population 300 and near Tomah, a reason to celebrate for more than 30 years. And the party keeps getting bigger.

The **Warrens Cranberry Festival** is the world's largest such event, fattening the town with about 100,000 visitors every September. **Carolyn Habelman** has been involved since the beginning.

"We sat around trying to decide how to raise money to build a fire station. We had nothing to have a festival about," she recalls. "Instead of another fish fry, we came up with this, because nobody else was really doing it." The timing was good: When the festival began, cranberries were becoming more than just a sauce for holiday meals.

The results have been impressive. Festival proceeds have helped build a town hall, ballpark and fire station during the past three decades. "We put in a $50,000 computer lab in our elementary school," Carolyn says. "How many towns our size have that?"

Now leaders in other small towns consult her about their festivals. Carolyn says it's important to involve younger generations, develop a sense of community pride, aim high with goals and keep trying new ideas.

The American Bus Association has ranked the Warrens festival—more than once—as one of the top 100 in the nation. So word gets around: Commercial bus tours—about 170 of them, from Kansas to Ohio—will make Warrens their destination in autumn. Some entries for the festival contests, such as best scarecrow or best cranberry hat/cap, "will come from the other side of the state—like Green Bay—places where they don't even know what a cranberry marsh looks like," Carolyn contends.

The three-mile stretch for the arts/crafts/flea/farm market will have vendors from at least two dozen states. Festival food will include cranberry pancakes, cranberry cream puffs and chocolate-covered cranberries—but not cranberry pizza. "We tried that one year, and probably should have used a crepe as the crust instead of pizza dough."

Cranberries, and the festival, have helped keep Warrens alive. "We were a lumber town, but when that industry moved out in 1898, people realized the soil was too sandy for most kinds of farming," Carolyn says. "Then the Depression hit, and we began to die."

A native of Washington, D.C., she and husband Robert moved to Warrens in 1948. He is a part of **Habelman Brothers Company**, a family business that has produced cranberries since 1906. The berries go to Ocean Spray's receiving station in Tomah.

"All these Wisconsin cranberries go into a bag with a Massachusetts corporate address on it," Carolyn says, bluntly. The biggest festival irritation, she acknowledges, is lack of parking and the slow crawl of traffic into town on County EW (these last three miles can take an hour).

•

Warrens Cranberry Festival
www.cranfest.com, 608-378-4200

Cranberries fit any meal.

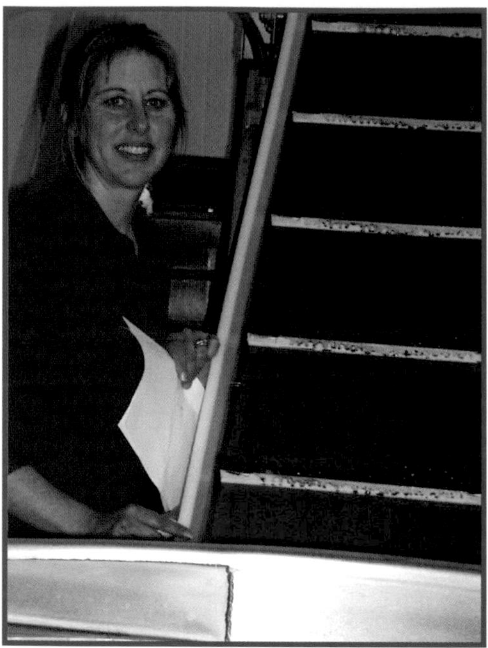
Cheryl Urban has a patent on a berry good process.

Urban Processing

Cheryl Urban's family used to just grow cranberries. Then they figured out how to dry and sweeten them naturally. Now she has a line of products, pancake syrup to trail mix, that simply keeps growing.

She passes over a cardboard box, and the chocolate candies in it look and taste like turtles, only denser because of the addition of dried cranberries to the caramel and nuts. One version has cashews. Another has pecans. All the candy needs is a name and the right packaging.

Urban Processing and its Urban Best line of cranberry products are an extension of **Bassuener Cranberry Company**, Wisconsin Rapids, which Cheryl's parents established after a land swap in the 1980s.

"When the cranberry industry pricing went down the tubes in the late '90s, we started to wonder what we could do with the berries ourselves," instead of being at the mercy of the market price for the raw fruit, recalls Cheryl, a former airport manager. "My son wanted to stay on the marsh, to work it. So we wanted to make this succeed, for him and as a family."

After much research and testing, a process was found and patented to sweeten and dry the berries, "similar to how I was doing it on my kitchen stove—only in massive quantities," she says. "It was a big risk. The process hadn't been proven when we took a big leap of faith."

The first batches of the dried berries were produced in 2001, the processing was refined "and we've been running ever since." It is a primary product, not a by-product of cranberry juice, and Cheryl says that's a part of what makes it superior to others on the market.

The goal was to sell 25-pound boxes of the kosher-certified dried berries to ingre-

Wisconsin produces about half of the nation's cranberries.

dient companies, and that was a challenge because Urban Processing had to find its way into the marketplace, then prove that product quality would be consistent.

As this was happening, a plant employee was putting partly dried cranberries on Twinkies during her lunch break. "This is good," she told her boss. "You should put it in a bottle."

That's the start of how sweet cranberry topping/filling became the next product. "This has been a collective effort," says **Steve Berlyn**, the company's CFO (and an outdoorsman who appreciates a good trail mix).

"So we came up with two kinds—manly and frou-frou," Cheryl says, laughing. "Because we are a small business, we can react fast to our customers' requests."

Gourmet Trail Mix has dried pineapple pieces and white chocolate. Outdoor Trail Mix has choc-o-buttons and almonds. Both have peanuts and the dried berries.

The berries also have been coated with white to dark chocolate, made into jelly, added to almond bark candy and a toffee crunch. There are product assortment trays and gourmet gift baskets, too.

Urban Processing is not open for tours, but its products are sold by many local retailers.

•

Urban Processing, 6011 Washington St., Wisconsin Rapids
www.cranberryproducts.com 715-423-5200

Fast Facts

Pittsville High School has the nation's only cranberry science class. During the fall cranberry harvest, the school's Future Farmers of America members give in-depth tours of cranberry harvest/production.

•

Wisconsin's **Cranberry Highway** map includes scenic routes for bicycling (24 miles) and self-drive (50 miles) tours in the Wisconsin Rapids area. There also is an optional, 17-mile loop route for viewing wildlife by bike or car. For more: **www.visitwisrapids.com, 800-554-4484.**

•

The Wisconsin Cranberry Discovery Center, Warrens, is a museum, gift shop, bakery and taste test kitchen. Go to **www.discovercranberries.com** or call **608-378-4878** for recipes such as this one:

Cranberry Salsa

1 cup fresh cranberries
Juice of 1/2 orange
1/3 cup sugar
2 red bell peppers, roasted, peeled, seeded and diced
3 tablespoons chopped cilantro
2 tablespoons toasted pecans, chopped
Zest of 1/2 lime
Pinch of salt

Blend cranberries, orange juice and sugar for 30 to 45 seconds in a food processor. Transfer to a mixing bowl and add remaining ingredients. Let salsa sit for 30 minutes or longer before serving.

You may have unusual winged visitors at the Stone Cottage.

Wisconsin Rapids: Timeless Pleasures

During a stay at **Phil** and **Mary Brazeau Brown's Stone Cottage**, on their **Glacial Lake Cranberries** estate, we were glad to cross paths with **George Archibald**, co-founder of the **International Crane Foundation** near Baraboo. George and friends were bird watching; the Browns alerted them to an unusual species spotted on their marsh earlier that day.

It was a glossy ibis and a rare visitor to Wisconsin, George decided, after seeing the creature. It was dark and long-necked, about 20 inches tall, with a slender and curved beak. The more likely habitat? Florida wetlands, we were told. Why here? Maybe it got off course because of hurricanes, speculated our enthusiastic ornithologist, also recognized as a world expert on cranes.

George likes visiting this part of Wisconsin because of its rich avian mix. That is particularly true during early fall, as bogs are flooded for the colorful cranberry harvest. Mary, who captured the ibis on her camera, knew the bird wouldn't be around long. "It will readjust and head home," she predicted. "It's like they have an internal GPS."

Watching birds and observing the natural world are timeless pleasures, easy to savor in a place that appreciates a slower pace. For another example, head a few miles northeast, to the **Little Pink Restaurant**, a few blocks from the Storo Enso paper plant,

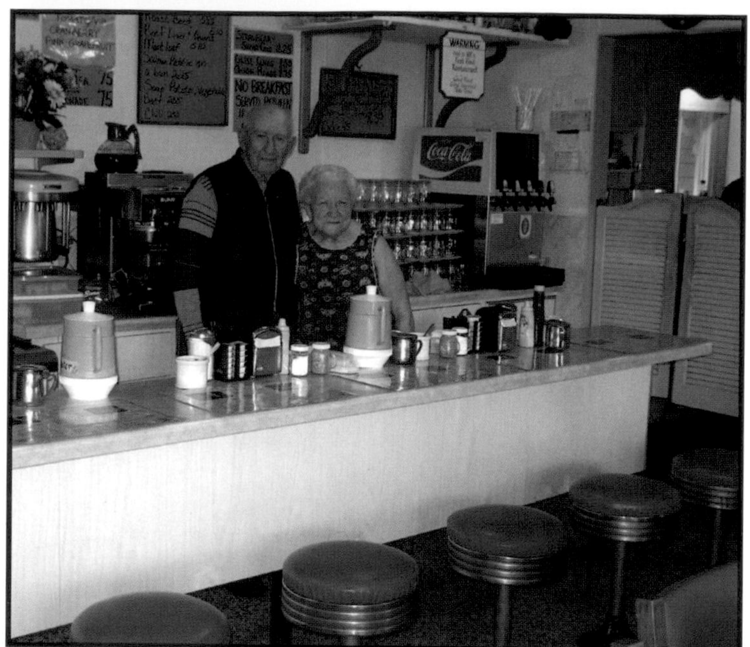

Melvin and Helen Ponczoch: It's all rosy at their restaurant.

where you'll find homemade bread and old-fashioned prices. **Melvin** and **Helen Ponczoch**, who have been married since 1942, still run the show.

For Helen, that includes baking a dozen giant loaves of bread each weekday. Get a slice with an egg for $1.75, or buy a whole loaf for $3.50. On Fridays, she makes cinnamon rolls, too, and you're advised to call ahead with your order. They go quickly.

"Do you ever go behind the counter?" Melvin is asked. "Never," he deadpans. "Helen won't let me get around the money." It's not unusual for her to arrive at the Little Pink, as the locals call it, by 3 a.m. to get a start on the day.

The restaurant, once you're in the neighborhood, is easy to spot. Just look for the brightest pink building that you've ever seen. It's open for breakfast and lunch on weekdays.

•

Glacial Lake Cranberries, 2480 Highway D, Wisconsin Rapids
www.cranberrylink.com, 715-887-2095

•

Little Pink Restaurant, 910 Dura Beauty Lane,
Wisconsin Rapids, 715-421-1210

DETOURS

Hungry for more? **Herschleb's** has been around since 1939, serving cherry phosphates and ice cream floats from its old-time soda fountain. Proprietors make their own ice cream and know how to use cranberries multiple ways in desserts. Burgers and plate dinners are served, too. It's near downtown Wisconsin Rapids, at 640 16th St. North.

•

Head north a bit, to Rudolph, for a quick taste of cheesemaking, something that's been an enduring craft in the Dairy State. **Dairy Cheese Company** on Highway 34 sells fresh squeaky curds—plain or flavored with herbs and spices. Climb a short flight of stairs and peer down on huge vats of cheese being made, or watch a movie about cheesemaking. Under glass, in cabinets downstairs, is a collection of antique covered platters for serving cheese and butter.

•

Another example of endurance: the **Rudolph Grotto Gardens and Wonder Cave**, the amazing and intricate work of **Father Phillip J. Wagner**. In 1928, he began construction of the first in this series of mini shrines—a way to show thanks for his answered prayers for improved health.

Butterfly weed is an enduring native species.

(next page) A light blanket of snow creates a maze of aerial patterns.

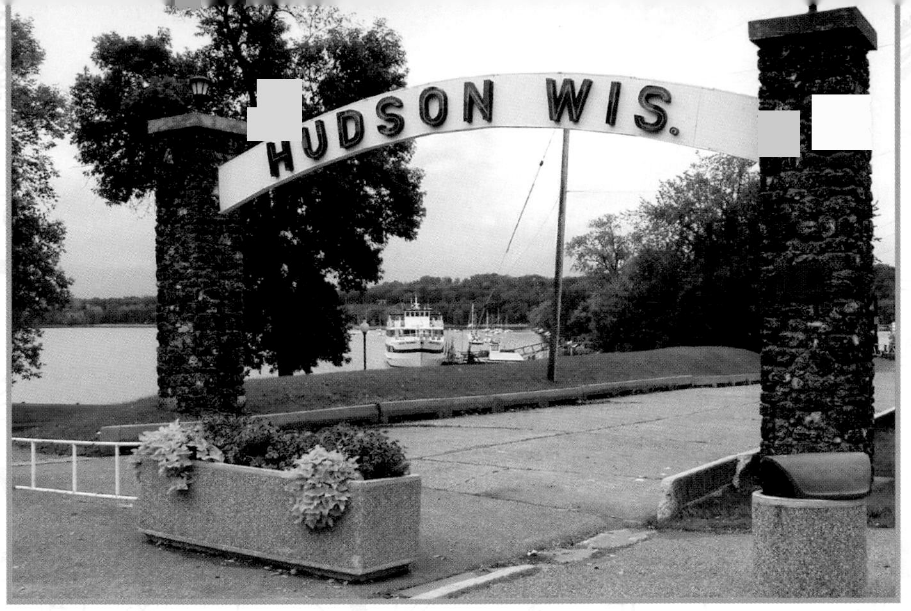

The St. Croix River has lulled and lured Hudson visitors.

Hudson Road Trip • Day 1

Hudson, on the St. Croix River and off I-94, is a charming community with an eclectic downtown that is experiencing a renaissance. Most downtown retail shops are operated by women, some who are Minneapolis transplants, and they are here partly because the cost of doing business in Hudson is far less than it is on Grand Avenue.

Minnesota Monthly magazine has praised Hudson and nearby Stillwater, Minn., as "the other Twin Cities," because of their rich character and potential to interest visitors.

1. Charge! **Grapevine Interiors, Et Cetera, Coco Bello, House Calls, La Rue Marché** and **Lavender Thymes**—all within two blocks on Second Street (Highway 35 North exit, off I-94)—are but a handful of examples of this growth spurt. Just park the car and stroll. Get a chocolate fix at little **Knoke's Chocolates**, 216 Locust St. (off Second), whose products are handcrafted.

2. Lunch Break. A fine lunch choice is **San Pedro Café**, 426 Second St., but not only if you crave spicy meats, *Rasta Pasta* or conch/corn chowder. Lobster enchiladas and brick oven pizzas stretch the menu in other directions, too. For appetizers, try Jerk Walleye Cheeks, pan fried. **www.sanpedrocafe.com, 715-386-4003**.

3. Gorge-ous views. **Willow River State Park** (5 miles northeast of Hudson; north on Highway 35, right on St. Croix Street, to Highway A) has hiking trails that overlook the St. Croix River Valley. Waterfalls, a beach, Willow River gorge and Little Falls Lake make it a full afternoon. (There is sledding and cross country skiing in winter.) **715-386-5931.**

4. Artful Meditations. **Hudson Hospital**, 405 Stageline Road (Highway A to Highway U, then I-94 West to Carmichael exit, left on Carmichael, left on Stageline), has an outdoor labyrinth, conducive to inner rejuvenation and surrounded by gardens and outdoor sculptures. The building also houses a growing, dynamic and varied art collection. Free public tours can be scheduled. **www.hudsonhospital.org, 715-531-6000.**

5. Return downtown to **Winzer Stube**, 516 Second St. (back to I-94 West, to Highway 35 North exit), whose specialty is German food from the Mosel, Rhein and Alsace regions. A specialty is marinated herring in sour cream, with onions and apples (an appetizer). The house band performs on the first Saturday of the month. **715-381-5092.**

6. Celeb support. Actress **Linda Kelsey** makes her home in Hudson and is a solid supporter of the **Phipps Center for the Arts**, 109 Locust St. (off Second), It is near the river and the hub of theater for the city. **www.thephipps.org, 715-386-2305.**

7. Sleep Tight. The **Phipps Inn**, 1005 Third St. (Second north, right on Myrtle Street one block), is a magnificent 1884 Queen Anne B&B, on the National Register of Historic Places and part of the city's historic district. Each suite has a fireplace and double whirlpool bath. Expect a four-course breakfast. **www.phippsinn.com, 888-865-9388.**

Day 2

8. Coffee Break. Before heading home, or to the Twin Cities, catch a cup of coffee (and maybe a slice of pie—who cares if it's 10 a.m.?) at **Dibbo's Café**, 517 Second St. A delightful diner, around since the 1950s, with an area in the back that became a hot nightclub with live music in the 1970s. **www.dibbos.com, 715-386-2782.**

9. Time for Lunch? Consider the hubcap chicken dinner at **Dick's Bar and Grill**, 111 Walnut St. (off Second). The dinnerware is just like it sounds. A live music venue, too. **715-386-5222.**

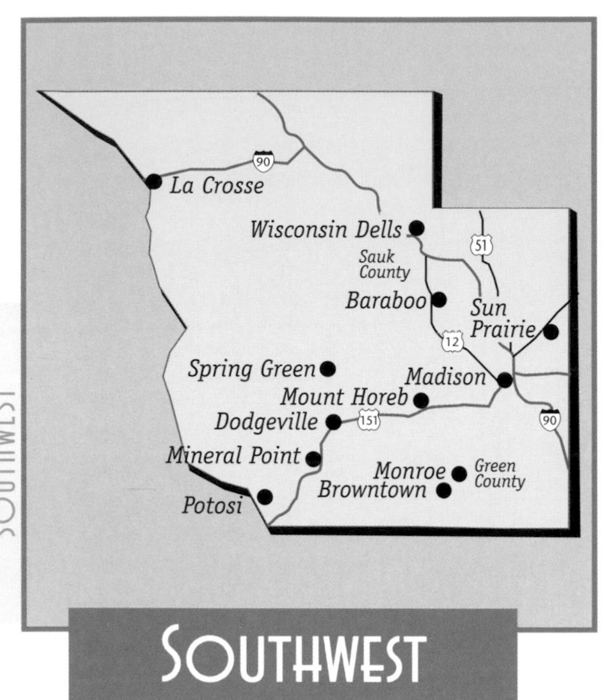

SOUTHWEST

Observation: Creative talent gets expressed in many ways, from music to mustard.

An old Cornish mining camp is transformed into an earthy and vibrant arts community. Risk takers turn a horse farm into an internationally known haven for cranes. A creative class of artists, dreamers and entrepreneurs express themselves with wacky lyrics, or a mustard museum, or a cheese that is a hit on both coasts.

(previous page) The glistening Wisconsin River.

BARABOO: SAVING CRANES

White-naped cranes are increasingly rare in their native eastern Asia due to habitat loss.

They call this strong and graceful bird a great ambassador, both for its own species and for generic conservation efforts. But that is not enough to make the work easy.

There are 15 types of cranes in this world—11 are vulnerable to extinction—and each is at the **International Crane Foundation**, on 225 acres off Highway 12, in Sauk County. Since its birth in 1973, ICF's work has ranged from the successful breeding of cranes in captivity to global efforts that enhance and protect their environment.

"Cranes are charismatic," explains **George Archibald**, co-founder of the organization with **Ron Sauey**, who died in 1987 at age 39. They met at Cornell University during their study of crane behavior.

"People think cranes are cool," agrees **Jeb Barzen**, ICF director of field biology. "It's that way wherever you go—people look at cranes and see value."

That attitude has been helpful as foundation staff and others work as far away as India and Russia to secure flyway space—a safe migration corridor—for Siberian cranes, the most endangered in the world. The effort—all to help reintroduce Siberian cranes to the area—requires the cooperation of countries that have been preoccupied with war. The list includes Pakistan and Afghanistan.

Black crowned cranes, the national bird of Nigeria, strut their stuff.

This is not George's only globally challenging project. Trips to Korea, for example, are efforts to strengthen conservation efforts in the country's demilitarized zone.

The area "is a wonderful refuge for cranes, but it's not really a protected area," he notes. "It's only protected because of the political tension" between North and South Korea.

Or, as Jeb describes it, "this has been a de facto conservation area since the Korean War. There is no agriculture. There are no people living here."

George's goal is for the ICF, the DMZ Forum (a group that wants the DMZ to become a World Peace Park and environmental laboratory) and the Koreans to bring the United Nations a proposal to develop a conservation management plan for the DMZ.

"It will be a long process" that can't be rushed, he predicts.

It's one thing to be interested in wildlife, and another to devote a facility, a worldwide effort or your life to the survival of a species.

"The cranes are just a passport in this complex world," George says of the Earth's oldest living family of birds. "If you concentrate on one particular thing, and do that well, you have to understand many other things, like fund-raising, cultural diversity and the sensitivities of international situations." Regardless of where the ICF makes its presence known, "we are kindred spirits" who are conservationists and do not wish to be political.

"Most people are like you and me," George says. "We have our role, our job." Although he remains a key player in global projects and works full time for the foundation, he stepped down in 2003 as chairman of the board and in 2000 as director.

The ICF has grown from being a no-budget entity on 40 acres, operated by volunteers, to having an annual operating budget of about $5 million and a staff of about 50 (with about 20 of these in other nations). The ICF headquarters has matured to include about 200 species of plants and 200 types of birds on about 150 acres of restored prairie, oak savanna, wetlands and forests. More than 100 people volunteer as crane caretakers, "chick parents," office workers and tour guides.

"It is a place for cranes, as well as other species that are declining," says Jeb, who includes the grasshopper sparrow, meadowlark and jumping mouse in this category.

When the ICF effort began in 1973, much of the world was closed off by the Iron Curtain, which meant "much of the world where the cranes were was closed off," Jeb explains. "There was a huge void of information, and a huge peril to the species."

The ICF is in Wisconsin because founder Ron Sauey's parents had a horse farm near Baraboo, and they were willing to let horse pens be converted to crane pens.

"People in this part of the world should feel proud that they have created an environment in which cranes can grow," George says, noting that most of the ICF's donations come from Wisconsin residents. "We have the values to support something like the Crane Foundation here. It represents healing and international goodwill at a time when some of the other efforts coming out of the United States certainly are not doing that."

A native of Canada, George says a critical point for the foundation came in 1978, when 16 cranes died of a herpes-like liver virus and "we thought our whole flock was contaminated." About 120 of the birds were on the ICF grounds at that time; eventually the virus was isolated, analyzed and eradicated.

There have been no major health alarms for the birds since that time, but Jeb is well aware of how well-meaning humans can affect the cranes' environment and health adversely. For example, the ICF has about 25,000 visitors per year, and for many it is a powerful experience. But double that total and "it would be a disaster to the site," he says. So this is a tiny part of the world where bigger attendance is not necessarily better for the cause.

The International Crane Foundation is working on a 10 year plan that includes improving the public facilities at its Baraboo headquarters.

"We hope to construct new bird exhibits, increase educational signage, add more outdoor crane art, and build a new educational facility," says **Ann Burke**, director of public relations. "We hope these plans will increase the number of visitors to our site."

Given its remote location, Ann says she doesn't believe that having too many visitors will ever be a problem. "If anything, we struggle to get people to visit."

•

International Crane Foundation, E11376 Shady Lane Road, Baraboo
www.savingcranes.org, 608-356-9462

Wild sandhill cranes search for frogs and invertebrates for lunch.

Fast Facts

Humans are the cranes' most dangerous predator. A dozen U.S. states have a sandhill crane hunting season. In other parts of the world, other types of cranes are hunted for food or sport.

•

Crane chicks—called colts—can grow up to one inch per day, or five feet in three months. The birds typically live 20 to 30 years when in the wild, or up to 80 years when in captivity.

•

About 100 of the 225 crane foundation's acres are restored prairie and oak savannah.

•

Tex—a whooping crane that laid her first fertile egg in 1981, after George Archibald's courtship dances with the bird enticed her to mate—died in 1982, after raccoons chewed through netting on the crane pens. Now electric wires on the top of the pen fences protect the birds from predators. Fences also extend two feet below ground, to prevent animals from digging underneath.

•

BROWNTOWN: SIMPLIFIED LIVING

John, Lisa, and Liam enjoy the simple life.

Lisa **Kivirist** and **John Ivanko** are taking the clutter out of their lives, but that hasn't made life simple. Nor is that their goal. What is clutter? It is things that take time, energy and resources away from personal priorities. The priorities, in this case, include a desire to conserve energy, preserve the environment, lessen stress and reconnect with people they cherish.

"Clutter stems from consumption of stuff and time: overcommitted social and volunteer calendars; overbuying shampoo and winter sweaters; more ornaments than fit on the Christmas tree." That's from the couple's book, *Rural Renaissance: Renewing the Quest for the Good Life*, (2004, New Society Publishers).

In 1996, they gave up jobs with a Chicago ad agency to buy a farmhouse on 5.5 acres between Monroe and the state line. Now they operate a laid-back bed and breakfast, **Inn Serendipity**, host workshops about renewable energy, and work to advocate responsible and sustainable lifestyle choices.

Their property is full of projects to decrease energy use, and they are key players in a network that encourages others to do the same.

"While our schedule today may be busy, it is a different—we'd argue healthier and more fulfilling—pace than we found in the corporate world," Lisa says. "We set our own schedule and work when we're most productive. We have consciously decluttered our lives, which has made a tremendous difference in freeing up our time and focus for projects we feel are important."

There no longer is a commute to work, so there is time to make homemade salsa and organize family reunions. There is no need for a business wardrobe, so there are

This B&B is laid back and understated.

resources to invest in energy projects that will save both money and the planet.

The family, which includes son Liam, has a television, but it's deliberately in an inconvenient location. The couple grow about 70 percent of the food they eat and have learned to preserve it several ways, from canning to freezing. They waste little, and for home projects they are the proud scavengers of doors, windows—whatever—that others discard.

"It doesn't make sense to save preserved fruits and vegetables for more than a year, so we try to eat through everything from last season," states a part of "Rural Renaissance." "Sometimes this 'use it up' mentality provides midwinter indulgences. We have a reason to break open the chocolate truffles someone gave us as a holiday gift....By the time spring rolls around, our cabinets have breathing room and we feel a bit lighter ourselves."

Lisa calls their farm—and the Inn Serendipity Bed and Breakfast—eclectic. "It's a philosophical place," she says. "Guests can experience a slice of our lives. We tend to attract people with the same values."

B&B revenue makes up about one-third of the family income. John also is a professional photographer and author of children's books. Lisa is a professional speaker and author. The two also co-founded the **Rural Renaissance Network**, which provides educational resources and information about sustainable living, through **Renewing the Countryside**, a nonprofit organization.

Inn Serendipity has been a stop on the recent National Solar Tour of Homes. It is an evolving project, one that has drawn national attention because of its alternative energy sources: solar hot water heating, photovoltaic system (it makes electricity from sunlight), wind turbine, EPA-certified woodstove (used for heat).

"We didn't have a huge master plan," Lisa says, about their mindset in 1996. "We just wanted to live on a farm. But by the time we got our solar hot water system in place, we were hooked. We started meeting other people who had projects; we began going to energy fairs. Funny how it happened. Once you start talking about what you want to do, the right mentors start entering your life."

A 1997 *Newsweek* story about "a new Yuppie class—Young Unhappy Professionals . . . sick of selling out but too high-powered to drop out" included this couple's story of transition. Inn Serendipity "reflects our philosophy that work and play should blend," Lisa told the magazine.

Too many cucumbers in the garden? Here is an Inn Serendipity recipe for turning them into a splendid summer soup:

Tasty Cucumber Soup

6 large cucumbers
3 medium onions
1 1/2 sticks butter (3/4 cup)
3 cups chicken or veggie broth
1 teaspoon salt
Pepper, to taste

Peel and de-seed cucumbers. Shred cucumbers and onion (easy, in a food processor). Sauté in butter until slightly brown. Blend in food processor. (If you're freezing it, freeze the "soup pulp" at this stage and add remaining ingredients before serving). Add broth, salt and pepper. Bring to boil. Serve hot.

That goal has only been reinforced with the passage of time.

Inn Serendipity was recognized as one of the "Top 10 Eco-destinations in North America" by *Natural Home & Garden* in 2005. Its proprietors received the 2004 Energy Star Small Business Network Award from the Environmental Protection Agency.

Another venture is **Inn Serendipity Woods**, a 30-acre wildlife sanctuary in **Vernon County** (near Hillsboro.) It has a simply furnished cabin that can accommodate six people overnight in its two bedrooms and sleeping loft. There is a fireplace, wrap-around porch and large kitchen. Open seasonally.

•

Inn Serendipity, 7843 Hwy. P, Browntown
www.innserendipity.com, 608-329-7056

Mike Gingrich with Pleasant Ridge Reserve—you, too, can own a Best of Show.

DODGEVILLE: Artisanal Cheese

A cheese that retails for $18 to $25 per pound—highly acclaimed and selling fast—is being produced by business partners who know how to challenge assumptions. The cheese is not pasteurized, it is made in small batches, and it comes from the milk of cows whose diet is 75 to 80 percent live grasses.

The product—Pleasant Ridge Reserve—earned Best of Show honors, out of 684 entries, at the 2003 U.S. Championship Cheese Contest. It was the American Cheese Society's Best of Show in 2001, after its first year of commercial sales, and again in 2005.

The producer is **Uplands Cheese Company**, headed by **Mike** and **Carol Gingrich,** and **Dan** and **Jeanne Patenaude**—couples who got to know each other because their children attended the same school.

Uplands follows a rotational grazing method of farming. About 270 acres of grassland (red clover, orchard grass and wild grasses) are split into 19 fields; about 200 head of cattle graze in a different pasture every day or two. The goal is to always provide grazing grasses of optimal height, 8 to 12 inches. That is when it is the most nutritious.

"In Europe, it's common knowledge that the best milk—that with the best flavor

—comes in spring, when the grass is new," Mike explains. Taller grasses aren't as palatable to the cows. Shorter aren't as nutritious. Baled hay is not as fresh.

"Once cut, flavors oxidize," he says. "It's important that they eat the live plant."

The best grasses at Uplands are the first grass of spring, the "full flowering of the meadows" (about four weeks later), and the second growth of grass that comes with fall rains. Up to 75 wheels of cheese, each weighing 10 pounds, can be made from a day's milk. When grazing is not possible, the Uplands cows get a diet of about 10 percent grasses and 90 percent grains/silage. That means their milk, although certainly acceptable for sale, does not meet the standard for Pleasant Ridge Reserve cheese production.

"So we made less than 20,000 pounds of cheese in 2003, about two-thirds of what we'd usually make," Mike says, acknowledging the effects of drought that year, which knocked out two months of cheese production. "We wanted to increase production by 50 percent."

The recipe for Pleasant Ridge Reserve is based on the Beaufort, a raw milk cheese that comes from cows that graze Alpine pastures in a specific part of France. Uplands couldn't duplicate that setting in Wisconsin, but University of Wisconsin researcher Bob Lindsay developed a formula and standards that are similar.

Thirty-two wheels of cheese—eight variations and each aged differently—were tasted before the farmers decided upon the winning formula.

Bob Wills, owner of **Cedar Grove Cheese,** near **Plain**, also got involved early. Mike, a licensed cheesemaker, uses Bob's factory to make the cheese.

"We'll drive behind the milk truck and make the cheese the same day that the milk arrives at the factory," Mike says. The next day, the cheese is taken to Spring Green for storage, until it is ready to be sold.

Each wheel of cheese is washed with brine daily during the first six weeks. As it ages more, the wheels are washed only every five days. The product is sold in three categories, based on the cheese's age: 4-8 months is "new," 8-12 months is "aged," 12-18 months is "extra aged."

The U.S. dairy industry "grew up differently" from Europe's, Mike and Dan contend. Large-scale cheese producers do not reward farmers for "doing it differently," Mike says. Although there are production standards, payment is based on quantity. As Dan sees it, a farmer's capital is judged more important than his ingenuity: "It is hard to retain talent in the industry, and there is no body of knowledge to draw from," to creatively manage "what nature gives us."

He and Mike take issue with the notion that "unpasteurized" means "unsafe."

"Pasteurization changes the flavor, kills the flavor potential of milk," Mike says, noting that the Food and Drug Administration has tried to eliminate the production of unpasteurized cheese. He also says the word "pasteurized" can give consumers false confidence about a product.

Mike used to operate a farm near Lone Rock and before that worked for Xerox in California. Work as a cheesemaker began in 1997. Dan has been a farmer during most of his life.

The Uplands partnership is an acknowledgement that it's not enough to farm with a small number of cows. The choices are to increase the size of the herd or come up with a way to specialize.

"Farming can be a hard life," Dan says. "We thought we could prove that we could make a good living with this scale of farm."

Mike notes that the average cheese consumption per person has increased, and that the specialty cheese market is growing faster than commodity cheeses. "There's a small group of consumers who want what they've tasted in Europe and are willing to pay a premium price for it," he observes.

•

Uplands Cheese Company, Hwy. Z, Dodgeville
www.uplandscheese.com, 888-935-5558

Wheels of cheese are aged to perfection.

Cheese Wiz

Pleasant Ridge Reserve has drawn the attention of chefs at some of the nation's finest restaurants.

The cheese plate at Alice Waters' Chez Panisse in Berkeley—called the best restaurant in America by *Gourmet* magazine in 2001—often includes Pleasant Ridge Reserve.

The cheese buyer at New York City's DANIEL restaurant—"There is no food in France better than what you'll find at DANIEL," says *The New York Times*—has selected 26 wheels of the cheese, each 10 pounds, for custom aging.

"Our fromager, Pascal Vittu, assures me that we absolutely order and use Pleasant Ridge Reserve cheese," says **Gail Simmons**. It is a part of DANIEL's cheese plate.

"Pascal says this is not a cheese he would want to cook with, as it is too good," Gail Simmons explains. "It is meant to be eaten on its own or with an exceptional wine."

Order a sandwich with cheese at the Savoy restaurant in Soho, and it also may contain the Dodgeville artisan cheese. Chef-owner Peter Hoffman says he put Pleasant Ridge on the menu after sampling it at a small gourmet cheese store in Greenwich Village.

"We are committed to cooking with local, seasonal and specialty products," he says. "This is a great cheese."

When author Laura Werlin of California was at **L'Etoile** restaurant in **Madison**, to rave about the quality of artisan cheeses in the United States, Pleasant Ridge Reserve got accolades. In her "All-American Cheese and Wine Book," she describes the semi-hard cheese as having "astoundingly deep, somewhat musty flavors, but at the same time it has a pleasant floral quality."

•

Follow the Factories

Although Uplands Cheese Company accepts online orders for its cheese, the business is a working farm with no tours or gift shop.

To get a free copy of "A Taster's Guide to Wisconsin: A Guide to Wisconsin Cheese, Beer and Wine," see **www.wisdairy.com** or call 608-836-8820. More than 100 places to visit are described and located on a state map.

GranQueso tops the Roth Kase line of Hispanic cheeses.

SOUTHWEST

MONROE: SAY "QUESO"

Wisconsin has quietly become a leader in the Hispanic cheese market, both in quantity and quality. It is in response to the nation's growing Latino population, as well as a non-Latino interest in becoming better acquainted with foods from other cultures.

The Wisconsin Milk Marketing Board provides these statistics:

• Twenty of the 46 plants that were making Hispanic cheeses in the nation in 2005 are in Wisconsin.

• Wisconsin produced 382 million pounds of Hispanic cheeses in 2004, which was 27 percent of the market nationwide.

• The amount of Hispanic cheese made in Wisconsin in 2004 was up 10 percent from 2003. It was more than twice of that produced in 1997.

Regarding quality: The GranQueso, similar to a Spanish manchego, has won national and world recognition for **Monroe's Roth Kase USA**. The firm and sharp, handcrafted cheese topped the fresh, unripened Hispanic cheese category in 2005 American Cheese Society competition. GranQueso also earned a gold during the 2005 World Cheese Awards in London.

The cheese, which costs about $9-10 per pound and can be purchased at the Monroe factory, has multiple recommended uses. It can be shredded onto a salad, melted in an omelet, matched with wheat beer as a snack.

GranQueso is one of the 11 cheeses in Roth Kase's Sole! line of Hispanic cheeses. It and the Panina (comparable to a Spanish queso), which rated first in another ACS Hispanic cheese category, were introduced around 2002. The other nine were introduced to the market in spring 2005.

Hispanic cheeses are "becoming more significant" in Roth Kase production, says **Kirsten Jaeckle**, marketing director. She represents the fifth generation of the family-owned company, whose heritage is Swiss.

The Sole! line is likely complete for now, she says, although other Hispanic products may be part of long-range plans.

A Hispanic cheesemaker is on staff, there are bilingual retail case cards, and chefs from Mandalay Place in Las Vegas to Chicago's Park Grill have crafted recipes that include the cheeses.

Roth Kase produces 30-40 kinds of cheese, aiming for authenticity in its ethnic products, although hybrids such as Fontiago (a fontina and asiago combo) are produced, too.

•

Roth Kase USA retail outlet, 657 Second St., Monroe
www.rothkase.com, 608-328-2122

SOUTHWEST

Other Big Cheeses

Who are the other significant Hispanic cheese players in Wisconsin? **Wisconsin Cheese Group, Monroe**, is described by the Food Institute as a leading manufacturer and marketer. There are 11 cheeses in its El Viajero line.

Specialty Cheese Company Inc., Lowell, donated its Pineapple Mango Fried Cheese for a first-time, large-scale sampling at the 2005 Wisconsin State Fair. About 1,000 samples were distributed in 40 minutes, says **Roxanne Pellen** of the **Wisconsin Dairy Promotion Board**.

Specialty Cheese operates four of the nation's oldest and smallest cheese plants. Its products are made from the milk that comes from about 60 small family farms.

Then there is **Mexican Cheese Producers**, based in **Monroe**, which makes only Mexican and Caribbean cheeses/creams. Founders **Miguel** and **Martina Leal** are from Guanajuato, Mexico.

Their work began in 1994 in Ohio, where Miguel perfected a recipe for Queso Cotija cheese, which is comparable to Parmesan. He would sell wheels of it to Chicago produce and meat wholesalers, the company explains online at **www.mexican-cheese.com,** driving there twice a week to make deliveries.

Now the company makes its products in a 40,000-square-foot factory in **Darlington**, but it is difficult to find out more. "Thank you for the wonderful opportunity," wrote **Christine Vincent**, marketing director, in response to a media inquiry, "however, we are just way too busy right now to assist you with a tour, photos and more information."

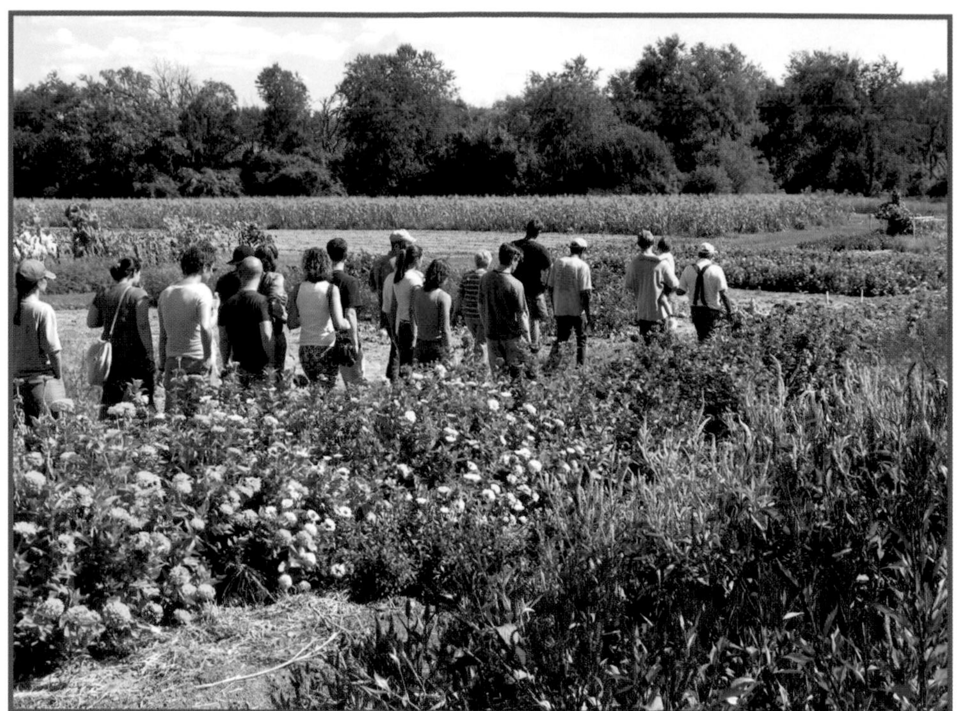

Culinary tours teach chefs the origins of fresh, nutritious and tasty food.

GREEN COUNTY: CULINARY TOURISM

New Glarus looks like a Swiss village. Cheese and beer are made in Monroe. It's easy to simplify and take places for granted, especially if they're close to home.

Green County businesses are putting a new and upscale spin on the packaging of their specialties. The result is "**Farm to Feast Culinary Getaways**," weekends that showcase the products and cuisine that make the area unique.

It is a local example of how culinary tourism is being nurtured and marketed. In Portland, Ore., the International Culinary Tourism Association was established in 2003 to acknowledge that there are advantages to having farms, chefs, food and beverage producers work in harmony.

The organization also notes that work already has been done in Australia and Canada to promote those countries as culinary hot spots. In Wisconsin, a Destination

Marketing Grant of about $30,000 was awarded to help establish the Monroe and New Glarus project.

What makes Green County unusual, besides having more cows than people? It has a concentration of Swiss-trained chefs, perhaps more than any other place in the United States.

"Farm to Feast" weekends are specialty tours for food lovers. One price includes two nights of lodging, meals, two cooking seminars, food/beverage samplings and walking tours of the area. The cost depends upon the type of lodging chosen. Group size is limited to 20.

Chefs who have participated in the cooking seminars include **Scott Stroessner** of the **Turner Hall Rathskeller, Monroe**, and a former sous chef at the Hotel Zurich in Switzerland; **Hans Lenzlinger** of the **New Glarus Hotel**, which he has co-owned with his wife since 1975; and **Mike Nevil** of the **Chalet Landhaus, New Glarus**, whose culinary training was in Unterwasser, Switzerland.

The first Monroe itinerary included a welcome reception with Swiss entertainment, tours of the **Roth Kase Ltd. Cheese Factory**, the **Historic Cheesemaking Center**, the **Joseph Huber Brewing Company** and the **John Wegmueller** dairy farm.

During a **New Glarus** weekend, participants visited the **Franklin Cheese Factory**, **Maple Leaf Cheese and Chocolate Haus**, **New Glarus Winery**, the **New Glarus Brewing Company** and the **Dan** and **Shelly Truttmann farm**.

Menus are up to the chef but may well include roesti potatoes, Swiss cheese pie, fondues or pork rahmschnitzel. Expect polkas, too.

This is not the first time for Green County foodies to work together to bring tourists into the area. The **Taster's Tour of Green County** was a more general marketing effort to make visitors aware of the county's food and beverage products.

•

Farm to Feast Culinary Getaways, 1505 Ninth St., Monroe
www.farmtofeast.com, 800-838-1603

Fast Facts

Green County has the nation's only cheese factory that makes 180-pound wheels of Swiss Emmentaler cheese. This also is the only place where pungent limburger cheese is made.

•

Cheese Days, the third weekend in September, is billed as the Midwest's oldest and biggest food festival. It's been a tradition since 1914.

•

For Bargain Hounds

Some of the state's best warehouse sales occur in south central and southwestern Wisconsin. Bargain hunters will love the annual:

- **Swiss Colony Warehouse Sale**—The mail order giant also sells overstocks of cheese, sausage and goodies listed in the **Monroe** company's other catalogs (Seventh Avenue, Midnight Velvet, Ginny's, Country Door, Monroe & Main, The Tender Filet). The annual spring sale is at the company warehouse, on Highway 69. There also is a Swiss Colony outlet store, open all year at 840 Eighth St., and that is the best way to get a handle on warehouse sale times and dates.

  Consult: **www.swisscolony.com**, **608-328-8572.**

- **Benefit Sale of American Girl Returns and Seconds**—Admission tickets to the mid July event in **Middleton** typically go on sale at 8 a.m. the first Saturday in June. About 13,000 dolls are sold, plus American Girl accessories, furniture, books, sleeping bags, bedding and little-girl outfits that match the dolls' clothes. Proceeds (about $12.5 million in 16 years) are split between the **Madison Children's Museum** and the American Girl's Fund for Children. For details: **www.madisonchildrensmuseum.org**, **608-256-6445.**

- **Lands End Warehouse Sale**—Returns, overstocks and slightly flawed home furnishings, clothing and shoes—for children as well as adults—are piled into a **Dodgeville** warehouse and sold for dirt cheap prices in early August. For details: **www.landsend.com, 800-963-4816**. The company's only **Not Quite Perfect** store in Wisconsin, small but with hefty discounts, is open all year at 411 State St., Madison.

- **Wisconsin Cheeseman Holiday Sale**—begins in early November at its outlet store, off Highway 151, **Sun Prairie**, about two blocks from the corporate headquarters. The mail order gift food company sells meats, candy and jams as well as cheeses. For details: **www.wisconsincheeseman.com**, **800-698-1721.**

- **The Lang Company Annual Thanksgiving and Christmas Sales**—Until 2005, the annual pre-holiday sale of cards, calendars, stationery, candles and collectibles was held in **Delafield**, the company's headquarters. Now there are year-round sales at 3600 S. Moorland Road, **New Berlin**. For sale are overstocks, discontinued and slightly damaged merchandise. There also is a corporate store at 606 Genessee St., Delafield. For more: **www.lang.com**, **800-967-3399.**

Lou and Peter Berryman celebrate the wacky sides of Wisconsin.

MADISON: ORIGINAL VOICES

The **Mabel Tainter** is an elegant old building in downtown **Menomonie** that is part church, part theater, part library and community center. Named after a lumber baron's daughter, who loved music and died in 1886 at age 19, its 313 seats come in four sizes: small to extra-large. The 1,597-pipe organ is a rare type, from 1890. Walls and fixtures are from a bygone world, too, carved and stenciled by hand.

It is grand and one of a kind. No wonder **Lou Berryman** of Madison calls it one of her favorite Wisconsin places to perform. She and **Peter Berryman**, her ex-husband, have spent the past 25 years singing about the Midwest's most peculiar and enduring qualities. Their disarming ballads and peppy folk songs—with topics from bowling to winter—are known for their clever lyrics.

A lot of professors—especially English professors—get to their shows, I was told before hearing the Berrymans for the first time in the early 1990s. That was not a drawing card for me, yet I quickly became a fan, too.

What's not to love? Consider the chorus to "Forward Hey," written for a video to promote Wisconsin:

"Oh hey, look at that! There's a fish on a hat!
"And we'd like to treat everyone here to a cow souvenir.
"There's a loon! There's a deer! There's a guy with a beer!
"There's the moon in the top of the trees,
"And it's still full of cheese!"

Their CD "Some Days" was released in time for deer hunting season. Everybody together, now, as we chime in with the chorus of "Dem Deer."

"Dem deer dey're here,
"Den dey're dere,
"Dey're here, dey're dere,
"Dey're everywhere."

It may play better in the Northwoods than the Manhattan basement cabaret where the Berrymans perform in spring, but that doesn't seem to matter much. The musicians have an odd repertoire of about 150 songs, on a dozen recordings.

If you live in Madison, as the Berrymans do, "Pflaum Road" is worth smirking about —but outsiders may sit clueless. "Cheese & Beer & Snow" and "Why Can't Johnny Bowl?" have a bigger geographic point of reference.

"We don't have aspirations to grow beyond ourselves," Lou says. "We're happy with the place we're at."

That said, critics elsewhere have found universal appeal to some of the ditties.

"Once in a while a song comes along that so successfully crystallizes familiar thoughts that you feel you could have written it yourself," writes the *San Francisco Chronicle*. "A lot of people feel that way about (the Berrymans') 'Why Am I Painting the Living Room.' "

"Lou & Peter Berryman write very eccentric, very funny satirical songs," writes the *Boston Globe*. "If Tom Lehrer had grown up in America's Dairyland, his songs might sound like theirs."

There are musical responses to social issues, too, ways "to voice our left-leaning principles," Lou says. Those play nicely "in all the little Madisons" around the country, like Berkeley.

This music has been presented in all kinds of unusual venues, including art fairs and food festivals, and small folk music gatherings to the state's biggest events. The musicians have sung on a hay wagon, atop the giant Hayward fish, before conventions of coroners and science fiction buffs (that's two events, not one).

The Berrymans will take their offbeat show just about anywhere.

Peter says they've also performed at "funerals, wakes, weddings, bars, folk clubs, restaurants, churches, barns, nature preserves, hospitals, living rooms, coffeehouses, libraries, city parks, bed and breakfasts, and just about every UW campus in the state."

He's loved it all, even the "gig on a small boat where no one could hear us over the roar of the engine."

It is not a high visibility operation, and a ticket to their show typically is $15 or less. The two just kind of go about their business, doing their thing, getting cited in Ph.D. papers and having people bring their song lyrics to shrinks, to explain how they feel.

"We absolutely love the fact that we can play at an opera house one night, then a women's banquet the next," Lou says. "And we're basically doing the same show."

She and Peter are good friends who met in high school, were married for a half-dozen years, divorced and for decades have been married to other people.

"I never know what to say about it," says Lou. "We were friends before we were married, and didn't make very good partners married. But we could be good friends."

•

Lou and Peter Berryman
PO Box 3400, Madison, WI 53704
www.louandpeter.com, 608-257-7750

Fast Facts

Who does what? From the musicians' website: Lou writes the music, Peter writes the words. Lou plays accordion. Peter plays 12-string guitar. They used to write new songs weekly, "many about the history, cheese, beer and strange politics of their home state."

Both of the Berrymans were raised in Appleton, played folk music together in high school and turned 55 in 2002. In 1999 and 2002, they were chosen as Wisconsin State Day representatives, performing at the Kennedy Center in Washington, DC.

Fans include Pete Seeger, Tom Paxton and Tom Lehrer, the duo say online. Their songs have been performed by Peter, Paul and Mary, Garrison Keillor and Peggy Seeger.

"Lou and I both use the audience as sort of a third writer," Peter told *Sing Out!* magazine in 2001. "When you play a song to a good audience, you can tell where it's weak and where it's strong, where it's working and where it's not working. That has always been very valuable to me. And we continue to do this."

While married, they lived in Canada for five years.

The Berrymans have gotten royalty checks from Jello Biafra and Mojo Nixon because both have covered a bar song from the first Berryman cassette, released in 1980. The song is "Are You Drinking With Me Jesus?" and lyrics include:

"Do you nestle by my barstool
"Makin' me so calm within?
"Have you touched me with your warmness,
"Or have I touched myself with gin?"

Here's the chorus:

"Are you drinkin' with me Jesus?
"I can't see you very clear.
"If you're drinkin' with me Jesus
"Won't you buy a friend a beer?"

MADISON: FOOD FETISHES

Robert Miller muddles an Old Fashioned for the thirsty and nostalgic.

Supper clubs with relish trays. Cheeses from rural factories. Sliced summer sausage. Friday fish fries. Grilled wursts. All shape Wisconsin's identity. These foods and food traditions have a home on the Capitol Square in Madison.

A trio of high-end and highly regarded restaurateurs—**Tami Lax** of **Harvest**, and **Patrick** and **Marcia O'Halloran** of **Lombardino's**—collaborated to create a more casual and lower-price spot for people who love the food and drink that define Wisconsin. The restaurant is called **The Old Fashioned**, after what is arguably the state's official cocktail.

It is a place for brick cheese from **Widmer's** in **Theresa**, 7-ounce sodas from **Seymour Bottling**, brats from **Meisfeld's** in **Sheboygan**, pickled beets from **Bea's Ho-Made** in **Ellison Bay**. At least 50 Wisconsin businesses that produce high-quality food or beverages are involved at one time. Many are obscure, unless you have a personal tie to the area.

"Somebody needs to do it right," says Patrick O'Halloran. It is not about pairing "the weakest drinks and cheapest fish" for a $6.95 all-you-can-eat. Tami calls this joint effort a way "to pay tribute to the foods and spirits that make Wisconsin famous."

The two other business founders—**Robert Miller** and **Daniel Momont**—are Wisconsin natives with extensive restaurant experience who are responsible for the day-to-day operations.

The Old Fashioned's most stunning feature is a 46-foot wooden bar; it and the wooden flooring are 175 years old, reclaimed materials from an out-of-state shoe factory. There also is booth and butcher block table seating for 120.

"We want this to be a warm, comfortable and welcoming place, with a feeling that it's been here for a long time," Tami says.

What else can customers expect? At least a half-dozen hand-muddled versions of the classic Old Fashioned cocktail, straight up to apple brandy. The bar brand? Korbel, of course. Wisconsinites drink more of it than anybody else in the country.

This also is where to order cordials of Cherry Bounce, Door County cherries infused with sugar and liquor. The mixture sits for six months before it is drunk.

Lazy Susans is a menu category; they are appetizer conglomerations that resemble relish trays and are meant to be shared. Think three kinds of wurst, with kraut, sweet gherkins and mustards. Another example: summer sausage, braunschweiger, bread-and-butter pickles, deviled eggs, coleslaw and rye bread.

Trios of cheese are sold as an appetizer or just to munch on at the bar. We're talking Hook's Colby from Mineral Point to Pleasant Ridge Reserve from Dodgeville.

Familiar nightly specials—fish fry Fridays, prime rib Saturdays, roasted chicken Sundays—have high-quality twists. Burgers are made on a wood-burning grill, and the House Burger comes with fried onions, aged cheddar, roasted garlic sauce and a soft-cooked egg.

The egg is an idea borrowed from the **Roxbury Tavern**; "it becomes a self-basting burger," Robert says. On the late-night menu are several specialty dip choices (including tiger sauce—horseradish and mayo) to match with munchies.

Possible entertainment: accordion music and polka bands on weekends. The restaurant is not designed as a sports bar, but three 52-inch plasma screen TVs are turned on for state sports events.

"We're not doing this to be trendy," Patrick says of the venture. "We want to build it to be an institution in the city."

•

The Old Fashioned, 23 N. Pinckney St., Madison
www.theoldfashioned.com, 608-310-4545

Asides

Madison takes pride in its independently owned restaurants and has a chapter of the **Council of Independent Restaurants of America** to promote them. There are 30-plus members of **Madison Originals.** See **www.madison.originals.org.**

•

The area also has ten distinctive **Food Fight** restaurants: **Bluephies, Eldorado Grill, Firefly, Fresco, Hubbard Avenue Diner** (Middleton), **Johnny Delmonicos, Market Street Diner** (Sun Prairie), **Monty's Blue Plate Diner, Ocean Grill**, and **Tex Tubb's Taco Palace**. See **www.foodfightinc.com.**

•

Always In A Food Mood

Terese Allen fights "fast food" thinking.

Terese Allen has a great appetite for food, both on and off her plate. It is her life—as a writer, teacher, recipe developer, cook, consultant, activist and researcher.

More than something to eat, she considers food "about everything in life. It's our health, our social connections, our environmental and political issues, our ethnic traditions."

She wants people to be more aware of where their food comes from, and thinks there should be a national food curriculum that begins in elementary schools, to fight "fast food thinking" and to get children interested in cooking.

The Madison woman is a fan of small-town bakeries and organic farmers, butchers and ethnic sausage shops.

"Every bite we take is something of a vote," Terese says, because of the wide-ranging impact of consumer buying habits. It is a serious observation from someone who also is fond of her state's casual and self-deprecating sense of humor.

Cheeseheads, cowpies and omnipresent brat frys? Only in Wisconsin will you find these "foodways," the term that academic folklorists use to refer to food traditions.

"I love the folkloric approach to cooking and food," she says. "It can tell you more about who you are."

Knowing her world as a child helps explain who Terese is today. The ethnic influence of **Emil's Bakery, Kaap's Old World Chocolates** and **Buddha's Sausage Shoppe** in **Green Bay** all made an imprint on her, the third youngest of 11 children in the family.

"We were one of the last families to get milk and cottage cheese delivered to the door," says the woman whose business card says "foodist." She was 4 years old when her mother died, which means siblings learned to take care of each other.

"As a big family, we couldn't afford to eat fancy, but we knew and appreciated fresh ingredients." She grew up around a lot of European pride and ethnic diversity. "There was access to wonderful food ingredients," Terese says.

Kielbasa. Belgian trippe (not tripe, but a pork and cabbage sausage). German brats. Swedish potato sausage. A sister, Mary, is the only other person in the Allen family who turned food into an occupation. She and her husband operate a Peruvian American restaurant in Sarasota, Fla.

"I always wanted to work in a small restaurant as a chef or manager," Terese says. And that is what she did, after training at the Restaurant School of Philadelphia. She was executive chef at two of Madison's former **Ovens of Brittany** restaurants, and *The Ovens of Brittany Cookbook* was the first book that she wrote, published in 1991.

Her cookbook *Wisconsin's Hometown Flavors* contains 130-plus specialty markets for food. Allen calls it a representative sampling, not a comprehensive guide, for the state. It is a book of recipes, people profiles, history lessons, ethnic preservation and small-town pride. It is a tribute to the "bakers, butchers and other small-scale food merchants" who "are undervalued in our culture."

It also is a statement about Terese's roots. She writes: "In memory of my mother Agnes, who filled a green box with hand-written recipes. Grandma Smallo, who fried long johns and made dandelion wine. Grandma Marlow, who did the dishes. Dad, who loved booyah and cream puffs. And Louie, who carved a painted cornucopia."

"The people who are doing this are doing it for more than the money," Terese says.

"Repertoire cooking" is a concept that she's been developing, perhaps for another cookbook. "I like to have 20 or 30 types of dishes that I know how to make," she says. "Then I apply ingredients that are in season."

So the beginning point of an entree, for any season, could be risotto (a plump Italian rice). Add asparagus, chicken and/or chives in spring. Try roasted sweet peppers or fresh soybeans in summer. Or squash in autumn. Garlic and Asiago cheese—or toasted hickory nuts—could be added in winter.

"The way the world is going, convenience will not be as important as flavor, nutrition or sustainability," Terese says. "We're beginning to consciously support the places that produce food" organically or to keep ethnic traditions alive.

•

Terese Allen is food editor for **Organic Valley**, an organic farming cooperative based in **LaFarge**. See **www.organicvalley.com**, **888-444-6455**.

Ellen Barnard—This is not your father's adult entertainment store.

MADISON: A WOMAN'S TOUCH

Porn vs. erotica. Intimacy vs. arousal. Genitals vs. brain. Toy vs. tool. Limitation vs. opportunity. The value of sexual resources is a matter of physical and emotional comfort. Some people are too embarrassed or offended to say the word "dildo," much less examine or use one.

This is a part of what makes **A Woman's Touch**, a business that opened in 1996, a mystery. It also is what has helped the sexual resource center—the first in Wisconsin with free professional advice and dozens of sex devices for sale—thrive.

The store in **Gateway Mall** is busy on a weekday afternoon. **Ellen Barnard**, a social worker, and **Myrtle Wilhite**, a physician, also own a store in Milwaukee. There are plans for stores in Minneapolis and Chicago.

Zoning ordinances are a hurdle. Restrictions on adult entertainment in Madison do not apply to businesses with materials that are instructional or informational. That's not so in Milwaukee. The Madison code allows no more than 10 percent of a store's retail space to contain sexually explicit merchandise, but that has not stymied A Woman's Touch. Things that vibrate or are meant to be thrust are only one part of the picture, in an over-18 area that is partly hidden by a colorful curtain.

As Ellen says, "This is not your dad's adult entertainment store."

There are gentle chimes, soft lighting, light jazz—and no posters or packaging that "assaults a particular image of sexuality that may or may not be yours." Games and coupon books about intimacy, aromatherapy candles and oils, edible body paints and stimulating books/videos tend to have "neutral packaging" that reveals neither the age, gender, status or ability of the intended user. Video content must be respectful of both sexes; only about 150 titles make the cut.

"It's about whole body pleasure," Ellen says, nodding toward the men's and women's lingerie. "Intimacy is about more than genitals." A top-of-the-line bustier costs $150. Sizes go up to 3X because "small, medium and large doesn't speak to half of Wisconsin."

Silk stockings—some sold as garter hose—can be enough to make some people feel frisky, "and that's a big part of it." A rack of greeting cards contains sassy to sentimental messages; "they are here because of our emphasis on communication."

The store's tone is feminine but not frilly. Men—as well as couples of all mixtures and generations—browse, too. Some are intense, some giggle, some come because of a doctor or therapist referral. "We serve as a resource for them," Ellen says, referring to her professional colleagues. "We speak their language."

Maybe you order cappuccino every morning, seek Thai food as a treat, tune in to the classics on Saturdays. Too bad we can't talk as easily about matters of individual taste that satisfy us sexually, she says.

"Sex is a basic drive, but we have a hard time admitting that we are sexual beings," Ellen observes. Of the dozen free brochures that she and Myrtle have developed, the most recent copyright goes on one titled "Vaginal Rejuvenation," a particular challenge for post-menopausal women.

"I struggle with people who expect to have sex lives like they were in their 20s," Ellen says. "We expect it to stay the same—quick and easy—all our lives."

There is no fast fix, she says. As people age, it will take longer to get aroused or reach an orgasmic state, so expectations need to be different. "I look at it as an opportunity to try new things, not as a disease to be treated" with a patch or pill.

The store's staff members have each completed 40 to 60 hours of training to help coach customers about how to make good choices for themselves. The co-owners also will take appointments; there is no fee and apparently no situation too hopeless to address. If there are no answers, there are ideas—such as when illness or disability appears to make intimacy prohibitive.

There is no "right way" to have sex or be intimate, Ellen says. "It's all about who you are, what you like" and being able to communicate what you need.

She and her business partner have dispensed their advice at college campus lectures as well as at a retreat for breast cancer survivors and a national conference for nurse practitioners. "We continue to be about sexual health as well as pleasure," Ellen says.

Answers to questions about sex and intimacy are posted online. In-store workshop topics have included chocolate tastings and the art of erotic dance.

•

A Woman's Touch
600 Williamson St., Madison
200 N. Jefferson St., Milwaukee, 414-221-0400
www.a-womans-touch.com, 888-621-8880

•

A Room of One's Own

Since 1975, local feminists have gladly gone to their Room. It is more than a place to simply buy a book, do business or plot a rebellion.

A Room of One's Own, in downtown Madison, was born as the Vietnam War was ending and as Bill Gates' Microsoft began. **Sandi Torkildson** was a recent UW grad who, with friends, opened this roost for feminists that continues to thrive today.

It has been a place for customers to browse, brood, rejoice, resolve, study and struggle to understand their world and themselves.

"Women and Their Bodies in Health and Disease" is a UW women's studies class that has 400 students each semester. Professor **Nancy Worcester** teaches it and always orders her textbooks from the Room. She likes the fact that many of her students keep going back for other reading materials, too.

Nancy does the same thing herself, because of the bookstore staff's dedication to stocking the best and newest resources/literature in women's studies.

"They often find a (new release) before I do, and it often is something that changes my life," she says. "It's finding the right book, at the right moment, that really helps you ask the questions that you want to be asking" during a turning point in life.

A Room of One's Own has a coffeehouse with an uncomplicated soup-sandwich-bakery menu (how about a tofu nut burger for lunch?). The store is a space for poetry readings and music performances as well as book club meetings and shopping.

•

A Room of One's Own
307 W. Johnson St., Madison
www.roomofonesown.com, 608-257-7888

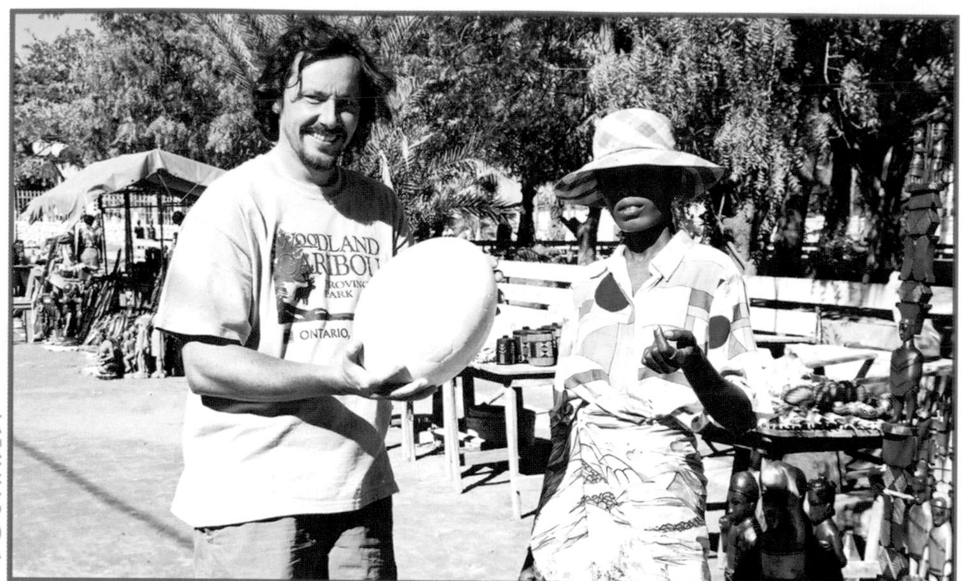

Is it a melon or an egg from the extinct Elephant Bird? Ask Andy Kammer.

Madision: Andy's Adventures

If you truly want to escape the world's turmoil, **Andy Kammer** can help by sending you far away. What's the logic in that? Andy's specialty is eco-tourism in remote locations: kayaking in Costa Rica, snorkeling in Panama, studying Mayan architecture in Belize, tracking lions in Zimbabwe.

From stays inside a Caribbean wildlife refuge to the African bush of Zambia, **Adventure Andy's Travel Company** offers customized tours for two to 12 people on some of the most beautiful, idyllic parts of the planet.

The cost, without air transportation included, ranges from about $1,500 to $6,000 for two weeks away. It all depends on the destination and lavishness of accommodations.

The excursions began in 1996, when Andy began leading wilderness canoe trips in northern Ontario, Canada.

His emphasis is on educational vacations instead of physically adventurous travel. "Safety has always been a huge issue" to potential customers, Andy says.

He grew up on a farm near Pardeeville and calls Kariba, Zimbabwe, his favorite place on Earth. It is a city whose 30,000 residents have learned how to live with wildlife, inside of a national park.

"Leopards will take your dog if you keep it out too long, and elephants will eat from your lemon trees," Andy explains. Still, "it is an Eden-esque place."

So does that kind of talk invigorate you, or make you want to stay home?

The protective bubble of a mainstream airlines' vacation package, he says, "is very good for safety but bad for experiences." There may be intense, magical moments—like being near a breeding herd of elephants, or getting closer to a hippo than expected—and they make for indelible memories.

"We are trained guides and we are entertainers, somewhat. What we have is nature as the show," Andy says. "Things that are not planned often become the highlights" of a trip. He participates in some tours and acts as the conduit between traveler and tour guide for others. He says there have been no injuries to any of his customers, whose ages have stretched from 18 to 80 years.

"I've never felt unsafe anywhere I've traveled," Andy contends, acknowledging that the worst experience he had was losing $50 to a pickpocket in Madagascar. "We have more violent crimes in the U.S."

He insists that he would never send anybody to a place he wouldn't go to himself —or use his energy to convert the overly timid. "If you're worried about this kind of travel, don't go," Andy says. "I'm not here to convince you."

Itineraries can have a lot of latitude. They can be rugged and physically challenging, or have more emphasis on comfort and learning.

Which of his trip choices is closest to home? Probably a walking safari to track polar bears in northern Ontario, or a trek to Canada's sparsely inhabited Northwest Territories to see its 750,000 caribou and other wildlife.

If this level of remote travel and adventure is not for you, maybe a slide show of it is. "I'll talk about this stuff anywhere I can," Andy says of his passion.

•

Adventure Andy's Travel Company
1906 E. Washington Ave. #1, Madison
www.adventureandy.com, 608-242-5166

Brian Kurth helps others blossom.

VOCATION VACATIONS

After **Brian Kurth** got laid off in 2001, he traveled around the country for six months, and that's how he learned something significant about people.

It didn't matter if he was having a beer in Boulder or hiking the Grand Canyon. When Brian asked strangers about their work, part of the answer tended to be the same.

"People apologize for what they do," the Madison native observed, and when they were pressed, they'd talk about their dream of doing something else for a living.

Brian eventually settled down in Portland, Oregon, began tracking dream jobs and now provides people an opportunity through **VocationVacations** to get a taste of other careers. The 2004 debut of VocationVacations quickly gained the attention of *Time* magazine, *CNN*, *USA Today* and the Associated Press.

For about $350 to $5,000 (not including transportation or lodging), a customer can spend one or two days with someone well-versed in another line of work—from innkeeper to PGA golf pro. It is one-on-one mentoring; the student learns about and experiences the work.

There are more than 150 vocational choices/locations, including a handful in Wisconsin. The plan was to have more than 500 by the end of 2006. More about that later.

Brian, in his 30s when he began the business, has had plenty of his own career adventures. A triple major at the University of Wisconsin-Madison (history, political science and international relations), "everybody else thought I'd go to law school, but I knew it wasn't for me."

He worked in retail management in St. Louis, helped set up an office retail store in the Baltic country of Estonia, was a phone company manager in Chicago, Budapest and Texas. The layoff was from an Internet security company near Chicago.

VocationVacations "was conceived on the Kennedy Expressway" during a traffic snarl that got Brian to thinking that "there's got to be more."

The job of horse trainer was the first dream job for which he found a match. The mentors were Rich Ovenburg and Mary Folberg of Four Mountains Ranch near Portland. Today the vocations range from film events producer to wedding coordinator; in the works are several other options, archaeologist to ocean fisherman. European mentors are being sought, too.

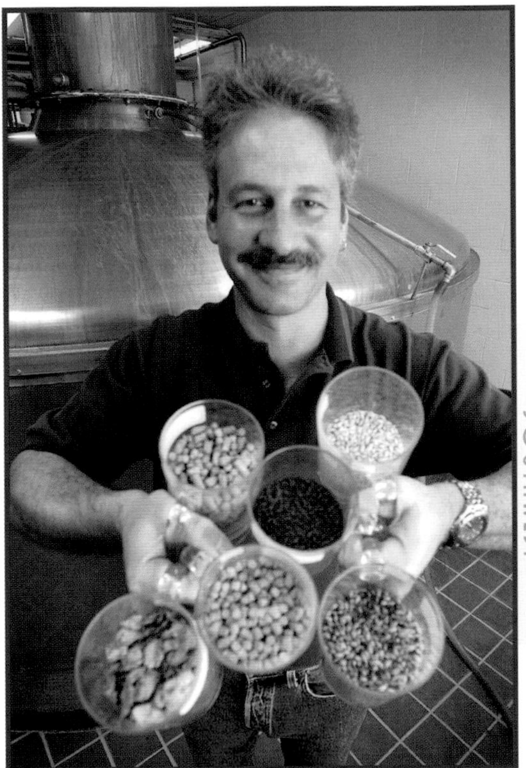

Learn the secrets of making great beer from Kris Kalav, Huber brewmaster.

The list is unlikely to include occupations that can be taught by enrolling in a traditional curriculum. Prospective mentors must have a product or service to sell and a Web site that potential students can study—before making a commitment—to better understand the business.

The goal is to give outsiders a realistic look at the work of others, and Brian says it's fine for somebody to conclude that the work is not for them. "What we want to hear is that we've fulfilled their curiosity," he says.

Wisconsin participants have included Christopher George of Slinger, who headed south to spend a day with **Kris Kalav** at the **Joseph Huber Brewing Company**, Monroe. Christopher, a project manager at Bank One, heard about the opportunity through National Public Radio. "It's a way for me to test-drive a career," he says. The expectations? "I'd just like exposure to what a brewmaster does all day, and what it would take for me to go down that road."

Christopher has been a home brewer for years. Kris, who is Huber's brewmaster, knows what it's like to change careers: He has also been a cellular biologist and has operated a sustainable fish farm.

Want to learn more about his work at the brewery, which has been around since 1845 and produces the Blumer (soda), Huber and Berghoff beer lines? It's $499 for the privilege of working alongside him, or brewmaster **Joe Karls** in Green Bay, of **Hinterland Brewery**.

Joe left the corporate life for a new career as brewmaster at **Hinterland Brewery**. The Maple Bock at Hinterland has been deemed a world champion; it is one of seven handcrafted beers made for Hinterland's restaurant and lounge customers.

The **Wisconsin Cheesecakery** was the third Wisconsin business in VocationVacations. Owner **Lisa Lathrop** produces appetizer to dessert cheesecakes. It's a challenging menu: Some selections are decadent; others are for vegan dieters.

Lisa stepped up plans for the business after her job with the state Department of Revenue was cut to part-time hours. She also has restaurant and hospitality experience that ranges from accounting to waitressing. It's $599 to spend two days with her.

What's next? Brian, the matchmaker, is pushing for the production of guidebooks that prospective students can use as a resource. "This Job's a Trip," a TV series based on VocationVacations, debuted on the Travel Channel in 2006.

•

VocationVacations
1631 NE Broadway #422, Portland, OR 97232
www.vocationvacations.com, 866-888-6329

Denny Berkery strikes a pose with his glass mosaics.

Bowling for Art

There can be an art to bowling. Just ask **Denny Berkery**. The proprietor of Madison's **Vinery Stained Glass Studio** offers a two-part class that turns bowling balls into glittering glass mosaics.

For 50 bucks and six hours of time, the balls go from collecting dust in the basement to attracting attention (and maybe birds) as yard art. They become gazing balls. The idea came from a hobbyist magazine, and dozens of balls were donated to Denny by local bowling alleys. One student paid for her class in bowling balls.

Students learn glass nipping, gluing and grouting techniques. Scraps of iridescent glass, mirror, ceramic tile and glass tile can be used. "The hardest part is coming up with the design, not the mechanics," Denny says. One of the trickiest times is before the balls are grouted—"there are sharp edges, and they must be moved carefully."

The bowling ball class is an example of how the business has evolved in the past few years. The Vinery, Denny says, started out as a retail plant store, with glasswork as a hobby. Then it became a stained glass business, "creation to repair, A to Z."

"People used to think of stained glass as being just for churches," he notes. "It took a while for glass to be looked at as an art form, and one that doesn't necessarily need to be functional."

Today his staff provides several options for students eager to learn about stained glass, including the bowling ball class, which Denny predicts will be phased out in a few years. But for now, it's trendy because "more people seem to want gazing balls in their yards" and "these balls won't go anywhere," regardless of wind, because of their weight.

•

The Vinery Stained Glass Studio
4317 W. Beltline Hwy., Madison
www.vineryglass.com, 608-271-2490

Some of Mineral Point's oldest buildings have a new life.

SOUTHWEST

MINERAL POINT: Shake Rag's Rebirth

The task, to raise $100,000 in three months, was daunting but it also sent the heart and soul of this artists' community soaring. And now look at what's become of that challenge. **Historic Shake Rag Alley**, part of a Cornish mining camp in the 1820s, came close to losing its public exposure in July 2004. That's when the *Wall Street Journal* featured Shake Rag and two other sites on the National Register of Historic Places as being for sale. Owners **Glenn** and **Harriet Ridnour**, antique shop operators, had put the Wisconsin property on the market after his heart attack. List price was $495,000.

A bid came in, just as **Sandy Scott** and **Judy Sutcliffe** were hosting the third annual **Woodlanders Gathering** at Shake Rag. More than 150 people—wood carvers, stone whittlers, mask makers, rustic furniture builders—from at least 17 states realized this might be their last visit to Mineral Point, where they had come to bond and philosophize as well as hone their art.

The prospective buyer intended to make the nine-building property a private residence.

Sandy and Judy, who operate the town's **Longbranch Gallery**, quickly found a banker and made a case that Shake Rag could become a successful, non-profit arts center. Then the women made their own bid on the 2.5-acre property, and it was accepted.

Some Woodlanders wrote checks. Others promised to come back to do landscaping, weaving, carpentry work. "We had a basket full of pledges," Scott recalls.

"I'm young but will do whatever I can do," wrote Mike Christensen, an Iowa farm boy, then age 14 and a Woodlanders student. "I want to work for you." He has been back each summer since.

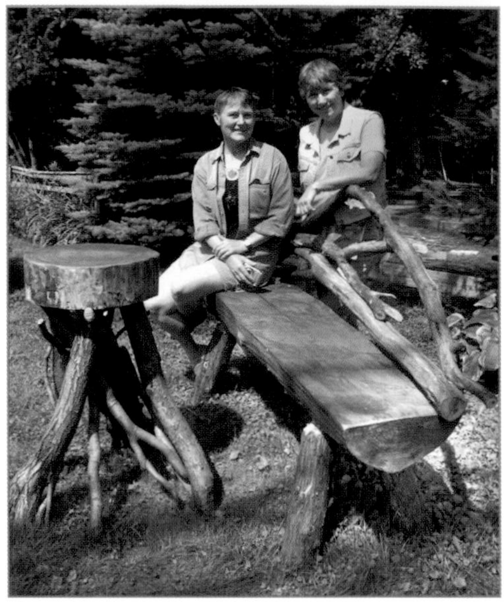

Judy and Sandy believe in Shake Rag's future.

Local residents fueled the effort, too, and the $100,000 down payment was raised in six weeks. Now called the **Shake Rag Alley Center for the Arts,** the grounds are used for all types of art workshops, for beginners as well as professionals, children as well as adults, the disabled as well as the physically fit.

"It captured people's sense of adventure," Sandy says of the project, "and it felt like we were saving something for the community."

The work and commitment continued. Although the Ridnours had made property improvements, previous owners let many of the nine Shake Rag buildings deteriorate from the showcase shape that they had been in during Madison florist **Al Felly's** ownership in the 1970s to 1990.

So roughly 40 volunteers donated time and materials to enhance the grounds and buildings. They roofed, decorated, weeded, rebuilt walkways and bridges. They put fresh flowers on outdoor cafe tables, constructed an office with cupboards donated from a local kitchen remodeling project.

"There is such a sense of ownership among the volunteers," Sandy says. When pressed, she acknowledges that "I try to look for the spark that makes people feel good and let them be all they can be." Her resume includes work with the disabled.

One building is dedicated to after-school and summer art programs for children. It is a multicultural approach: The kids learn to sing in Japanese, drum to African music, use puppets and dance as "warm-ups" to other expressive arts projects. About 100 students (most in elementary school) participated the first year; the town's population is merely 2,500.

"It has been a way to engage young families and young people," says Judy, "so another generation is becoming involved with Shake Rag."

Cafe space has been leased to local caterers who also serve breakfast and lunch here on some days. Above offices are three bedrooms that are being rented to tourists and visiting artists. There also is a computer lab, for digital photo and other workshops, plus studio space in several of the other Shake Rag buildings.

The oldest, a log cabin built in 1828, is Mineral Point's oldest standing structure.

Sandy and Judy are both from small towns in Iowa but did not meet until living in California, where Sandy was a public television producer and Judy was a tile muralist. The friends decided to retire to the Midwest, where the cost and pace of life could be slower. Or so they thought.

Now they've hired someone else to run their gallery, not because they don't want to work, but because the art center is taking up more of their time.

Surprises and good timing continue, such as a benefit concert donation from Christopher Finkelmeyer, an acclaimed concert pianist in Chicago whose great-grandparents lived at Shake Rag.

Volunteer workers got permission to salvage a beautiful old barn that was about to be bulldozed in Sun Prairie. They took down 15- and 20-foot panels of weathered, tongue-in-groove barn board that was recycled as walls in Shake Rag's largest classroom.

DETOUR

The Cornish pasty—a meat and vegetable filled pastry, once considered "peasant food"—has been a longtime menu item at **The Red Rooster Café** and other Mineral Point restaurants. **Pendarvis**, near Highways 151 and 18, is a place for documenting and interpreting both Cornish and lead mining history. For more: **www.wisconsinhistory.org/pendarvis**, 608-987-2122.

•

An intimate restaurant-brewpub is right behind the bright red doors of the **Brewery Creek** building in Mineral Point. Upstairs are five B&B rooms, each with a fireplace and double whirlpool bath. The setting is a restored 1854 limestone warehouse, and the bar/restaurant close by 10 p.m., so people can get some sleep. For more: **www.brewerycreek.com**, 608-987-3298.

Pendarvis is a fine example of historic preservation—hard work and a "passion to preserve".

A longer-term goal is to combine the use of studio spaces throughout Mineral Point, as well as Shake Rag's, for creative arts endeavors of all kinds. The hope is to have a strong, ongoing curriculum from May through December, and ultimately become self-sufficient.

"We are hoping an angel finds us and believes, as we do, that Shake Rag Alley is an extraordinary, magical place—with a worthy vision for our community and for our region—and has the resources to help make it so," Sandy says.

Shake Rag acting/directing/screenwriting instructors have included a creative advisor to Robert Redford's Sundance Film Institute and a former acting coach for "Seinfeld." They donate their time, says Sandy, who predicts they will bring more Hollywood pros with them in the future.

•

Shake Rag Alley Center for the Arts, 18 Shake Rag St. Mineral Point
www.shakeragalley.com, 608-987-3292

'A Passion to Preserve'

Robert Neal and **Edgar Hellum** toiled and sacrificed in the 1930s to preserve the deteriorated stone cottages that eventually became **Pendarvis**, one of nine state-operated historic sites, in Mineral Point.

They salvaged building materials that others had discarded, hauled rock, laid shingles—and later would put on aprons to serve tea and saffron cakes to wealthy, out-of-town visitors. It was high-class teas and antique sales that paid for much of the restoration work on "the slummiest street in town."

Pendarvis, arguably, wouldn't exist if these men hadn't become involved. Historic preservation, now a noble effort, was considered frivolous back then. This was, after all, the rural Midwest—and the work was that of two gay men.

Their sexuality and work—the subject of jokes and ridicule among the locals, and their perseverance, is but one chapter of *A Passion to Preserve: Gay Men as Keepers of Culture* by Will Fellows. Literature about the historic preservation movement exists, and so do studies about gender identity. Now Will has linked the two topics.

These are stories about men who know how to use a hammer but also read *House Beautiful*. They mix cement and restore antiques, confound neighbors as they improve the look of their neighborhoods.

"For many people, gay men are viewed as non-contributors of the culture, although I'd like to think that segment is shrinking," says Will, a gay man who was raised on an Evansville farm and now lives in Milwaukee.

"The gay contribution to preservation has been largely obscured, if not obliterated from the record," Will writes. "Many historic sites and house museums carry on the tradition of concealing and denying the gayness of the men who have had so much to do with the preservation of those places."

Passion to Preserve documents some of these contributions and argues it is no coincidence that these preservationists were gay.

Wisconsin is well represented in this book, including recollections from several gay men who rescued tiny **Cooksville**, in **Rock County**, from architectural neglect.

The restoration of Cooksville, which is unincorporated, began in 1911, when a teacher named **Ralph Warner** paid $500 for a weathered brick house there. The work of "a brotherhood of gay men," as the author describes it, eventually was enough for the town to be designated a historic district on the National Register of Historic Places.

•

Another Will Fellows book, *Farm Boys: Lives of Gay Men From the Rural Midwest*, was a resource and inspiration for the 2006 Academy Award winner "Brokeback Mountain," confirms movie producer James Schamus.

•

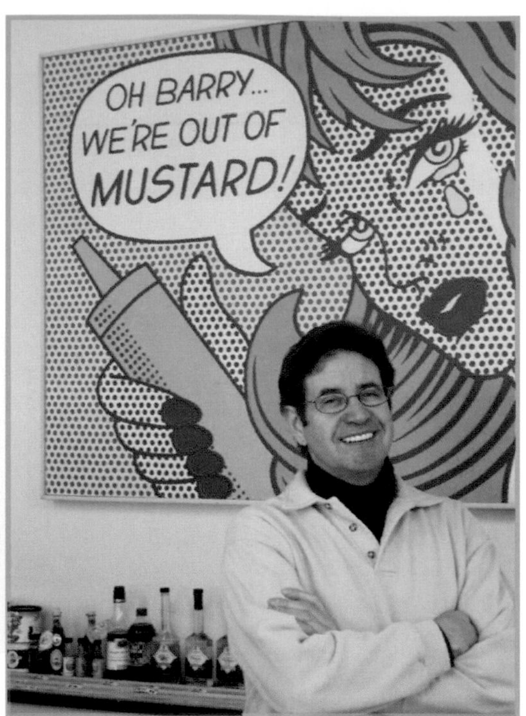

Barry Levenson—proud to be yellow.

MOUNT HOREB: MUSTARD RULES!

In a corner were the fruity recipes: the tart, the sweet, the zesty. Another table was all herb/veggie combos: the dills, the onions, the garlic. Segregated elsewhere was one honey of a collection, literally. All the fuss was about mustard, 15 categories of it.

This was an eclectic food sampling project, one part of three rounds of the **Mustard Festival's World-wide Mustard Competition** at the **Mount Horeb Mustard Museum**. About three dozen judges dipped and swizzled hundreds of pretzel sticks into the entries, all sold on the market somewhere in the world. It was a blind taste test.

Within four hours, I sampled at least 60 of the 300-plus products being judged by chefs, food critics, cookbook authors, food fanatics and average consumers.

One of the smallest catgories was yellow mustard—maybe it's what you use the most, but the field sure has gotten a lot more competitive and complicated in other ways.

There are coarse grained mustards, jam-like spreads of tiny mustard seed balls that burst with flavor when bit. There are deli browns, classic hots and even spirit mustards—those made with some kind of booze, tequila to champagne.

One of the more popular categories was all about salad dressings, marinades and barbecue sauces made with mustard.

The Wisconsin museum is an excellent match for the judging, which has been done here for about a dozen years (there were only 25 entries the first year). Since 1986, museum owner **Barry Levenson** has devoted himself to collecting and advocating this condiment. He is an attorney whose specialty is food law issues. Both he and his wife, **Patti**, have a funny, clever and savvy way of marketing their venture.

Want a souvenir that won't be slathered onto your next platter of grilled meats?

Enough mustard to suit every palate and plaster.

Consider the museum's Poupon U collection of sweatshirts, baseball caps, pennants and other varsity-like merchandise.

The Levensons also have two versions of the "Poupon U Fight Song." One is sung to the tune of "On Wisconsin":

"On our hot dogs, on our bratwursts, mustard is so cool...." The other tune is for Notre Dame fans.

Think there's not enough to know about mustard to fill a museum? This place has more than 4,500 kinds—the world's largest collection—from more than 60 countries.

Ready to diversify your condiment cabinet? More than 800 kinds of mustard products are for sale online; about 500 also are sold in the museum gift shop.

Mount Horeb puts on a National Mustard Day bash every August; it is an extraordinary family event that has gotten the attention of the **Food Network**. Kids use mustard to make paintings. **Culver's** mixes up a batch of Mustard Custard. There is Mustard Bowling, Mustard Ring Toss.

Oscar Mayer rolls in the Wienermobile and donates dawgs for everybody to eat. Just don't ask for ketchup—that's not appreciated here.

Chef **James Jens**—then with the **Old Feed Mill** in **Mazomanie**—served his first Mustard Champions Dinner, multiple courses of gourmet fare, each matched or made with its own award-winning mustard from the festival.

Olivier Cognac Mustard was the marinade for a duck breast entree. Old Spice Gold Honey Mustard was mixed into almond ice cream for dessert.

Near this community of 6,000 are vineyards, the **Tyrol Basin** ski area, **Blue Mound** and **Governor Dodge state parks**, **Cave of the Mounds** and **Little Norway**. So mustard isn't all you need to have on your mind to make the trip.

•

Mount Horeb Mustard Museum, 100 W. Main St., Mt. Horeb, WI 53572
www.mustardmuseum.com, 800-438-6878

Tomorrow's History

Brian Bigler believes history is dynamic. As such, he sees chronic wasting disease as more than an ailment with devastating consequences to whitetailed deer today. In the future, it will be seen as a significant part of local history.

That's one reason he collects hunting paraphernalia—hunter outfits, deer tags, DNR alerts and signs posted on farmland about chronic wasting. Brian is president of the **Mount Horeb Area Historical Society**, and he is a believer in intentionally gathering pieces of the present, for the benefit of future generations.

"History just doesn't stand still," says Brian, and he is proactive in his efforts. A press release to the *Mount Horeb Mail* newspaper, for example, solicits specific donations for archives and exhibits, from phone books before 1975 and high school annuals after 1980, to contemporary team sports uniforms for children and adults.

There also are boundaries set: "All items must have been used in the townships that comprise the historical society's collecting area."

The project intends to attract "those who would like to make a permanent mark on local history," Brian says, contending that any sized community can do the same kind of thing.

Here is advice about what to collect:

Time and place—What's important to the majority of a community? What items best represent its everyday life? What symbolizes a community's image? For Mount Horeb, some of the answers are specific, like wooden trolls and mustard jars. Others are more generic, yet can remain personal.

The late journalist **John Newhouse** took and donated 100 photos of local people in their daily routines. Kids stand on hay bales. A gas station switches to self-service. Grocery clerks work the checkout counter.

The scenes won't be seen as mundane—especially decades from now, as fashion and technology change.

"Collect materials that are common to the identity of the community," Brian advises. Celebrated local residents include painter **Peggy Flora Zalucha**, who has contributed work to the **Mount Horeb Area Museum**.

Cause and effect—Any community can collect artifacts that show a community's reaction to changes in technology or social justice issues. "What's the local impact to an outside situation?" Brian asks.

Social justice statements can be shown through protest buttons, brochures, lapel ribbons with American flags, newspaper pictures and articles. "We don't make judgments," he says. "We let the objects comment on themselves."

Change over time—In Mount Horeb, maybe it's an exhibit about ironing that

A farm boy and his dog on a hot summer day—photos of everyday events are an important legacy.

includes a disposable paper dress, a permanent-press shirt and irons that require coal, gas, steam.

The theme also can be how a community's vision of itself has changed, or how it has changed physically.

Impact and significance—Whether it's a local athlete who wins a gold Olympic medal or a community's reaction to *9-11*, Brian says milestones, achievements, tragic events and notable growth can and should be documented while materials are easily accessible. A part of that has practical implications: assigning a number and filling out a form for each donation made "helps personalize the acquisition," he notes.

•

"Your Treasures, Your History: 1875-2005" is an exhibition that celebrates the museum's 30th anniversary and its diverse collecting policy. It will be in place through December 2007.

•

Mount Horeb Area Museum
200 S. Second St., Mt. Horeb
www.mounthoreb.org, 608-437-6486

A once-dormant brewery (left) has new life as the site of a national museum.

POTOSI: SUDS IT UP

My office is full of suds, and it has nothing to do with the laundry that's clinking around downstairs. Wherever I turn my head, I am reminded of our state's great love affair with beer. I have brewery memorabilia and press releases about beer tours, tastings, beer anniversaries. All of this, regretfully, no longer is uncommon. The proliferation of microbreweries from one coast to another tends to water down Wisconsin's reputation as the nation's beer state, but that should change before this decade ends.

Thanks, **Potosi**.

The town of 726 people, in southwestern Wisconsin, has elbowed out Milwaukee and St. Louis to be the site for a national beer museum. Up to this point, Potosi's biggest fame was a **1941 Ripley's Believe It or Not** assertion that the town had the world's longest Main Street without an intersection.

Yes, it is long and narrow, a community built between two bluffs. How did it get the attention of Ripley's? "I don't know," says **Frank Fiorenza**, village president. "That was the year before I was born."

The **Potosi Beer Museum** is a joint project with the **American Breweriana Association**, a nonprofit group for people who love brewery history and advertising. They signed an agreement to pursue the museum project right around the time of **Catfish Days** in 2004, the annual fundraiser for the Fire Department that is held during the second weekend of August.

Craftsmen for Potosi Brewery hoist their product.

More than a ton of catfish are cooked, and this is Potosi's biggest event of the year. Now there's once again enough Potosi Light to wash it all down, thanks to the **Joseph Huber Brewing Company** of **Monroe**, which took over production of the hometown label—one of at least two dozen kinds of beer that used to be made here.

Other labels of the past include Holiday, Peerless, Monarch, Bohemian Club, Alpine and Augsburger. The latter brand is a German lager that is owned by Pabst but since 2003 has been brewed by **Stevens Point Brewery**.

Potosi is a place with a deep love for its beer heritage, Frank says. **Potosi Brewery** operated for 120 years, until 1972, and the building—although in disrepair—is on the National Register of Historic Places.

Soon it will be restored because of $2.8 million in grants and private donations. Among the local contributors, Frank says, was one person who pledged $100,000 and another who has given $80,000.

Did he realize that people of such generous means live in this modest and remote town? "Yes," the retired language arts teacher responds, "but it still was a nice surprise."

Roof work quickly became the priority. By 2008, the old brewery will be a place to exhibit, catalog and restore beer production artifacts from around the country. Potosi also will gain a microbrewery, restaurant and beer garden, plus a local beer museum.

Tourists learn the excitement of bottling at the Potosi plant.

Some of the artifacts will come from the national breweriana group (see **www.americanbreweriana.org**). Others, like **Dan Durley**'s vast Potosi beer memorabilia collection, will be local donations.

There is talk of making room for antique brewing and bottling equipment, plus items as small as bottle openers and beer coasters.

"It's like walking," Frank says, with regard to the overwhelming scope of what needs to be done. "One step at a time."

"We are rural, but we aren't isolated," Frank says, to explain why Potosi is a great location for this project. He contends that one-fourth of the nation's population is within a day's drive. "I'm excited for both the village and the tri-state area" of Iowa, Wisconsin and Illinois.

If the project brings in 30,000 to 40,000 visitors per year, he says it will revitalize the economy. A gift shop and antique shop already have made plans to open.

•

Potosi Brewery Foundation
PO Box 177, Potosi, 53820
www.potosibrewery.com, 608-763-2261

DETOURS

What else is there to do in Potosi and neighboring **Tennyson**, which used to be rival lead mining towns? **Grant River Canoeing and Tubing** are options; the tube float lasts an average of three hours as you meander down the Grant River.

•

There also are tours of the **St. John Mine**, which has been around since 1827 and is named after Willis St. John, the first to establish a mine in the area (although there also are written records of American Indians mining in the 1600s). See **www.grantcounty.org** or call **608-763-2121.**

•

One of the biggest craft beer festivals on the continent occurs in **Madison** on the second Saturday of August, and all 5,000 tickets to it are sold more than three months before the beer flows. **The Great Taste of the Midwest** features more than 400 types of beer from about 100 beer producers. The five-hour event is in a city park. Designated drivers pay a nominal fee to get on the grounds and drink pop; the others pay more to taste all that beer, 2 ounces at a time. The sponsor is the nonprofit **Madison Homebrewers and Tasters Guild**. See **www.mhtg.org**.

Aldo Leopold's shack was the incubator for his land ethic.

SAUK COUNTY: A SENSE OF PLACE

Halfway between **Baraboo** and **Wisconsin Dells**, on a frigid but sunny morning, tree branches glisten from a light coating of frozen rain. The turnoff is unmarked, the road rugged and slick. The landscape is bare, the mood quiet. Even the three curious chocolate Labs that trot over to greet and sniff their visitor are silent.

A massive amount of wood has been cut and stacked in the back yard of this stone and wood house, which is set back and on a bit of a hill. Inside, the view from huge windows is of nothing—and everything—on a single-digit winter day.

This is home for **Nina Leopold Bradley**, octogenarian daughter of the legendary wildlife ecologist. "One of the luxuries of old age is having the time to do so many things," Nina says. "The older I get, the more I realize what a privilege that is."

There is a strong sense of affection for family, and an equally strong sense of mission, to follow the principles of patriarch **Aldo Leopold**—conservationist, scientist, philosopher and author of *A Sand County Almanac*—who died in 1948.

What gives somebody a sense of place, a personal attachment to a piece of land, and what cultivates the priority to respect and nurture the Earth? "You plant and you work, and you have failures and successes," Nina explains. "Pretty soon, you are a part of this land, and you are connected."

She starts talking about the famous **Leopold Shack**, less than a mile away; she and most of her four siblings were introduced to it as teenagers. "That chicken coop was knee deep in manure, on worn-out farmland" that had been depleted of its nutrients, she recalls.

Nina Leopold Bradley still gets her hands dirty "grubbing in the land."

Restoration of the 80 acres to its natural state was an example of subtle teaching and meaningful lessons. "We're going to the shack—anybody want to come?" her father would ask. It was always an invitation, not a demand.

Then developing the **University of Wisconsin Arboretum**, he had been working to create "an example of what Wisconsin looked like before white man took it away from the Indians," Nina says. It was natural for her father to want to take the work a step further—to do the same thing to his own land.

The learning that began back then will never finish, says Nina, who spent many of her working years in Montana as an educator and ecological researcher. In 1976, she and her husband, the late **Charles Bradley**, ventured back to live at the **Leopold Memorial Reserve**.

The family began the Leopold fellowship program after their retirement. Each year, a half-dozen graduate students examine the area's character—its geology, soils, birds, amphibians.

"The most important thing is the hands-on work—collecting prairie seeds, the grubbing in the land," Nina says. Similar to gardening, it creates a personal connection: a personal investment between human being and dirt, a personal awareness of how interdependent one part of the natural world is on another.

"With our urban society, it's harder to get that point across," she acknowledges. The science of the future, she contends, will be the science of relationships: understanding why a hawk needs to swoop down on a chickadee, understanding why the health of snail darters is worth caring about.

"We have to teach children how to bond with the land before we can expect them to heal its wounds," she surmises, then mentioning "two theories that lean on each other: loving and being loved, and knowing that we live in a web of relationships that define and sustain us."

In a roomy office that is heated with a wood-burning stove and filled with plants that thrive in a window-filled alcove, Nina produces a file that quotes Kathleen Dean Moore, a philosophy professor at Oregon State University.

"Aldo Leopold," she reads, "brought together nature and culture, emotion and intellect, philosophy and science, the abstract and the concrete."

Would he be proud of the Leopold Memorial Reserve, now 1,600 acres? "He'd be pleased to see the kind of people who are being attracted to it," the daughter believes.

•

The **Aldo Leopold Foundation** conducts environmental programs, heritage and work tours. During the growing season, there occasionally are night seminars about conservation issues. Tours of the Leopold farm and shack, which last 90 minutes to two hours, include a walk through restored woods and prairie. The presentation is about the conservationist's philosophy as well as the land's history. Reservations are required.

Work has begun to recognize the Leopold Shack as a National Historic Landmark, a project that involves stopping the deterioration of the building. There also are plans to construct the **National Aldo Leopold Legacy Center**, to be a hub for education, research and Leopold archives.

•

Aldo Leopold Foundation, PO Box 77, Baraboo
www.aldoleopold.org, 608-355-0279

Fast Facts

Aldo Leopold's legendary *A Sand County Almanac*—about his respect for nature and goal to protect it—was not published until 1949, one year after his death. The writing had begun in 1937.

The author had a heart attack and died while battling a grass fire, one week after he got word that Oxford University Press would publish his essays. The book's original title was "Great Possessions."

•

Jura Silverman likes to mix her media, combining handmade paper, printmaking and copper.

SPRING GREEN: ABUNDANCE OF ART

Jura Silverman became smitten with the picturesque and peaceful nature of Spring Green, so the paper and print maker moved her art studio from Chicago in the 1980s. She has not regretted the decision.

Jura was the first artist to set up shop there, and now her business, Jura Silverman Gallery—a former cheese warehouse, built in the early 1900s—showcases the work of 70 Wisconsin artists. Her own studio is a former ice storage room.

Spring Green, population 1,500 and near the Wisconsin River in Sauk County, slowly has turned into a haven for art: visual, architectural and performance.

"We get quite a few people who are interested in the area because of other things that are related," Jura says, mentioning **Taliesin** (architect Frank Lloyd Wright's estate) and **American Players Theatre** (great theater, especially Shakespeare, on an outdoor stage amidst 110 wooded acres).

But it wasn't always that way.

Tours of Taliesin did not resume until five years after Jura moved to Spring Green,

A bird waiting to be freed by woodcarver Bob Russell.

and APT was struggling financially upon her arrival. Now the area is flush with art venues and artists. Several have creative workspaces, from old schoolhouses to barns.

The art studios typically aren't open to the public, but the third full weekend of October is an exception. About 50 artists from four communities participate in the free **Fall Art Tour**.

Visitors can use a map of the sites to drive from one studio to another; maps are online and at each tour stop. Artists and gallery owners in Spring Green, Baraboo, Dodgeville and Mineral Point display their work and demonstrate how it is created.

It's 35 miles from Baraboo to Spring Green, 18 from Spring Green to Dodgeville and seven from Dodgeville to Mineral Point. The event tends to coincide with the peaking of fall colors, making for a great weekend drive.

"It's hard to survive as an artist," Jura notes. The decision to locate in a remote rural area is an additional hurdle. Semi-isolation can nurture the spirit or challenge it. "Somehow, beautiful rural areas make for the creation of beautiful art," Jura says. "But it's harder for the artist to survive."

Spring Green has hosted the **Midwest Rural Arts Forum**, which helps motivate, inspire and advise people in rural areas who want to promote the arts.

"It's good to see histories of people who have started where there is nothing," Jura says, noting that rural artists tend to collaborate more, out of necessity.

"The more you have for people to enjoy, the more likely everyone will benefit from the effort."

For more about the annual Fall Art Tour, see **www.fallarttour.com**. "It's big-city quality combined with small-town atmosphere," said the *Chicago Sun Times*.

•

Jura Silverman Gallery
143 S. Washington St., Spring Green
www.springgreen.com/jsgallery, 608-588-7049

American Players Theatre actors in rehearsal.

Fast Facts

Spring Green used to have one other cheese distribution warehouse. Today it is the **Spring Green General Store**, 137 S. Albany St., which sells housewares to natural/organic foods, clothing to vitamins. It's a popular hangout for locals, with a comfortable café that serves burritos to quiche. **Bob Fest**—an open mike tribute to Bob Dylan—draws a crowd on the Sunday of Memorial Day weekend.

www.springgreengeneralstore.com, 608-588-7070.

•

Use **www.portalwisconsin.org** to learn more about arts events, classes, resources and artists in Wisconsin. That's also the place to sign up for a free newsletter about the arts in Wisconsin, delivered electronically.

•

Organic products from West Star Farm, near Stoughton, are showcased at a Home Grown Wisconsin tour.

SUN PRAIRIE: CHEFS ON TOUR

Customarily **Brandon Wolff** works in a crisp white chef's jacket—not a blaze orange Oklahoma State T-shirt and Nikes. He is one of Milwaukee's culinary leaders, having set the standard for high quality at **Dream Dance**, then **Bacchus**, then **Carnevor**.

Recently I saw him and more than a dozen other upscale restaurant chefs plucking raspberries, wandering through prairie grasses, feasting on fresh melon, sampling micro radishes and Laotian vegetables. The day ended with Brandon and his sous chefs grilling a simple meal of free-range poultry and newly picked veggies—eggplant to zucchini—while standing between fields of beans and strawberries at the **JenEhr Family Farm** near **Sun Prairie**.

This was a feast for the chefs, as well as the farmers whose products help give the restaurants their fine reputation. These culinary experts are far from identical, and you can say the same about the four Wisconsin farms that they visited. The tour was organized by **Home Grown Wisconsin**, whose 20 members are certified organic farmers. Many of them are vendors at the weekly **Dane County Farmers' Market**, which is considered to be one of the best in the nation. *Gourmet* magazine is among those who describe the market this way, both because of the range of products sold and the scenic Capitol Square setting.

Even Wisconsin's smallest cities seem to have at least one weekly farmers' market in summer. Each is a reminder of how good and fresh locally grown food can taste.

It is one thing to buy fresh produce from a booth, but quite another to see where it is grown and hear about the challenges of producing it. Our caravan of vehicles traversed Rock, Green and Dane counties—past the bright patches of goldenrod and sunflowers, the clank of bells on Brown Swiss cows and the hum of tractors at work.

Paul Maki of **Blue Skies Berry Farm**, **Brooklyn** sells 100 pounds of beets and carrots (including cosmic purple) per week at Chicago's Green City Market. There also is a pick-your-own option at the farm, for eight types of raspberries.

Scott Williams, at **Garden to Be** (on the Little Sugar River, near **New Glarus**), makes sustainable farming practices a priority. A walk-in cooler is insulated with "bricks" of straw. A corn burner warms the hoop house in winter, less expensive than propane.

Some crops are planted for the good of the soil, instead of the human appetite. Specialty crops include micro vegetables and herbs, tiny in size but powerful in flavor. Restaurants already buy them by the flat, and Garden to Be produces 250 flats per week, on top of its more conventional garden harvest.

Four miles from Stoughton is **West Star Farm**, 40 acres of organic vegetables, fruits and flowers. **George Kohn's** operation includes a tented farm stand that is open daily. Come fall, there will be a ton of salsify to harvest. It is a root vegetable with a Mediterranean history, one with ornamental as well as purported medicinal value.

"My favorite herbicide is called 'hoe,' " **Ruben Yoder**, a Mennonite who farms near Hillsboro, was telling a colleague later in the day. The farmers were full of stories and had an appreciative audience.

"We can tell our customers that our ingredients are from a small Wisconsin farm," notes **Jon DeCamp**, chef at Thyme in Chicago. And do they care? "They love it," says Jon.

It also was a great way for chefs to meet and compare challenges. **Dave Swanson** introduced us to **Braise**, a restaurant in Milwaukee's Third Ward. His restaurant is named after one of the first cooking procedures that culinary students learn.

"It is about getting back to basics," he says of the cuisine. "People have gotten so disconnected from their food" as preparations have become overly complex and elaborate.

Brandon Wolff prepares fresh organic vegetables for the grill.

Tory Miller, executive chef and co-owner of **L'Etoile Restaurant** in Madison, said "It makes sense for us to talk to each other about our business and our producers. When they do well, we do well."

•

Home Grown Wisconsin
PO Box 6171, Madison 53716
www.homegrownwisconsin.com, 608-341-8939

Fast Facts

Don't look for bananas or papaya at the **Dane County Farmers' Market**. Although it is the state's biggest, with about 300 vendors, all are required to sell products made in Wisconsin and related to agriculture. The outdoor market, around the **Capitol Square**, had only five farmers when it began in 1972. Today the county has at least one farmers' market in operation on almost every day of the week, but the Saturday market downtown continues to be the largest and has a three-year waiting list of prospective vendors. **www.madfarmmkt.org**, 608-455-1999.

•

Produce sold at the Dane County Farmers' Market must be fresh and local.

Come August, when most people are gnawing on sweet corn, fresh and locally grown *huitlacoche* makes an appearance at $5 an ear. Pronounced *wheat-la-CO-chay*, the corn fungus has a pleasantly mild and nutty flavor. Considered a delicacy in Mexico, the corn mushrooms/fungus are picked off, sautéed in garlic/olive oil/onions and added to tacos or quesadillas. The annual harvest at the **Troy Gardens** community farm, Madison, is 100 pounds or more.

What happens to make the vegetable huitlacoche, also known as Mexican truffles? The ears are injected with a fungus around the time that corn silk appears.

•

VALTON: THE PAINTED FOREST

We don't know how old **Ernest Hupeden** was when he was wrongly convicted of bank embezzlement in Germany, but he spent eight years in prison, until the real criminal confessed from his death bed.

What kind of mark does that leave on an innocent man? It was enough for him to move in 1878 to the United States, where he lived the rest of his years as a drifter, a drunk—and an incredibly prolific, obsessive and distinctive painter.

Self-taught while in prison, Ernest later would paint the bottles of alcohol that he had emptied, plus the plates and pie tins of people who had fed him. He'd create murals on house walls and the outside of barns, in exchange for a place to sleep.

Painting was a way to earn his keep while walking from New York to Wisconsin, which took him almost 20 years, and it is here where his most public work survives. Now a small, rural building—drenched with Ernest's people and landscapes, slices of life and fraternity, dark and serene moods—has become a site to inspire Madison art students and scholars nationwide.

The Painted Forest, a former Modern Woodmen of America lodge in the Sauk County town of **Valton**, has become the property of Edgewood College, thanks to the generosity and restorative work of the **Kohler Foundation**, which also has helped build a nearby art studio and study center for the college to conduct workshops.

The artist spent about two years (1897-99) painting the inside of the 60-by-33-by-24-foot white frame lodge, almost every square inch of it. That includes the arched ceiling.

"It is truly a Wisconsin treasure," says **Terri Yoho**, executive director of the **Kohler Foundation**, "and it hasn't been seen by enough people."

The work is a classic example of outsider art, that which is created by people who are self-taught and typically unheralded until after their death. The foundation has restored the Valton murals to their original condition, and Yoho is heartened by the enthusiasm and respect Edgewood has shown for the property.

Edgewood's attention to outsider art has been longstanding. There have been lectures, exhibits and advocacy that have involved—among others—the **Dr. Evermor** outdoor sculpture park near **Baraboo**, the late **Mona Webb's** Williamson Street art in **Madison** and the found art sculptures of northern Wisconsin's **Hope Atkinson**.

The **Valton lodge**, also called **Camp 6190**, is open for public tours but not routinely used for other events. "There is some fragility to the art," Yoho notes. And although heating and air conditioning have been added, there are no bathrooms.

The Painted Forest reveals a part of its creator's soul, as well as the values and activities of the organization that paid for his work. Modern Woodmen of America, since 1883, has been all about resilience through financial and fraternal stability.

The Valton lodge contains blue skies and lush forests as well as brutal scenes of injury and death, happy families as well as blinded victims. "Woodmen clearing the forest for mankind" was a part of the brotherhood's desired image as well. Death was inevitable; insurance was necessary.

Modern Woodmen—a business that sells life insurance and other financial services—also has long been an outlet for families to socialize, support each other, stay wholesome and do charitable work.

That makes the end of Ernest's life story even more ironic. After finishing his work in Valton, the painter began to wander and work elsewhere in Wisconsin. In 1911, his body was found in a snowbank near Hillsboro. His burial site is unknown, but historians speculate that it is a pauper's grave. *(See painting on page iii.)*

•

The Painted Forest, near Hwy. EE, Valton
608-663-4861 (Edgewood College)

SOUTHWEST

Fast Facts

The **Kohler Foundation** is known for its preservation of folk architecture and art environments. After restoration, a site typically is given to an entity that will keep it accessible to the public.

"The medium for many self-taught artists is both literally and figuratively free—a home, a yard, a building, a hillside," states **www.kohlerfoundation.org**, which explains other preservation projects. "Some build chapels and grottos, others create murals that encase entire buildings or hundreds of sculptures to populate a landscape. To visit one of these sites is to experience the boundless soul of the artist."

•

The Painted Forest is mentioned in *Miracles of the Spirit: Folk, Art and Stories from Wisconsin* (University Press of Mississippi) by **Don Krug** and **Ann Parker**.

•

Edgewood College maintains an art studio and study center near the Painted Forest. It "provides studio space, a sleeping loft, a small kitchen and bathrooms —all things that were not available" at the art-filled building, says the Kohler Foundation. The new building is where art events typically are held.

•

Snow sculpting is a matter of art, logic, physics and luck.

WISCONSIN DELLS: FROSTY FLASHBACKS

In my office are pictures of people who have influenced my life. They are great reminders of where I've been, and of where I'd like to head next. One of the images is of a guy who is sporting a huge grin, plus a cap dusted with snow and medallions. His name is **Mark Shully**, I have long cherished his friendship, and the picture was handed out at his memorial service.

Full of life and humor, Shully died of an aneurysm three days before Christmas in 2000.

My buddy spent a part of his last year in the picturesque Dolomites of Italy. Snow sculpting is what brought him to these mountains; his three-person team from Cudahy represented the U.S. in international competition there. To hear Shully talk about it, the event was all about goodwill and hospitality. It was one big welcome party, oozing with cultural richness.

Less than 10 years earlier—on a whim—he and co-workers at Poblocki Sign Company, Milwaukee, decided to enter a Wisconsin Dells contest and see what they could carve out of a 10-foot block of snow.

They liked the challenge, the setting and the camaraderie of other sculptors. So year after year, they honed their technique and strategy. Their working reference would be a clay model of the design, about one-tenth the size of the final sculpture. Then it became a process of strategy and extraction, deciding what to remove, how and in what order. The shoveling, sawing, drilling and chiseling would take roughly 48 hours, about 10 hours per day for each of them.

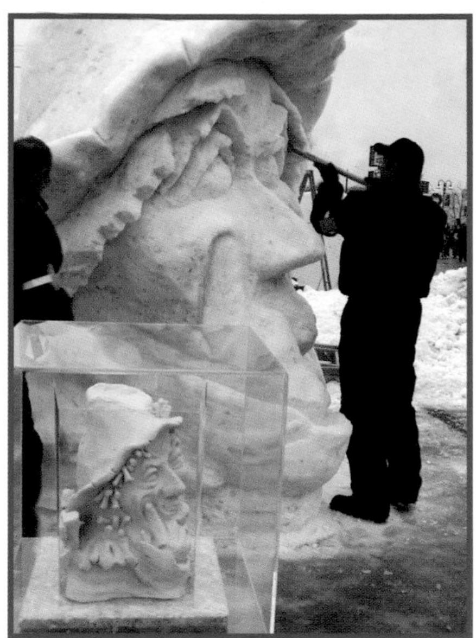

Competitors use 1/10 scale maquettes to help them keep in proportion.

Their biggest challenges? Sunshine could do more damage than a warmer temperature. Snow could change to slush and double in weight.

The Cudahy guys eventually won state, national and international contests with sculptures of a coral reef and fish. **Mark Mayzik** has a fine arts background and came up with design sketches. **Greg Moerner** is an industrial designer who can turn a sketch into a larger and three-dimensional work.

And Shully? He used to joke that he was in charge of the grunt work—the heavy lifting and the shoveling. For his teammates, though, it was much more than that. "He was always able to maintain a certain spirit and appreciation for what was going on," Mark says. The mental challenges aren't to be underestimated.

"It's really a marathon, a test of endurance. It's a matter of staying interested, staying focused, and not going too far too early. The sun can destroy you if your work is done too early.

"As a team, you have to keep your own opinions in check, to a point, and be open to criticism. The wrong emotion can disintegrate the momentum."

Mark and Greg continue to sculpt snow in winter. Their teammate has been **Jim Schmitt**, another Poblocki employee, who grew up with Mark Shully.

•

Flake Out Festival, Wisconsin Dells
www.wisdells.com, 800-223-3557

•

Fast Facts

Wisconsin Dells is the world's waterpark capital, but plenty of other diversions will keep you dry.

The **January Flake Out Festival** contains the only state-sanctioned snow sculpting event; the winner goes to **Lake Geneva's** national competition during **Winterfest** in February. Consult: **www.lakegenevawi.com** and (800) 345-1020.

Shannah Bass, who organizes the Dells event, prefers teams with experience. How do you get it? Watch competition sculptors, notice the tools used and ask questions. Find an empty cardboard appliance box, pack it with snow, then remove the box and hack away. For inspiration, go to **www.sculptor.org**, an online forum for sculptors of all kinds.

•

Wisconsin Dells is best known for what it does with water that is not frozen. The city has become the Waterpark Capital of the World, because of the high concentration of these hydro extravaganzas.

All told, there are 21 waterparks in the Dells, and they have more than 200 waterslides. The biggest outdoor waterpark is at **Noah's Ark** (70 acres), and **Kalahari Waterpark Resort** has the largest that is indoor (125,000 square feet).

What's the biggest indoor/outdoor combo? It was **Wilderness Hotel & Golf Resort**, until two properties merged into **Mt. Olympus** in 2005.

"The credo here," according to press materials, "is that if it isn't the biggest, tallest, fastest, newest or wettest then we're not interested in building it."

So it's likely that these statistics already are outdated. Before the end of 2005, the Wilderness had announced a $150 million expansion. **Great Wolf Resorts**, the world's biggest waterpark resort company, has been expanding as far away as Tennessee.

The nation's first indoor waterpark was at the **Polynesian Resort Hotel & Suites**, in 1989.

•

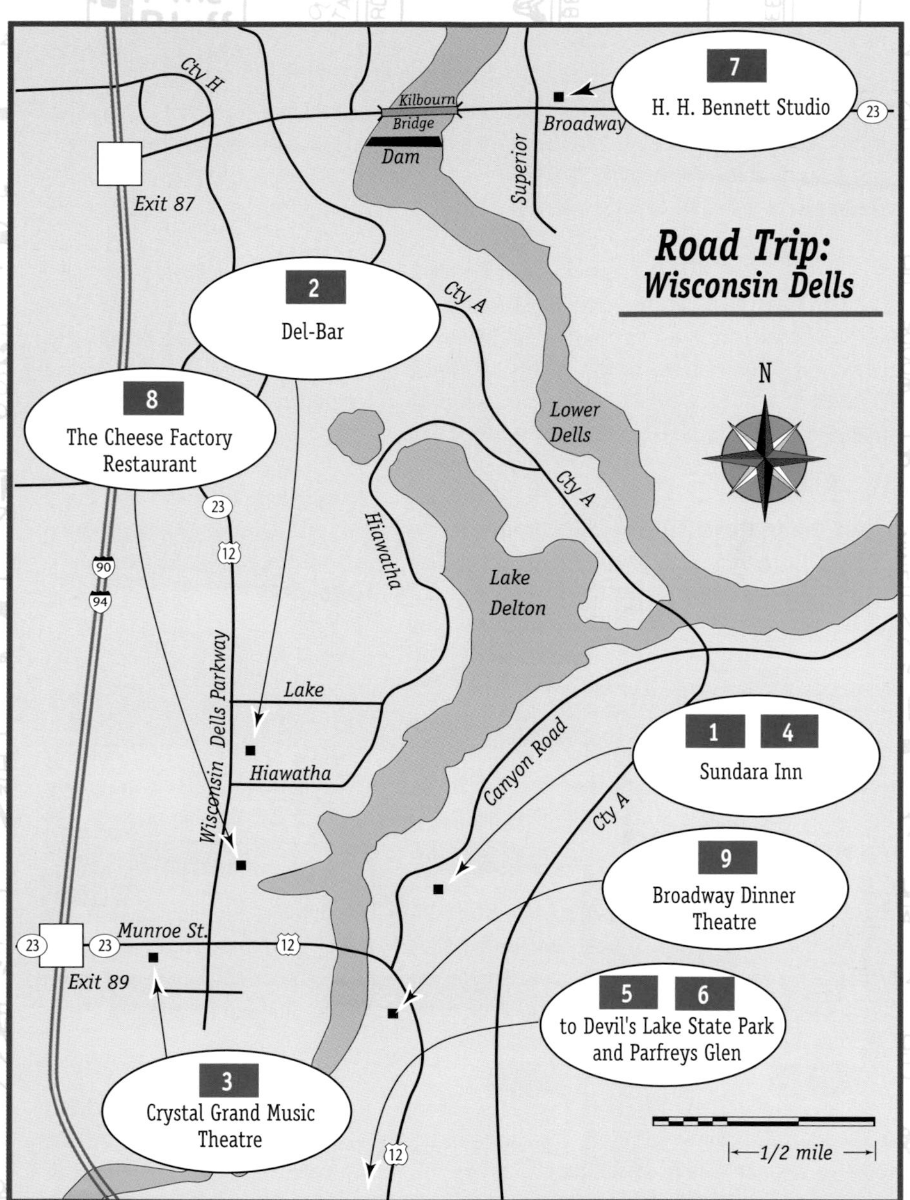
Road Trip:
Wisconsin Dells
7
H. H. Bennett Studio
2
Del-Bar
8
The Cheese Factory Restaurant
1
4
Sundara Inn
9
Broadway Dinner Theatre
5
6
to Devil's Lake State Park and Parfreys Glen
3
Crystal Grand Music Theatre
Kilbourn Bridge
Dam
Broadway
Superior
Cty H
Exit 87
Cty A
Lower Dells
Lake Delton
Hiawatha
Lake
Wisconsin Dells Parkway
Canyon Road
Munroe St.
Exit 89
23
12
90
94
N
1/2 mile

Dells Road Trip • Day 1

1. Enhance Romance. Turn the Dells into a destination for two by checking into **Sundara Inn & Spa**, 920 Canyon Road. Pack a swimsuit, not for the area waterparks, but for the steamy purifying ritual that precedes spa treatments. **www.sundaraspa.com, 888-735-8181**.

2. Dinner with Frank. Like **Frank Lloyd Wright** architecture? It's two miles (southwest on Canyon, right on East Adams, right on Hwys. 12/23) to the **Del-Bar**, 800 Wisconsin Dells Parkway, which got its name because it is between the Dells and Baraboo. Renovations to this 1930s log home were designed by **James Dresser**, a Wright protégé. Steak eaters, splurge for a topping of asparagus, crabmeat and hollandaise sauce. **www.del-bar.com, 866-888-1861**.

3. Show Time? Call it a night, unless you snag tickets for a show at the **Crystal Grand Music Theatre**, 430 Munroe St. (go south on Hwys. 12/23, right on Munroe). In the lineup are well-known celebrities, the comedy of Bill Cosby to the music of Sawyer Brown. **www.crystalgrand.com, 800-696-7999**.

Day 2

4. Easy Does It. Lounge, year-round, at Sundara's outdoor infinity pool while having breakfast, or after beginning the day with a massage or body wrap. Too much exertion? Simply stare at the fireplace in your room, while kicking back on the featherbed.

5. Take a Hike. **Devil's Lake State Park** is a straight shot south, (left on East Adams, left on Hwy. 12 East, left on Hwy. 159, right on Highway DL to Park Road). A superb place for serious rock climbers as well as sunbathers, snow and water skiers. Expect sultry ballroom dancing, too, at the lakeside Chateau on summer Saturday nights, overlooking the lake.

6. Cool It. **Parfrey's Glen** is eight miles east, in the Baraboo Hills near Merrimac and on Highway DL. It is a cool and pretty respite, no matter what the thermometer elsewhere says. It is a narrow ravine with sandstone walls, with great shade and scenery for the hiker and nature enthusiast.

H.H. Bennett Studio and History Center explains how tourists found the Dells.

7. History Lesson. Head to the **H.H. Bennett Studio & History Center**, 215 Broadway St. (backtrack to Highway 12 West, then west on I-90/94, north on Highway 13). Now that you've seen the Dells' natural beauty, find out more about the first photographer whose landscape work brought a huge migration of tourists to the area. Guess he gets the credit/blame for what the area is today. **www.wisconsinhistory.org/hhbennett, 608-253-3523.**

8. Time for Dinner. Not a meat eater? No sweat. **The Cheese Factory Restaurant**, 521 Wisconsin Dells Parkway South, has a vegan menu, too. (Take Broadway/Highway 23 West, then left on Highway 12/Dells Parkway). Rattlesnake Tofu is a signature dish; it is seasoned tofu, charbroiled and served with barbecue sauce. Hours are abbreviated in winter. **www.cookingvegetarian.com, 608-253-6065.**

9. Final Act. The Dells has a big-time theater playbill, too, with the opening of **Broadway Dinner Theatre** in a new $10 million, 600-seat facility at 564 S. Wisconsin Dells Parkway. **www.broadwayinthedells.com, 888-998-7469.**

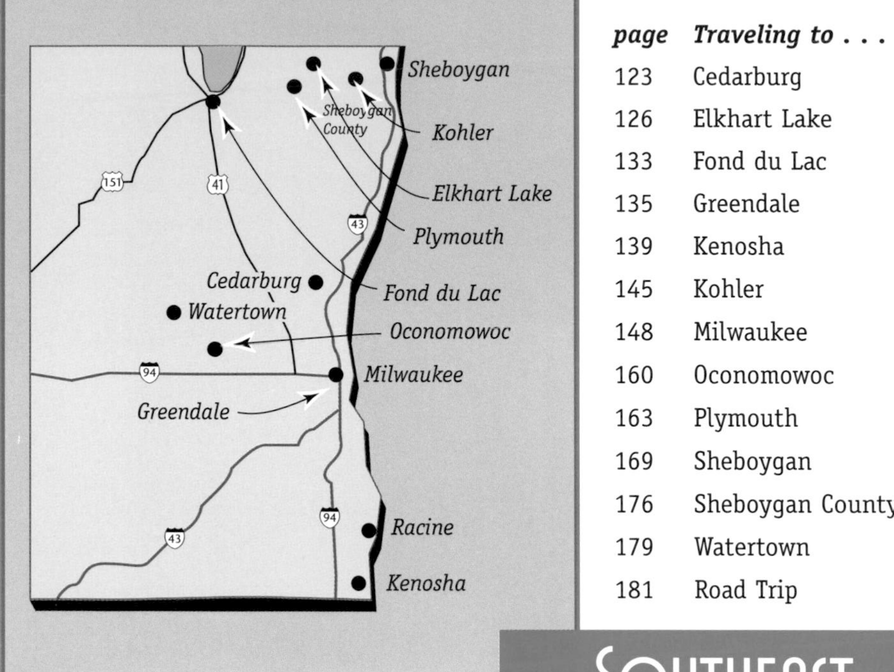

SOUTHEAST

Observation: Local color and caring communities create an authentic "sense of place."

That's how Hispanics in Milwaukee, golf courses near Kohler and car racing in Elkhart Lake are making their mark nationally. The combination of tradition with a fine human touch is sustaining old-fashioned businesses—an Italian market in Kenosha, Danish bakeries in West Racine. What used to be commonplace is increasingly seen as a treasure, from locally produced ingredients in fine restaurants to the stitchery and recipes of home cooks and housewives.

A historic farmstead showcases quilts and textiles.

CEDARBURG: HISTORY IN STITCHES

Wisconsin Museum of Quilts and Textiles makes its home on 2.2 acres in Cedarburg, a former German Four-Square farmstead at the corner of Struck Lane and Portland Road. Some of the seven farm buildings contain exhibition space, a gift shop and resource library. This also is where special textile shows occur during the community's biggest celebrations.

The museum exists because of **Wisconsin Quilt History Project Inc.**, which is passionate about its purpose. Founder **Luella Doss** says that includes preserving and improving awareness of the historic farmstead, whose 1850s-1870s buildings include a lambing shed, icehouse, carriage house and smokehouse-summer kitchen.

"It is a matter of saving the stories as well as promotion and education," says **Maribeth Schmit**, volunteer coordinator. "We'd like to preserve several types of textiles," hooked rugs and weavings as well as quilts.

An annual event is the **Spring Fling Tea and Bed Turning**, on a Saturday afternoon in mid May. Maribeth says about three dozen quilts are stacked on one of three propped up beds in the farm's 1850s barn. One at a time, the quilts are folded back, to reveal the one underneath it.

"We'll talk about how old it is, the fabrics and pattern used, the story behind it," she says. Such documentation began in 1987, and the results were the basis for the 2001

Textiles, preserved in a homespun setting.

book *Wisconsin Quilts: Stories in the Stitches* by the state's first poet laureate, **Ellen Kort** of Appleton.

The quilt historians want the museum to attract visitors from across the country.

Textile arts have long been a way to tell family stories, teach about life, provide an outlet for creativity. There are social statements to be made, too.

The stitchery—be it by hand or machine—helps preserve the history, ethnicity, artistry and craftsmanship of everyday and gifted people. They are works that combine the practical and the aesthetic.

Volunteers in the Wisconsin Quilt History Project have documented a history and description for about 7,000 Wisconsin quilts. The process involves finding out about the quilter—from name, age and occupation—as well as the fabric content and dimensions of each quilt that has been produced. Among the best-known Wisconsin quilters is **Diane Gaudynski** of Pewaukee, a self-taught quilter whose work began in 1980. See **www.dianegaudynski.net** for workshops that she conducts.

•

Wisconsin Museum of Quilts and Textiles, PO Box 562, Cedarburg 53012
www.wiquiltmuseum.com, 262-546-0300

Asides

Since 1988, quilts and other textiles have been documented during Cedarburg's annual **Strawberry Festival**. For a nominal fee, the handmade item is described through a photo and written history which are secured, computerized and filed into the Wisconsin Quilt History Project's archives. A numbered label is sewn onto the textile product, so it can be tracked by future generations. Researchers also can investigate the history of older quilts that have changed hands.

If you want to arrange a tour of the Wisconsin Museum of Quilts and Textiles when it isn't open, contact the **Cedarburg Woolen Mill** at **262-377-0345.**

•

What Else?

What else brings people together in quaint Cedarburg, a city that is proud of its historic preservation work?

Locals let loose during **Winter Festival**, which is the first weekend in February. Most events are free.

Ice seems to matter more than snow. It is a tradition for speed-skating teams to pull beds on runners, down the frozen creek, then around a barrel. Wooden barrel races require the kegs to be rolled through the same course. Without ice, both types of races are moved to city streets. Bed runners come off and are replaced with wheels.

The annual Alaskan malamute dog weight pull also proceeds, regardless of weather. The **Ice-Burg Open Golf Tournament** proceeds with yellow balls, to show up against snow.

In summer, berry lovers migrate to Cedarburg for the **Strawberry Festival** during the last weekend of June. Berries are sold by the quart. The **Strawberry Pancake Breakfast** is on Sunday morning. **Cedar Creek Winery** produces Strawberry Blush Wine.

Be it schaum tortes or strawberry slush, the **Berry Big 5K Run/Walk** or bubblegum blowing contest, Cedarburg puts all of its berries into one basket for this annual celebration, which began in the 1980s.

For more: www.cedarburgfestivals.org, (800) 237-2874.

Elkhart street races began in the 1950s.

ELKHART LAKE: A RACER'S DREAM

Ask me about **Road America**, and all kinds of memories are quick to return. When I was a kid, the constant buzz of the racing car engines was easy to hear at our farm, about five miles from the competition.

While in college, several friends found future husbands during race weekends—if not at the track, then at Sportsman's Bar in Elkhart Lake.

When I was a waitress, some summer tips would be pit passes that bought access to the rolling racetrack's inner sanctuary. Restless resort staff would be motivated, year after year, by rumors that Paul Newman was booked for a stay. That never happened, as far as I know (he apparently preferred **The American Club** in Kohler).

Much in my life has changed since those easygoing years. The family farm has become a haven for wildlife, pheasants in particular. Sportsman's Bar is gone, too, replaced by a restaurant called **Lake Street Cafe**, with white linens and a menu that the locals call "California food."

What stays the same? Road America, in a way. The facility is more than half a century old, and its 640 acres continue to be a car racer's dream.

"One of the dynamic things is that the big track has stayed the same," says **George Bruggenthies**, Road America president and general manager. "That says a lot about the foresight and design of the track. It remains one of the drivers' favorites."

Called the fastest road course in the world, its average lap speed is 148 miles per hour. One lap is four miles, and there are 14 turns.

The toughest? That might be Canada Corner, where the drivers take a hard right after a fast track straightaway. Or Corner 5—it's a 90-degree left hand turn, which also comes off a long straightaway.

The thought freshens another memory: the smell of grilled brats, the heat of the sun, the flow of cold beer, the squeal of car tires and the crowd. None of that has changed either.

Although the actual track is the same, George says crowd access has improved because of the addition of bridges and viewing areas. "It's more like a park than anything," he says. "It's not a dusty oval."

This track is used about one-half of the year. Newer and smaller tracks (a motorplex, especially for racing karts and hybrid motorcycles, and adventure tracks for ATVs) make it possible for the facility to operate in all seasons. These are sites for corporate escapes and team-building outings, as well as training grounds for would-be professional racers.

The seven adventure trails are in Road America's wooded areas. They go over rock walls, trees and ground holes. "It is a low-speed adventure that involves a lot of balance," George says. "You're almost proceeding at a crawl, during some parts."

What is Road America's biggest challenge? "It's a small business," the general manager says, "and that means it's hard to keep pace" with the industry. NASCAR, he notes, does two road races per year, but the waiting list to host such an event is long.

"Maybe it'll come back someday," George says. NASCAR last raced at Road America in 1957. Auto racing began in Elkhart Lake when the village and the Sports Car Club of America organized street races in 1950. The routes went through town and around it.

The area had been a magnet for Chicago vacationers—including gangsters—since the mid 1800s. Trains used to stop there; the terrain of the Kettle Moraine glacial area was both a scenic tourist attraction and ideal for racing.

The final track design, wrote Everett Nametz, in Road America's first official program, embodied "practically all the normal driving hazards that one might encounter in any section of the country." Elevation changes several hundred feet from one part of the course to another.

The intent was to establish a racetrack "with terrain so different from all other racing circuits that after the course was built it would continue to hold the esteem of racing fans and respect of competition drivers down through the years."

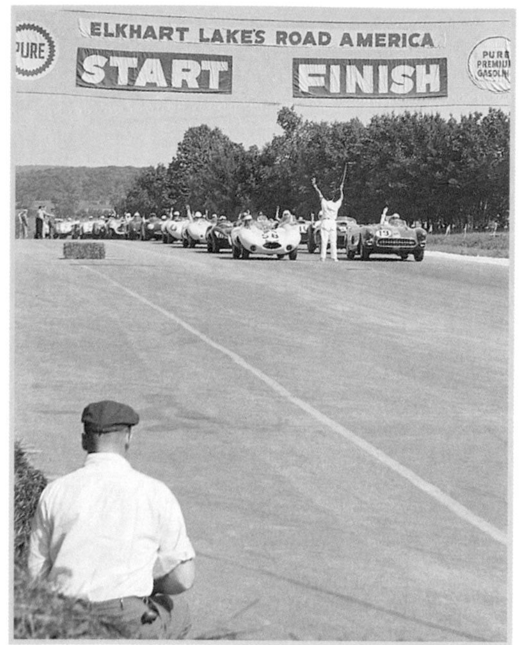

Some of the nation's most legendary car racers, including **Mario Andretti** and **Brian Redman**, returned to Road America in 2005 to celebrate the track's 50th anniversary.

•

Road America
N7390 Hwy. 67, Elkhart Lake
www.roadamerica.com
800-365-7223

SOUTHEAST

DETOUR

One of the least expensive ways for families to enjoy Road America is to attend the **Community Tailgate Party** there in mid May. There typically is vintage sports car racing, a Big Wheel Race for children, pony and carnival rides, car show, music, food and beverage samplings, tours of the track facilities and helicopter rides. Admission is free, as are many (but not all) activities. Enter at Gate 2, off Highway 67.

•

A cheap way to pass the time in summer is to laze at **Fireman's Park**, 411 S. Lake St., or let the sand ooze between your toes while wading far out into the clear water. Admission to this public beach is cheap. Sundays are especially peaceful; no motorboats are allowed. Afterward, take a stroll and order an old-fashioned phosphate at **Gessert's**, a soda fountain that has been around since the 1920s, but hours of operation are minimal.

•

Eclectic decor at Back Porch Bistro.

Food Artistry

Back in the 1970s, I spent five summers at the Schwartz Hotel in Elkhart Lake, working as a waitress to pay my way through college. Those are fond memories, even though we'd get only one meal off—not a full day—during the busiest summer weeks.

College students from as far away as England would come to work until Labor Day, and it was the first time this farm girl got an inkling of what people and life could be like away from home.

The resort has since seen other owners and gotten other names. Today it is the **Victorian Village Resort**, and it's undergoing a transformation.

One part involves the massive restoration of the Grand Victorian Lady, a worn, gallant and turn-of-the-century hotel building that has become a condo complex with dramatic lake views. Another is development of a dining niche that is good for farmers and the environment as well as the chef and his customers.

•

Jesse Salzwedel bakes artisanal breads daily.

Jesse Salzwedel is a self-taught chef who operates the **Back Porch Bistro**, one of the few Wisconsin restaurants that are members of the **Chefs Collaborative**, an organization founded in the 1990s "to promote the virtues of local, seasonal and sustainable ingredients within the restaurant community and to the greater public."

About 90 percent of foods served at the bistro are from Wisconsin, says Jesse, who continues building upon this culinary emphasis. The goal is "to buy the highest-quality ingredients I can for my menus."

The Back Porch, Elkhart Lake's oldest lakefront restaurant, has huge windows and an inviting decor that is both eclectic and nostalgic. Outdoor dining is available in summer. There is an occasional "Taste Wisconsin Series," a fixed-price meal "to showcase the very best of what is available that month from Wisconsin."

For details, go to **www.vicvill.com** or call **877-860-9988**. Jesse is in good company; Chefs Collaborative membership includes some of the nation's most acclaimed restaurants.

"It is a challenge to be in an organization with chefs at such a high level," he says. "It can raise people's expectations.

"I don't claim to be an equal to many of these members. I am, however, proud of them for laying the groundwork to start Chefs Collaborative. Many of them are inspirations to me and have helped to shape my career path and goals."

There are about 160 restaurant members. Others in Wisconsin include:

L'Etoile, 25 N. Pinckney St., **608-252-0500**, in downtown **Madison**. Previously owned by Odessa Piper, a three-time James Beard Foundation award winner, it is now owned by the brother-sister combo of chef **Tory and Traci Miller.** "We choose local, organic and naturally raised ingredients whenever feasible," the restaurant's menu states. Many ingredients come from "a large network of small-scale farms," many of which are listed at **www.letoile-restaurant.com.**

Roots Restaurant and Cellar, 1818 N. Hubbard St., **Milwaukee**, **414-374-8480**. One of the city's newer restaurants, it is in the renovated Brewers Hill neighborhood. "We believe Milwaukee is ready for something new and creative," says **John Raymond**, the chef/owner. The business also includes an organic garden and a greenhouse, to produce

Jesse Salzwedel says most of his restaurant's recipes are handwritten. He shares two—this gazpacho and Purple Potato Salad—that "would work great as part of a summer picnic, maybe out at the track."

Cucumber Almond Gazpacho

2 1/2 cups almonds
10 slices of day old bread
1/2 cup olive oil
3 quarts vegetable stock
9 garlic cloves
3/4 cup white wine vinegar
Salt
8 cups skinless, seedless, cubed cucumber

Blanch the almonds for two minutes, cool and remove the skins. Lightly toast the almonds in the oven. Lightly fry the bread with a little olive oil in a fry pan. Soak the bread in the vegetable stock. In a food processor, grind the garlic and almonds. Add the soaked bread and process to a smooth puree. Add the rest of the olive oil and white wine vinegar. Consistency should be a thick liquid. Add salt and cucumbers.

food served at the restaurant. This is "American regional cookery with contemporary world-fusion cuisine celebrating the seasons." For more: **www.rootsmilwaukee.com.**

Sanford Restaurant, 1547 N. Jackson St., **Milwaukee, 414-276-9608.** Well-regarded and in an east side Italian neighborhood, this restaurant has been a four-diamond AAA property for more than a decade. Chef and owner **Sanford D'Amato** works in a building that used to be the family-run grocery store. His claims to fame include being one of a dozen chefs selected by Julia Child to cook for her 80th birthday. The family's more casual restaurant is **Coquette Cafe**, 316 N. Milwaukee St., in the city's Third Ward. For more: **www.sanfordrestaurant.com.**

•

Chefs Collaborative, 262 Beacon St., Boston, Mass.
www.chefscollaborative.org, 617-236-5200

•

Another longstanding dining option in Elkhart Lake is **Siebkins**, a quaint and turn-of-the-century resort that is open seasonally. Dine on the screened porch, then meander to the tavern for a nightcap, music or chocolate-cherry cake.

For more: **www.siebkins.com, 888-876-2600.**

Purple Potato Salad

5 pounds purple potatoes
3 cups thinly shaved fennel
1 cup diced red onion
1 cup diced celery
1 cup fresh tarragon
Dressing
1 cup mustard
1 cup crème fraiche
1/2 cup red wine vinegar
1/2 cup olive oil
1/2 cup lemon juice
Salt

Boil potatoes in their skins until just barely cooked through. Be careful not to overcook. Peel and cube the potatoes. Blanch the fennel in boiling water for 2 minutes. For the dressing, mix mustard, crème fraiche, red wine vinegar, olive oil, lemon and salt together.

Toss the fennel, onion and celery with the potatoes, add tarragon, then mix in the dressing.

Elks Lodge 57 has a secret.

FOND DU LAC: BOWLING PARADISE

The good people of Fond du Lac are quietly protecting a piece of history that is deemed significant in the world of bowling. They have the country's oldest sanctioned and continuously operating bowling alley in the basement of **Elks Lodge 57**. Who knew? You wouldn't guess it, from the outside.

This Elks lodge, a monstrous Queen Anne Victorian downtown, cost $40,000 to build and furnish in 1903. It retains much of its grandeur, with a lovely round bar, wall panels of imported Italian woods, an inviting fireplace, carved trim and floors of maple.

The Elks also had slot machines into the 1930s, taking in 5 to 25 cents per pull.

"The most important job of the bartenders was to determine when to hide the three machines," write lodge historians. "Sometimes the police came into the lodge three times a day. When the 'heat was on' the bartender quickly slid a false wall across the front of the machines."

Manager **Chuck Balnis** is glad to conduct tours of the property, but it's important to call instead of just show up. Visitors can't simply walk in; a buzzer announces their

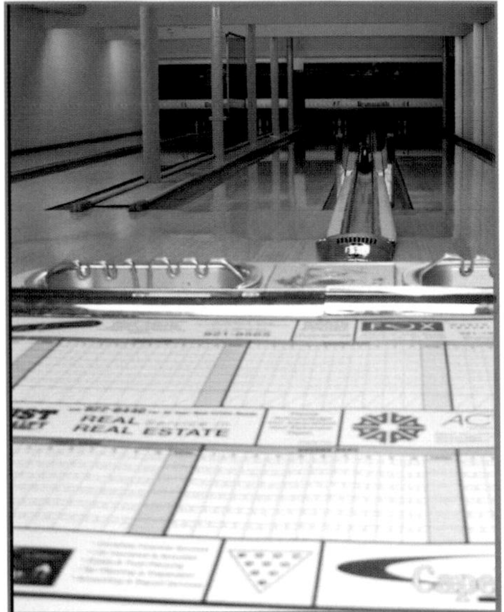

arrival and clearance.

"We'd love to open it to the public, but we have tax-exempt status as a private club," says **Stan Plageman**, exalted ruler of the lodge.

The basement bowling alley has its own bar, making it an ideal place for private parties. Scoring still is done by hand, but machines now set the pins.

"Bowlers used to toss a half-dollar or quarter down the lane, to get the pin setter to stay for an extra game," Chuck says.

The lanes are old but they are not outdated. New synthetic surfaces increase the potential for good scores.

The bowling lanes have been certified since 1909. That means 40 criteria must be met, having to do with things like lane width and length, bowling pin weight and tilt.

You have to be an Elks member (from any city), or the guest of one, to bowl here—or eat lunch or a Friday night perch fry in the lodge dining room. That's not as hard as it may sound.

Membership is $110 per year and open to women as well as men. Prospective members need a sponsor but don't need to live in Fond du Lac.

"I think all fraternal organizations are seeing a decline in membership," Chuck says, regarding lodge loyalty. The peak was 1,000 in the mid 1980s.

Nationwide, there are more than 2,100 Elks lodges, and the group is known for its work with at-risk youth: mentoring, anti-drug programs, scholarships. The Fond du Lac lodge is one of 33 in Wisconsin.

•

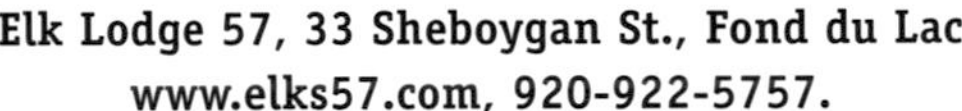

Elk Lodge 57, 33 Sheboygan St., Fond du Lac
www.elks57.com, 920-922-5757.

For more about bowling leagues in Wisconsin or places to bowl, go to **www.wibowl.com**.

Joylyn Trickel (left) and Sue Megonigle, at work in the Taste of Home *test kitchen.*

GREENDALE: MAKING IT FROM SCRATCH

There are 1,000 from-scratch cooks (from each state and throughout Canada) who are volunteer field editors for ***Taste of Home***, a bimonthly publication with 4 million paid subscribers. This is the biggest cooking magazine in the world.

"It's like a recipe exchange for good home cooks," according to **Ann Kaiser**, managing editor. **Reiman Publications Visitor Center** in downtown Greendale was developed, Ann says, because "people wanted to come and see us."

It is an orderly three-ring circus. Food stylist **Joylyn Trickel** prepares and arranges ingredients for chicken tostadas. Sheets of cookies are in the oven. Kitchen assistant **Sue Megonigle** uses a rolling pin to flatten miniature Tootsie Rolls, for shingles on a gingerbread house.

Taste of Home contains no outside advertising, and 80 percent of the written content comes from readers. The field editors get a free magazine subscription, quarterly newsletter and good deals on cookbooks—but no salary—for their recipe contributions.

Ann Kaiser has an army of 1,000 and legions of fans because she knows how to listen.

How does the loyalty and strong sense of ownership happen?

Founder **Roy Reiman**, of Reiman Publications, has long made it his priority to pay attention to customers' interests and to respond to their concerns. His publishing empire in 2002—12 titles at that time—was sold to *Reader's Digest* for $760 million.

Taste of Home, a 68-page glossy with fetching food photos, is the eighth-largest circulated consumer publication in North America. It has been around since 1993.

"We view our role as selling a service, not a product," Roy says. He unabashedly calls this "the good news company," one that helps people "feel proud about who they are."

So 65,000 recipes are sent to this Milwaukee suburb each year—about 15,000 of them for *Taste of Home* recipe contests. Hundreds of recipes are tested in one of three kitchens.

Taste of Home uses 85 recipes per issue. Fifty recipes per reader contest are tested. There is a kitchen staff of about 20—home economists, dietitians, assistants—plus four or five stylists and two photographers.

"We look for recipes with readily available ingredients," Ann says. "No unusual spices or other items that are hard to find." The recipes also must be easy to make and understand.

One reader recipe contest will generate 1,000 to 10,000 entries, depending on the topic. "Root vegetables," for example, isn't as popular as "pies." If a recipe is sent in by more than one reader—"we may get 25 to 30 of the same thing"—it will be credited to the one which arrives first.

"We also have a database that lets us check recipes by their ingredients or name," Ann says. She will work with kitchen staff to screen recipes and select finalists before testing begins. They are deliberate about coming up with a good mix of both states and food types.

What if a recipe tastes fine but doesn't look appealing? "A lot of times, good garnishes can go a long way," says Joylyn, the stylist. Recipes that make it into the magazine are prepared at least twice, first for tasting, then for photographing.

Six people read proofsheets before the magazine is printed; recipe errors are not acceptable. A picture of the cook, as well as the food, appears. There also often is a brief, personal comment about the recipe's origin.

The recipe mail is in addition to the 500-800 e-mails and 100-200 snail mail letters that arrive each week. Editors answer basic, unusual and complicated cooking questions —from "What are day-old bread cubes?" (day-old bread that is sliced into cubes; if using fresh bread, put the cubes in a 300-degree oven for 10-12 minutes) to "Can I make mashed potatoes ahead of time, then keep them hot in a slow cooker?" (yes, if on a low setting for no more than two hours).

What has Ann learned from her readers?

"The readers direct our focus," Ann says. "If they want more of something, we try to work that in."

When a food trend seems especially strong, spin-off publications are considered. That's what brought about *Light & Tasty*, for health-conscious cooks; *Quick Cooking*, for time-pressed cooks; and *Cooking for Two*, for empty nesters.

It's also how *Taste of Home* got established. Roy began the tabloid *Farm Wife News* in 1971, after noticing that farm publications were dropping their women's sections because there wasn't enough advertising to justify them. The name was changed to *Country Woman* in 1986, and *Taste of Home* was an eventual spin-off.

Ann has been editor of *Country Woman* since 1971, and she is not the only Reiman staffer to have more than one job title. She's sampling food from reader recipes on almost every workday and, no, she really doesn't need to pack a lunch.

The combos might be odd—first a spinach recipe, then a chocolate bundt cake—but the mission is satisfying, partly because of the readers' support and loyalty.

Now some people are even having *Taste of Home* parties or luncheons, potlucks at which everybody brings something from one of the magazine's recipes.

•

Taste of Home Cooking School hits the road from coast to coast, with home economists conducting two-hour sessions that involve food preparation, recipes and generic cooking advice. It is typical for guests to get a gift bag of product samples, coupons and a Taste of Home cookbook. More than 300 of these events occur annually, often in school auditoriums.

•

Reiman Publications Visitor Center
5602 Broad St., Greendale
www.tasteofhome.com, 414-423-3080

SOUTHEAST

The *Best of Country Chicken* cookbook by Reiman Publications includes this recipe from Polly Lloyd of Burlington, who says the herbs "make great seasonings for the vegetables, too."

Thyme Herbed Chicken

3/4 to 1 cup water
1 tablespoon chicken bouillon granules
3/4 teaspoon dried thyme
1/2 teaspoon dried marjoram
1/4 teaspoon lemon-pepper seasoning
1 broiler/fryer chicken (3 1/2 to 4 pounds)
1 pound red potatoes, halved
2 medium onions, cut into 1/2-inch pieces
1 1/2 to 2 cups fresh baby carrots

Combine 1 cup water, bouillon, thyme, marjoram, and lemon-pepper; pour into a roasting pan. Add chicken; arrange potatoes, onions and carrots around it. Cover and bake at 350 degrees for 50 minutes. Uncover; bake for 20-30 minutes or until vegetables are tender and chicken juices run clear. Yield: 4 servings

Stand-up comedians at Mike Bjorn's place are part of the show.

KENOSHA: OFFBEAT FUN

I would have never expected to find Jimmy Carter, Jesse Jackson and Sylvester Stallone shoulder to shoulder in downtown Kenosha. And I was amazed, just a block away, to meet the gaze of Oprah Winfrey, next to Walter Cronkite, before sunset the same day.

This is a city that is proud of its celebrity natives: Don and Alan Ameche, Daniel J. Travanti, Al Molinaro, Concetta Tomei, Mark Ruffalo. One native son—Orson Welles—wanted to be forgotten here; he once referred to his birthplace as a "nasty Midwestern city."

Nasty? Hmmmm. Maybe in a former life.

The longtime industrial wasteland that swallowed Kenosha's downtown Lake Michigan shore has now been replaced by a pretty museum campus and generous marina. Restored electric streetcars follow a two-mile loop that is both scenic and practical. New condos, in this heart of the city, are a good base for generating retail and entertainment growth.

So Kenosha has begun an extreme makeover that eventually will include dinosaur,

Civil War and lighthouse museums, plus a second downtown theater restoration. What a pleasant accompaniment to the rich variety that already exists in Kenosha.

Within two blocks are three businesses—a diner, a gallery and a clothing store—rich in character and spirit. Well, maybe "attitude" is a better description of at least one of these offbeat emporiums. You won't find anything quite like them anywhere else in Wisconsin.

•

The Garbage Plate is great at Franks Diner.

My first choice for lunch, ever since I worked as a copy editor at the *Kenosha News* in the 1980s, is **Franks Diner**. Big deal, you say? Yes, because of the history and the atmosphere. This railroad lunch car was pulled into town in 1926. Today the place looks like a homely box on the outside, and the original diner sits inside of it. A narrow alley of booths—an add-on—runs parallel to the original grill and stool-counter seating.

While restoring the interior in 2005, workers uncovered "Franks Diner" lettering under decades of paint. A new arched and rich wood ceiling is another sign that the place is getting spiffed up. What next, ghosts of Liberace and Duke Ellington? They're reputedly former customers.

Great bread, desserts and soups, particularly the velvety smooth Hungarian mushroom, make for a decent dining experience. Lippy remarks from the waiter and menu ("Whining is unattractive. Tapping is even worse.") make the meal worth talking about later. Best bet for breakfast is the Garbage Plate: hash browns, eggs, veggies and ham. Half an order will fill most of us.

•

Local artist **George Pollard's** work is on display at **Pollard Gallery & Gifts**, in the **Rhode Center for the Arts**. It's one impressive magic show.

What do we mean by that? George—"Portrait Artist to the Famous"—knows how to take 10 years and 20 pounds off of any subject, and they have ranged from Mother Teresa to Bart Starr, Oprah to Kareem, Tommy Thompson to Dwight Eisenhower. Also notable is wife Nan Pollard's fun illustrations for children's books and Walt Disney projects.

Clothing suitable—or not—for any occasion.

People like the inherent humanity that always colors and informs Pollard's work, and his subjects love the flattering likeness. About 175 examples of his portraits, as well as Nan's bright illustrations, are always on exhibit. Visitors also can read accolades from several of the portrait subjects.

It is a grand showcase that also includes the work of other artists. Admission is free, but donations are appreciated.

•

A Madison friend started to grin when he heard that I'd be visiting Kenosha. "You gotta see the tuxedo museum," he said.

That threw me, but it didn't take long to find out that he was referring to **Mike Bjorn's Fine Clothing & Museum**, a serious men's clothing store with a lot of good humor and a rebellious nature.

This is where tuxedo-clad mannequins look like celebrities because of their rubber masks. It's Hillary and Mr. T, comedians and kung fu artists perched near the ceiling and leering down on the shoppers.

Cut-outs of Clint Eastwood and Peewee Herman get mixed into the merchandise. Mingled in front of and above the racks of clothing are a team of gold carousel-like horses, an old accordion described as Lawrence Welk's first, a wooden plane propeller described as Amelia Earhart's last.

"Truly?" I ask, incredulously. "Not truly," Mike replies.

At the check-out counter, a ragged eagle with spread wings seems ready to swoop. It is the real thing, and the cause of much cackling among new customers, a couple of whom have alerted the authorities—police and the DNR.

You can tell that the proprietor—a guitar player and former art teacher—loves the commotion. He says the bird is more than 100 years old and of unknown lineage, a friend's cast-off.

The zany retail theater has a mix of traditional and contemporary men's wear, plus the outrageous. Think zoot suits to full-length fake furs in wild colors. There are ties and cummerbunds for less than a buck, outfits that can be rented as well as owned.

"We're not Blah-mart," Mike says, the understatement of the day. Here and there, laminated news clips dangle. Many are about the deaths of old-time celebrities.

They represent treasured characters that can't be replaced; it is this way with the business, too.

Mike and **Judy Bjorn** had $10,000 to open their Sixth Avenue store in 1981. "We were so undercapitalized," he says, "but we've had fun doing this" and reinventing the business as competition changed.

Strip malls and discount chains have taken customers from many downtowns, not just Kenosha's. "I don't think business is good for anybody, anywhere," Mike says. "I'm just glad the house, inventory and this building are paid for."

He points to an odd mobile of clothing hangers, each from a men's clothing store that has closed. Mike has been keeping tally. There are 84—and counting, from Chicago to Milwaukee to Monroe, of which he is aware.

"It keeps me humble, dear," he offers.

•

Mike Bjorn's Fine Clothing & Museum, 5614 Sixth Ave., Kenosha
www.tux-a-rama.com, 262-652-0648.

•

Pollard Gallery & Gifts, 514 56th St., Kenosha
www.rhodeopera.com, 262-657-7529

•

Franks Diner, 508 58th St., Kenosha, 262-657-1017

SOUTHEAST

Fast Facts

Kenosha is undergoing a makeover that involves a suburban area as well as its downtown. The city, long known as an outlet shopper's haven, remodeled and expanded **Prime Outlets** at **Pleasant Prairie** in 2006. What else is Pleasant Prairie known for? Free tours and samples at the **Jelly Belly Center**, one of the candy company's two distribution centers nationwide that is open to the public.

•

The downtown is gaining three museums: the **Dinosaur Discovery Museum** (with a 40-foot T-rex named Stan) completed in 2006, followed by **Southport Light Station & Maritime Museum** (2007) and the **Civil War Museum** (2008), devoted to the wartime roles played by the Upper Midwest states.

•

The Lure of Italian Food

Cosmopolitan cheeses grace the space at Tenuta's.

A gallon of virgin olive oil is one of the oddest holiday gifts I've ever given, and it was bought on a whim while shopping in Kenosha a few years ago. It came from **Tenuta's**, an engaging and massive Italian deli/market that has been around since 1950.

John and **Lydia Tenuta** moved to Kenosha from their native Italy in 1920. Their first business, a jam-packed ice cream parlor and deli called Tenuta's Confectionary, was less than the size of a two-car garage. Son **Ralph** grew up with the business and eventually took it over.

"When people told us they wanted something, we'd find it and add it," notes **Chris Tenuta**, the current owner and one of Ralph's seven kids ("all have helped from the time they were old enough to sort bottles," the family says online).

Longtime customers have included TV actors Al Molinaro of "Happy Days" and Daniel J. Travanti of "Hill Street Blues."

Now the store is 17,000 square feet, the stock is extensive and claims are slightly bold. Want pasta? "If we don't have the cut you want, you will not find it anywhere," the Tenuta family proclaims.

A family recipe that is four generations old is used to make the Italian sausage here; mild to hot spicing is available. Giardiniera peppers, also mild to hot, can be and are purchased by the case.

There are many types of domestic and imported cheeses, including fresh mozzarella. Feta choices are Greek, French, Bulgarian, domestic (slightly drier, milder and less salty). The half-dozen provolones range from smoked to "extra extra sharp."

A trademark sandwich is the Muffo-Lotta, a play on the word muffoletta, which means "a bread, a salad and a sandwich." This version contains mortadella (a bologna), ham, capicolla (seasoned, cured pork), salami, pepperoni, provolone cheese, lettuce, mild

Tenuta's whets the appetite for everything Italian.

peppers, vinegar and oil dressing. Ingredients are stuffed into thick, pita-like bread that's specially made by a local bakery, then sold by the slice.

There are dozens of other treats here, from eggplant Parmesan to freshly filled chocolate cannoli shells. I used to make a beeline for the chicken tortellini, but this is one labor-intensive item that no longer is stocked regularly.

•

Tenuta's
3203 52nd St.
Kenosha
www.tenutasdeli.com, 262-657-9001

Sculptor Berit Naeseth has used Kohler factory space to create her art.

KOHLER: THE ART FACTORY

SOUTHEAST

Arts/Industry is a part of the **John Michael Kohler Arts Center** of **Sheboygan**. The program is introduced with this quote, attributed to Victorian writer and philosopher John Ruskin: "Life without labor is guilt. Labor without art is brutality."

More than 350 artists have had two- to six-month residencies at the Kohler Company since the Arts/Industry program began in 1974. Typically, four people are in residence at a time; some return for a second residency. They come from around the world.

The agreement is that artists will spend 40 hours per week making art. All the Arts/Industry artists share a home behind the plant. Although they own the art that is produced, the expectation is that each artist will donate two pieces to the factory and arts center.

Sculptor **Berit Naeseth** happily spent a summer inside the Kohler company's pottery division, working in 90-degree heat. At Kohler, she had access to the technical expertise and equipment that she could not afford, operate or accommodate in her Middleton studio. That is one of several advantages of being here.

"The potential to reinvent yourself is huge," Berit said. She had 24-hour access to this part of the plant, to work, wander and "just look at things." It's the largest pottery in the world, a place that is "spooky and wonderful" late at night, when there is "so much space and so few people around."

"The artists were so excited about this," recalls **Ruth Kohler**, director of the John Michael Kohler Art Center. Few had knowledge about clay slip casting and molding. "We concentrate a lot on emerging artists," Ruth says, and program value is multi-dimensional. The artists get access to new techniques and expertise. Kohler Company gains exposure and, on occasion, a new product.

Kohler and Sheboygan gain public art: Dozens of pieces are on display indoors and out; there is a walking tour map. Seemingly different work worlds intersect, too. As artists and factory workers interact, they gain mutual respect for each other's work.

Artists in Europe, who worked in glass and clay factories, tended to be factory employees whose work was monitored and owned by the company. Arts/Industry has a much looser leash; artists decide what to create.

The makings for at least three projects emerged from Berit's studio space at Kohler. A dozen oblong, volumetric clay forms—large, hollow shapes—resemble wafts of factory smoke. One is covered with shiny porcelain. Others take on vastly different textures, depending upon how she carves the material.

One artist, **Ann Agee** of Brooklyn, left behind a mural in the pottery casting shop; it shows many of the people she came into contact with during her early 1990s residency. Ruth Kohler says: "It is a wonderful memory piece," as some employees in the mural have since retired or died.

One of Ruth's favorites is a life-sized deer with a fiberglass back that can be lifted off, turning the deer into a cast iron grill. There also have been a couple of rabbit sculptures that serve a dual purpose as hibachi grills.

Arts/Industry projects are on display at the Kohler Design Center, a facility that is about history as well as art, design and cutting edge decorating. Free admission, and open daily (except Thanksgiving, Christmas). It is adjacent to The American Club, the Midwest's only five-diamond resort.

Kohler Company factory tours are free, last 2 1/2 hours and are offered on weekdays. The guides are retired factory workers; they lead visitors into the pottery, brass and foundry departments. Reservations are required; call **920-457-3699**. For more: **www.destinationkohler.com**.

•

Kohler Arts/Industry Program
www.jmkac.org, 920-458-6144

•

Seasons in the Kitchen

People in the Kohler tourism business are beginning to think of late fall and winter as the "culinary season" instead of the "off season." That is because of all the ways in which food is showcased in and near **The American Club**.

A 2006 experiment, which will be repeated annually in winter, is the **Kohler Five Diamond Dine Around**. It is a progressive meal, each of five courses—matched with wines from California to Tuscany—at a different property, at an introductory rate of $95 per person (including tax, gratuity and transportation from one place to the next).

The event gives the Kohler chefs a chance to experiment on a small (up to 30) group, getting feedback as well as making themselves available to answer questions. It feels a bit like an in-house culinary competition, too, and it is the diners who win—big time.

Here is a sample menu:

Welcome reception at **The Greenhouse** (best known for the ice cream it serves in summer): Mushroom Strudel, Crab Cakes with Cajun remoulade, Nori Rolls with ginger and wasabi, Beef Tenderloin Carpaccio.

First course at Cucina (at The Shops at Woodlake): Handmade Ricotta and Veal Ravioli, with porcini mushrooms, fava beans, Pecorino Toscano cheese.

Second course at **Blackwolf Run Restaurant** (the golf course lodge): Coconut Almond-Fried Shrimp, with spicy fruit relish, vanilla cream sauce.

Entrée course in the **Wisconsin Room** (at The American Club): Lake Superior Walleye with crab and tomato hollandaise or Grilled Tenderloin of Beef with béarnaise and horseradish mashed potatoes.

Dessert course at the **Winery Bar** (at The American Club): Poppy Seed Lemon Tartlet, with lemon ice cream, raspberry coulis. Plus, coffee and a nightcap of Amarula or Limoncello liqueur.

The community experiments with your appetite in other ways, too. Kohler chefs present culinary demonstrations at **The Shops at Woodlake** on Saturdays, typically November through April. Call **920-457-8000** to make a reservation.

Nationally known wine experts and specialty chefs lead three days of lectures and demos at multiple Kohler locations every October, during the **Kohler Food & Wine Experience**, co-sponsored by *Food & Wine* magazine.

•

The American Club, 419 Highland Drive, Kohler
www.destinationkohler.com, 800-344-2838

Our Lady of Guadalupe shrine sits in a beautiful and peaceful setting.

MILWAUKEE: Hispanic Pride

Milwaukee's Hispanic population—nearly 100,000—has one of the strongest peer-support systems in the nation. One of the toughest, poorest and least scenic parts of this city—off I-94 and National Avenue—is being transformed, through about $25 million in building investments and a tremendous range of programs and services that both benefit the ethnic residents and introduce the public to authentic Hispanic cultures.

Centro de la Comunidad Unida (United Community Center) averages contact with more than 1,000 people per day. It includes a school for about 850 preschool, elementary and middle school students, plus a senior center that serves meals, educates and entertains. There are English classes for adults and field trips for kids learning Spanish.

This also is a place to learn salsa dancing, to get a haircut for $5, to exercise with weight machines, to hear Latino music (in an auditorium that can seat 350). A restaurant (**Cafe El Sol**) specializes in Puerto Rican and Mexican food. A gallery is devoted to the work of well-known Hispanic artists.

"It is one of the best models of community development and intergenerational partnership," says **Libby Burmaster**, as state superintendent of public instruction.

It is not unusual for children to walk down a hall to get after-school tutoring from a senior citizen, or to see four generations of a family going in four directions at the facility.

Bruce-Guadalupe School has one of the state's first kindergartens that is open to 3-year-olds. "The sooner we can begin, the better," **Ricardo Diaz**, executive director, says of the education process at the bilingual charter school. In addition, **Sixth Street Academy** is for at-risk middle-schoolers.

The center has operated since 1970, starting as an after-school program for hard-to-reach youth, run by volunteers in a burned out storefront. That makes it among the oldest Hispanic community centers in the nation, says **Lisa Navarrette** of the National Council of La Raza, which is like an NAACP, but for Hispanics.

Milwaukee Hispanics "recognized very early that they needed institutions to integrate with the larger community," Lisa says, calling the center "among the strongest and most respected in the country."

"This is the community center of the future," says **Walter Sava**, executive director of **Latino Arts Inc.**, which leases space there. Enlarged, vintage photos of local families cover the lobby walls.

More than $20 million was raised to expand the center from one 40,000-square-foot building (a former church) to several blocks of facilities. That includes housing for the elderly—first apartments, then assisted living.

Programs can be short, like a three-hour workshop about heart health or buying a home. Or they may be as extensive as residential treatment for people with substance abuse problems. A youth center has both pool tables and a "kids bank."

After-school options include a mariachi class, which has 60 students, and a strings program. "We buy the violins and the uniforms," says Walter, who grew up poor in Argentina in the 1950s and has a doctoral degree in Spanish literature.

"It is unusual," Ricardo says, of the center. "There may be a place that has a better school, or one that has more housing, or better athletic programs. But there is no place else where all this comes together under one roof."

Basic education involves neighborhood adults as well as children. "We have a huge number of parents with little more than a third-grade education," Walter says. That is because they were raised in rural Mexico, where ranch work was a higher priority.

"The agency has grown as a result of some practical solutions to real and perceived social problems," Ricardo says. "With growth has come vitality, a can-do attitude. There is great interest in family, and keeping family together."

•

Centro de la Comunidad Unida, 1028 S. Ninth St., Milwaukee
www.unitedcc.org, 414-384-3100

Maria Hernandez shows off a colorful handmade quilt.

Asides

Café El Sol, which is open to the public, serves a Latin-style fish dinner buffet on Friday nights. It is an ethnic adaptation to the traditional Wisconsin fish fry, accompanied by Latino music. The colorful restaurant also serves authentic Puerto Rican and Mexican food on weekdays. Reservations are appreciated.

•

Latino Arts Inc. coordinates seasonal theater and music events, featuring award-winning performers from North and South America. There also are seasonal art exhibits, and classes that are open to the public, at Centro de la Comunidad Unida. The gallery is the only one in Milwaukee that is devoted to the works of Hispanic and Latin American artists. For more: www.latinoartsinc.org.

Latino Arts also welcomes student field trips. Matinee performances, tours and meals can be arranged for Spanish classes and others.

•

The two-day **Latin Music Fest** is in mid-September at State Fair Park, West Allis. There also is Latino food, art and other merchandise vendors, plus activities for children. For more: **www.latinmusicfest.org.**

•

Carol Kosakoski has heard many stories about the lion at her bar and bowling alley.

Little Pin, Long History

Koz's Mini Bowl** isn't in the Yellow Pages, because the owner considers that a waste of money. Word gets around fine on its own. In the heart of south Milwaukee, it's a smoky but charismatic, unusual and unpolished tavern in a blue-collar, Polish-Hispanic neighborhood.

"The epicenter of Milwaukee bar culture" is how Jim Atkinson described Koz's in his book, *The View From Nowhere: The Only Bar Guide You'll Ever Want or Need.*

Visitors from Escanaba to Japan have signed proprietor **Carol Kosakoski's** guest books. They come to gawk or bowl, using 4-pound balls that are the size of grapefruits to knock over battered, wooden pins.

Pin boys, ages 15 or 16, break a sweat behind the alley, aligning the tenpins by hand, then jumping atop a carpeted bench before a preschooler or grandmother lets the next ball fly. It's $3 per person, per game.

"Because it's a small place, there's a lot of camaraderie," says Carol, who with husband **DuWayne** began raising five sons on this income in 1977. He died in 2002.

"This was DuWayne's baby, his idea," the widow says. "He enjoyed it and brought the people here."

Bowlers at Koz's use duckpin-sized balls and pins on a 17-foot alley. If it were genuine duckpin bowling (more common on the East Coast), Carol says the alleys would be 60 feet long, and the bowler would throw three balls per turn instead of two.

The bowling area easily turns into a party room without pretense, for families, youth groups, corporate execs from Miller Brewing or Allen-Bradley. This is where bachelor parties and wedding showers sometimes begin.

Customers bring their own food. Children are welcome until 7 p.m.; after that, Carol says it's not an appropriate place for them.

The building was a restaurant and boarding house (some say bordello) before the four bowling alleys were added in the mid-1950s. There used to be league play every night; now it's just two days a week.

The league secretary was a pin boy in the 1950s.

Carol has gotten offers to buy and haul away the alleys, but she declines: "My sons would never forgive me." Now grown men, this is where their friends reunite, and a son in Ripon helps her run the place.

•

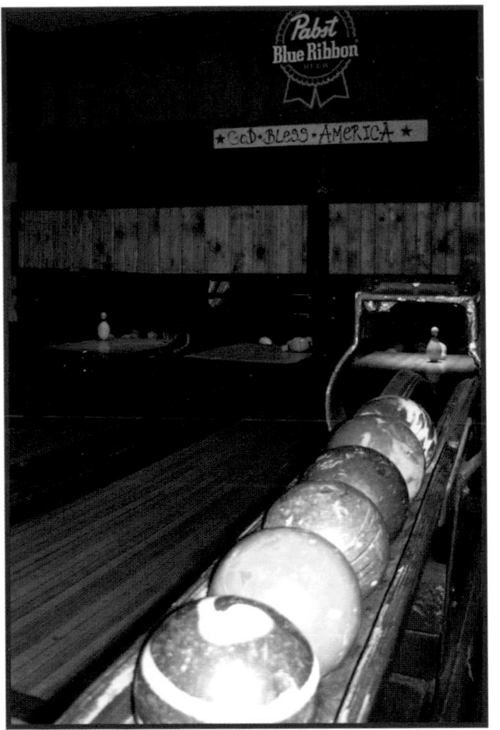

Head two blocks south—following Kosciuszko Park—to **St. Josaphat's**, 2333 S. Sixth St., Wisconsin's only Catholic basilica. (See **www.thebasilica.org** or call **414-645-5623.**)

•

Koz's Mini Bowl
2078 S. Seventh St.
Milwaukee
414-383-0560

(left) Bowling balls are the size of grapefruits.

(next page) Bowl and pray: St. Josaphat's basilica is a short hike from Koz's Mini Bowl.

TO MIEJSCE ABY TAM IMIĘ MOJE BYŁO NA WIEKI AŻEBY TAM TRWAŁY OCZY MOJE I SERCE MOJE

Visitors are invited to add to the collection at Holler House.

Just Holler for More

At the corner of West Lincoln and South 20th Streets are two Milwaukee landmarks—one sprawling and dignified, the other tiny and irreverent. Both attest to Wisconsin's identity.

Forest Home Cemetery is the resting place of the sausage maker Usinger and beer brewer Pabst, actors Alfred Lunt and Lynn Fontanne, a handful of governors, numerous other politicians and industrialists. Its 200 acres are on the National Register of Historic Places. The first body was buried at Forest Home in 1850.

Across the street, on West Lincoln Avenue, is **Holler House**. From its ceiling hang skimpy bras and dusty boxer shorts, many autographed by their former owners. There is a box of hats for customers to wear while they sit at a worn but stately wooden and mirrored bar.

"We have fun here," says **Marcy Skowronski**, who has run the place since the 1950s. Her in-laws built it. The outside looks like a home, and a part of it is. It also is a dying breed of neighborhood bar, and in the basement is a bowling alley—one of the oldest in the nation. The first pins flew in 1910.

League play is leisurely. That's because pins are set up by hand; Marcy says she bribes her grandson, or other kids down the block, to do the work. Even after the season ends, bowling ball bags remain stacked on wall shelves next to a few trophies. And the underwear? First-time women visitors are encouraged to leave a little something behind.

What about the guys? "They just watch," says Marcy, although a few—including seminary students, she says—have made their own donations. It's a place typically frequented by those in their 20s to 40s, although "the old people get foolish, too."

To bowl at Holler House, call a couple of days ahead of time, so Marcy has time to find a pin setter.

•

Holler House, 2042 W. Lincoln Ave., Milwaukee
414-647-9284

(From left) Business owners Jennifer Hemberger, Stephanie Sherman and Elissa Elser are three reasons why the Historic Third Ward thrives.

Third Ward Reborn

Jennifer Hemberger co-owns the upscale **J. Bird** boutique in Milwaukee's ripening **Historic Third Ward**. Almost one-half of the retail businesses here are at least partly owned by women.

A noticeable number of the entrepreneurs, like Jennifer, are first-time business owners who are in their early 30s and without children. They have decided to run their own show because job satisfaction and independence are priorities. They realize they will be at work for more years than their parents and grandparents.

The movement is turning this musty warehouse district—the city's oldest center of commerce—into a retail showcase that intends to rival the finest Chicago and urban coastal shopping districts. The targeted demographic tends to be professional women, ages 20-50 years, some of whom shop with their mothers or daughters.

Who has noticed? *Women's Wear Daily*, for one. The cutting-edge fashion publication featured the Third Ward in 2005, declaring that the city is moving away from its "Laverne and Shirley" reputation.

It has become "a hip metropolis that has been receiving more attention for architect Santiago Calatrava's $100 million addition to the Milwaukee Art Museum than the city's breweries and cheesehead hats," writer Rebecca Kleinman observed.

The *WWD* headline: "Brewing to Boutiques: Milwaukee's Style Evolves."

If Oliver Twist denim, Hanky Panky lingerie or Flora and Henri outfits for newborns get your attention, the Third Ward has become the place to shop. Ann Taylor and Liz Claiborne will seem tame to this level of clientele.

Mel en Stel clothing appears on "The Apprentice," and at the **Lela** women's boutique here. Two blocks away, in a shop called **Blush**, is New York's Paula Dorf cosmetic line; the makeup artist's celebrity patrons include Jessica Simpson and Sandra Bullock.

This venture is Hers.

Stephanie Sherman and **Carrie Arrouet** were among the first retailers to take a chance on the Third Ward, in October 2003, when they opened Lela. "We knew what we weren't able to shop for locally," says Stephanie, who worked for nonprofits for seven years. "We saw the need and were at the right point in our lives" to do something about it.

"The right point," to some, means having health benefits because of a spouse, but not the responsibility attached to motherhood. Lela's owners opened in the Third Ward, Stephanie says, because "we love the architecture and the feel of the neighborhood—it is like the meatpacking district of New York."

Elissa Elser agrees. The owner of **Hers** boutique has degrees in merchandise management and accounting. She worked at Barneys New York and Scarborough Fair in the Chicago area before opening her own shop.

"Since I was 16, I've wanted to open a women's boutique," she says. It also was a matter of measuring what the community needed against personal interests and expertise. "There are certain things you just know."

Jennifer is a former national sales manager for a jewelry design company. Success, she says, has been a product of building relationships with customers and working cooperatively more than competitively with other Third Ward business owners. "My sales reps use us as a role model for their customers in Chicago," she says. "I will send customers to the other shops here. There's a lot of camaraderie."

Sarah Brucker owns Blush.

Stephanie agrees. "Elsewhere, it's pretty cutthroat," she says. "Here, it's the feeling that we're all in this together. It would be horrible if one of us failed."

These business owners take turns wheeling back their clothing racks and hosting Pilates classes at the end of the day. There also are cross-promotions, private shopping parties, self-defense workshops and round-robin events.

A newer Third Ward retail player is **Deanna Innis**, whose **Freckle Face** boutique of children's clothing opened in mid 2005. There is a small play area, and complimentary animal crackers and diapers in the infant/toddler fitting room.

Inventory is sizes 0 to 7; at the high end, an outfit will cost $200.

"I just love baby clothes—they evoke so much emotion" and are "such a symbol of innocence," says the New York native, who is single and moved here to help develop a children's clothing brand for Kohl's. She also has worked for the Gap, in product and fabric development.

She has "been blown away by the number of young entrepreneurs" around her, and the quality of life in Milwaukee. "I went from a one-bedroom box, paying $1,650 a month, to paying $675" for an apartment here.

The area's biggest needs? A boutique hotel and shoe and men's clothing boutiques are on the retailers' wish list. So, for some, is a Pottery Barn, Gap or Banana Republic, an anchor to fuel business in a bigger way.

Their biggest challenges: attracting suburbanites to the area and deciding what potential customers want. "I didn't realize Milwaukee would be as fashion-forward as it is," Elissa says. So there have been surprises.

•

Historic Third Ward Association
219 N. Milwaukee St.
Milwaukee
www.historicthirdward.org, 414-273-1173

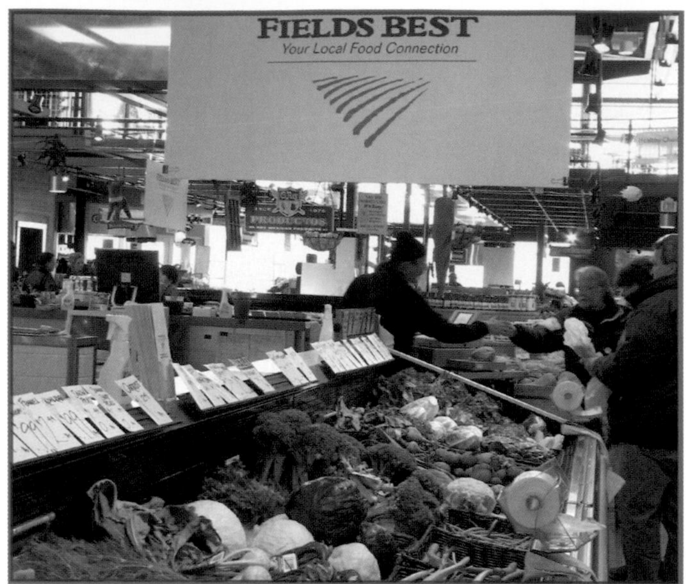

Fields Best sells the bounty of several Wisconsin farmers.

SOUTHEAST

DETOURS

The **Eisner American Museum of Advertising & Design**, 208 N. Water St., is associated with the **Milwaukee Institute of Art & Design** and is the only museum in the nation dedicated to the connection between design and advertising. The space is roomy and exhibits are both educational and fun. Full of nostalgia, with changing topics, from the Red Cross to the circus, Harley Davidson ad history to analyses of what consumers buy.

For more: **www.eisnermuseum.org, 414-847-3290**

•

The **Milwaukee Public Market**, 400 N. Water St., gives people another reason to check out the area. It's artisan bread and fresh sushi under one roof, with ethnic and locally grown products sold year-round. More than one dozen farmers sell from a booth that has been rented by the **Michael Fields Agricultural Institute**, East Troy, whose priority is sustainable farming. A demonstration kitchen has seating for 55, and cooking classes are conducted by notable regional chefs.

For more: **www.milwaukeepublicmarket.org, 414-336-1111.**

Take a stroll along Milwaukee's RiverWalk—and find intriguing architecture on the way.

Take a RiverWalk

Milwaukee's **RiverWalk** follows the Milwaukee River about eight blocks downtown, from Juneau Street on south. The next step is to connect this walk with four blocks of the Third Ward (south of the I-794 bypass). The entire area is becoming a place to congregate, listen to music, watch crew races and take boat tours. "We used to turn our back on the river," notes RiverWalk spokeswoman **Marsha Sehler**, who says city planners learned a lot by studying what San Antonio, Cleveland and Chicago have done with their rivers.

•

Fast Facts

The Historic Third Ward benefits from **Summerfest** and multiple ethnic festivals, which bring 2 million people to the nearby Milwaukee lakefront annually, but the neighborhood also books its own events to draw a crowd. They include a **Gallery Night and Day**, four times a year, which involves 60 Third Ward businesses and East Town galleries. **Summer Sizzle** is an early August jazz festival, and **Artscape** is an outdoor sculpture walk in October.

•

This also is the home of **Skylight Opera Theatre, Theatre X** and the **Milwaukee Chamber Theatre**. The area's boundaries are I-794 to the north, the Milwaukee River to the west and south, and Lake Michigan to the east.

•

About 70 buildings are on the **National Register of Historic Places.** The neighborhood association has a Historic Walking Tour booklet that describes the historical significance of these sites.

Oconomowoc Rediscovered

Oconomowoc is one of the state's few five-syllable cities and probably the only one with five Os. In the shadow of Wisconsin's two largest metro areas, this burg off of Interstate 94 has been overlooked as the urban growth of others has sprawled.

That's a shame, and that likely will change. A large part is due to the city's largest development ever, about 1,500 acres held by the Frederick Pabst family since 1906. At I-94 and near Highway 67, this farmland eventually will be turned into retail boutiques, a business park, about 900 homes, and more.

It has been controversial, with greenspace preservation, big-box retailers and a strategic zoning change all fodder for debate.

What's apparent is that Pabst Farms represents a significant part of Oconomowoc's future. But drive downtown—toward Lac La Belle and Fowler Lake—and it's clear how the lavishness of the past has molded the city's personality and pride.

Way back in 1837, the Indians named this city Coo-No-Mo-Wauk, which means "where the waters meet." La Belle and Fowler are two of 39 lakes within a half hour's drive. These waters have been both popular fishing holes and picturesque scenery.

The city historically has attracted the wealthy, first as a resort area, then with the development of huge summer homes. Retail magnate Montgomery Ward and meatpacker Phillip Armour are among those who used to live here. It's been a playground for beer barons and bootleggers, gangsters and millionaires.

Overnight guests can enjoy a glass of wine at the Inn at Pine Terrace.

"Newport of the West" is what Oconomowoc was called during a prosperous era that began in the 1870s and lasted until the 1930s. Draper Hall, an imposing hotel, had Presidents Taft, Grant, Cleveland, Coolidge, McKinley and Teddy Roosevelt as guests before being razed in 1967.

One of the stately Victorian mansions, built in 1879, has been turned into an exquisite, 12-room country inn. Named the **Inn at Pine Terrace**, it is on the National Register of Historic Places, and a national B&B publication has selected the inn as the best place for wine tasting.

The city is still small enough to get excited about its high school homecoming weekend. Downtown merchants let students decorate their storefronts; locals lug lawn chairs to the parade route, clogging traffic and sidewalks on a warm but windy October day.

In summer, it is the beach—and the music from the **American Legion Band** in the downtown band shell—that will attract a crowd.

The city also is large enough to count the plush, 256-room **Olympia Resort and Conference Center** as its own. The Olympia's outdoor facilities include an 18-hole golf course (one of three in the city) and downhill skiing on the Highlands, a man-made hill that is 235 feet high. Snow can be manmade, too.

Large enough to have a train depot, but not to have a train stop there, the Oconomowoc depot has been turned into a restaurant.

In the 1990s, the city gave its armory to the local historical society. So now it's the **Oconomowoc and Lake Country Museum**, a thoughtful compilation of local history that includes an impressive "Streets of Old" gallery that is similar to the Milwaukee Public Museum's "Streets of Old Milwaukee" exhibit.

There also are artifacts from a Victorian home, dentist's office, barbershop, print shop, general store, medical clinic, railroad and old-time classroom.

Since just under 100 millionaires had lakefront estates here at one time, during warm weather there are guided walking tours around **Fowler Lake**. Old Mail Boat tours of **Lac La Belle** also can be arranged.

•

Oconomowoc Area Chamber of Commerce
152 E. Wisconsin Ave.
Oconomowoc
www.oconomowoc.org, 800-524-3744

DETOURS

Holy Hill National Shrine of Mary, on Highway 167 at **Hubertus**, can be seen for miles. After reaching the hilltop, 1,350 feet above sea level, it is 178 steps to the observation tower's top. This national landmark is within 400 acres of woodland; an Ice Age Trail hiking path crosses into it. People picnic here; others consider it a serious pilgrimage. The building dates from 1863; today there are at least two Masses daily—plus fantastic pies and breads for sale in the cafe's bake shop.

For more: **www.holyhill.com, 262-628-1838.**

•

Also nearby is **Honey Acres**, a fifth-generation honey production business that began in 1852. There is a honey museum on these 40 acres, as well as a place to buy honey creams, mustards, candy, fruit bars and other sweet gifts. It's on Highway 67, near **Ashippun**.

For more: **www.honeyacres.com, 800-558-7745.**

•

An unlikely location for one-of-a-kind handcrafts from more than a dozen countries—especially Germany—is **The Weather Vane**, in business since the 1970s. The rural shop is north of Oconomowoc, at 8233 Pennsylvania St. Yes, there are weather vanes for sale, and shop owner **Jane Tremaine** also has a penchant for the German "smoking men" incense burners.

For more: **www.weather-vane.com, 800-873-4413.**

A family legacy can be humble, yet significant.

Plymouth: Always a Homecoming

Perhaps you think that your dearest possessions—a locket, a family picture, a love letter, a child's toy—are of little value to anybody else. That's not necessarily true.

Hundreds of local historians in Wisconsin are passionate about rescuing and preserving pieces of the past for their museums, research centers, historical archives and local history books. Most are volunteers who live in the state's tiniest communities. They have little to gain, except the satisfaction of helping future generations understand their heritage.

In 1998, I was moving my parents off of their Sheboygan County farm and into an assisted living facility. It was a flurry of transferring, discarding, donating and boxing decades of accumulations.

This included a massive American Indian artifact collection that my dad compiled in 75 years, while walking the plowed fields of his land and that of his neighbors. It was important to him that the collection be kept intact. It was important to me that the collection go to an entity that would respect it.

I sent various letters, to gauge local interest, and was pleased when **Jim Stahlman** of the **Plymouth Historical Society** promptly replied. After dozens of volunteer hours, and consultation with Wisconsin Historical Society staff, our family's donation became the lead exhibit at the Plymouth Center, a combination museum/Chamber of Commerce office/art gallery/performance space.

My dad died before the exhibit opened, but his picture still is on a wall of the Plymouth Center. The exhibit has since gotten a bit smaller, to make room for more recent donations, but it remains a great testimonial to him and the area's American Indian heritage.

I stop by a couple of times a year, to read the complimentary reactions of kids,

Billy Bergin compiled a museum-quality collection of artifacts.

farmers, former neighbors and strangers from far away. For me, this has been a tremendous gift, and I can't over-emphasize the passion and dedication of the volunteers who made it possible.

It is one of many examples. Each year, several individuals and organizations receive recognition from the Wisconsin Council for Local History, an organization of 339 historical societies.

A few years ago, I had the good luck of crossing paths with **Joyce and Bill Menzel**; she was a winner because of her Early Settlers Quilts project in 2002.

Joyce is from Springbrook, a dozen miles west of Hayward, off Highway 63 and in Washburn County. It is a town that doesn't show up on some state maps, and its sole tourist attraction is the **Springbrook Church Museum**, a former Catholic church that contains extensive church records and local artifacts.

As a millennial project, people with Springbrook roots were encouraged to use a quilt square to create a symbol of family history. Contributions came from as far away as New Mexico and Oregon.

The handiwork depicts many things, including farmland and one-room schools. We also learn that "Old Abe" the war eagle had a link to Springbrook, and that a Springbrook resident was an honor guard at Abe Lincoln's funeral.

The museum is open seasonally, two days a week. Does that mean its contents have less value? Not in the least. It all counts in the preservation of our past.

•

Plymouth Historical Museum
420 E. Mill St., Plymouth
www.plymouthhistoricalsociety.com, 888-693-8263

RACINE: SHOP THE NEIGHBORHOOD

Cindy Bendtsen's kringle defines the neighborhood.

Jerome Boulevard was an average neighborhood two decades ago. Our Racine bungalow was a good starter home, with not much—besides the lime green basement walls and floor—to set it apart from others on the block.

But I've yet to live in another place where neighbors left plates of homemade bakery on the doorstep, to welcome you into the fold. Or had wintry Sunday mornings where it was too awful to drive, but always worthwhile to trudge around the corner to the same cozy restaurant for breakfast.

On one end of the block was **Christiano's**, just a box of a grocery store. At the other end was **Hammes Tavern**, operated by the same family since Prohibition ended in the 1930s. Both places remain in business, but evidence of these close-knit communities is getting rarer. Today I realize there is added value here, and wherever else independent businesses can thrive.

Cindy Bendtsen understands. Since 1982 she has been selling kringle—a buttery, flakey, circular and fruit- or nut-filled Danish pastry—at Racine's oldest family-owned bakery. The dough is rolled by hand; "this is not a cookie cutter system."

"If you have something to talk about, they don't know you and don't care to hear about it" at the big discount stores, Cindy says. "You don't feel special" as a customer.

Bendtsen's Bakery has been in the same place since 1934, a four-generation family business that is part of the three-block West Racine retail area on Washington Avenue. It used to be known as Kringleville.

The nickname stuck because of all the Danish-owned businesses, but today the neighborhood's cultural uniqueness belongs to little more than the Bendtsen's and Larsen bakeries. The latter makes sinful Seven Sisters coffeecakes, and sweet cheese crescents, as well as kringle.

These are not Racine's only or biggest kringle producers, but they have avoided neighborhood decomposition because of their unusual merchandise and personable customer service.

The same can be said for the nearby **Nelson's Variety Store**, which has a cluttered five-and-dime feel, dull wooden floors—and an impressive selection of Packer and Badger merchandise (near the artificial flowers and hot popcorn bin).

We also had no problem finding unusual gifts for a friend's birthday party. It is a sea of disarray that contains treasures, as does the otherwise ordinary neighborhood, whose residents seem to appreciate the hometown feel that I used to take for granted.

Do the merchants in your downtown encourage Girl Scouts to decorate store windows for the holidays? That's a part of the deal in West Racine, where moms sip steaming coffee and take pictures as the window painters work on a crisp November Saturday.

"You're fighting these big conglomerates," Cindy Bendtsen explains. "It's hard to compete with the pricing. Sweet rolls, breads—you can get them anywhere. But the kringle is something different," and so is the small-business owners' ability to respond to customer requests and address them by name.

What, besides national chain competition, threatens the retailers' survival? The declining health of the old buildings, Cindy says, and the younger generation's lack of interest in taking over business.

At **Larsen Bakery**, proprietor **Ernie Hutchinson** died in 2004, the same year that his widow, **Patricia**, lost a son. But the baking has continued; a daughter and son are involved.

"It's a lot of work," Patricia says. "A lot of bookkeeping" besides baking.

Up to 40 people are employed to handle seasonal business spurts; orders for Christmas are taken only until Dec. 1. The 30 varieties of kringle are made from an old Copenhagen recipe; sales make up more than one-half of the bakery's business, and pecan kringle is the top seller.

•

Bendtsen's Bakery, 3200 Washington Ave., Racine
www.bendtsensbakery.com, 262-633-0365

•

Larsen Bakery, 3311 Washington Ave., Racine
www.larsenbakery.com, 262-633-4298.

•

Nelson's Variety Stores, 3223 Washington Ave., Racine
www.nelsonsvarietystores.com, 262-633-3912

Racine's other kringle makers include **Lehman's Bakery**, 2210 16th St., and **O&H Bakery**, with two locations: 1841 Douglas Ave., and 4006 Durand Ave. O&H reports that the original kringle of the late 1800s was pretzel shaped, with an almond filling.

A striking exterior makes the museum a sculpture, too.

RAM: Museum as Sculpture

The **Racine Art Museum (RAM)** began to earn acclaim way before its opening in 2003. The building has received all four design excellence awards that the Chicago Chapter of the American Institute of Architects offers. That's a first in the organization's 50-year history.

The $6.5 million Racine project pretty much gutted a building that had been donated by M&I Bank. Ceilings were lifted and light used strategically to create a Zen-like and airy atmosphere. The remodeled site includes subdued lighting, recessed lighting, skylights and huge windows with dynamic lake views.

Also notable is the exterior lighting of a "continuous wrapper of translucent acrylic panels" that make the museum glow at night.

"We're trying to treat the building as a sculpture," says **Bruce Pepich**, museum executive director, of Brininstool + Lynch's architectural work.

The unusual siding—similar to what is used in skylights and roofs of greenhouses—covers "a brutal limestone facade put up in the 1960s," Bruce says. The approach is both theatrical and practical, given budget limits.

Fine art is defined in non-traditional ways. "Star Series" glazed stoneware by Toshiko Takaezu.

"People forget that this is not new construction," he says, noting that financial restraints "made us a lot more creative" in executing a practical and appropriate design. The project, he believes, "is one example of how you can have true excellence in design without spending $900 per square foot."

RAM houses significant collections of contemporary crafts (ceramics, fibers, glass, metals, wood), the type of artwork that is snubbed in some fine art circles.

"We are still a fine art museum," Bruce contends, and he says development of these collections as an art niche is working to Racine's advantage. As Bruce puts it, "We're not just collecting artwork, but collectors" who believe their donations will be treated more seriously at this facility than at larger ones. It all fits well with the heritage of the geographic area.

"This is a community in which people have traditionally made things with their hands, be it through construction or farming," he notes, so there tends to be an easier appreciation of the artists' efforts.

Visitors "aren't going to look at any of these objects and think 'my 6-year-old could have done this.'"

The Racine facility's contemporary crafts collection is considered the fourth most significant nationwide, following the Museum of Arts and Design in New York City, the Renwick Gallery in Washington, D.C., and the Mint Museum of Craft + Design in Charlotte, N.C.

RAM's 46,000 square feet include 10,000 square feet for exhibits. That allows several pieces of furniture to come out of museum storage at a time. Subdued lighting showcases textiles, baskets and works of wood—artwork that can't be exposed to intensive light.

There's an outdoor sculpture garden, and an art library that is open to the public by appointment. Most artwork was moved from the Charles A. Wustum Museum, which continues operations, but with an emphasis on outreach programs and regional artwork.

•

Racine Art Museum, 441 Main St., Racine
www.ramart.org, 262-638-8300

SHEBOYGAN: CULINARY BLISS

Chef Biró and his students sample quenelles, awash in rich consomme.

In a world where nobody seems to have enough time to cook, Marcel Biró simply shrugs. We do what we can, but there is good reason to try harder.

Watch. Try. Smell. Taste.

The master chef—one of the youngest in European history—joined an elite group in 2006, after cooking dinner for about 75 at The Beard House in New York City. Compare it to a musician being asked to play Carnegie Hall. James Beard, an acclaimed chef and food writer who died in 1985, helped define good eating in America.

The June event was the most recent Wisconsin culinary presence at The Beard House, says **Sandy D'Amato** of Milwaukee's **Sanford Restaurant**. Beard chefs include Sandy; Odessa Piper, founder of Madison's L'Etoile; and chefs from Kohler's American Club and Milwaukee's three Bartolotta restaurants.

Marcel was born in 1973 and raised in East Germany, before the fall of the Berlin Wall, and he was a personal chef for German Chancellor Helmut Kohl. So Marcel is accustomed to challenges, and this part of Wisconsin has presented a new one because it was "a largely untapped market, unfamiliar with high-end European cuisine."

Or, as a press release from his company, **Biró Internationale**, notes: "Brats, beer and cheese are the holy trinity of Sheboygan cuisine, and Friday night fish fries are the hottest ticket in town."

"High end" does not mean "pretentious" in this case, but it does require an appreciation for the labor, techniques and quality ingredients involved.

At a Biró soups and stocks class, seven students made beef, fish, chicken and vegetable stocks from scratch. That's as in skinning the fish, roasting the beef bones, skimming impurities from the top of simmering chicken carcasses and ditching the vegetables after stock is strained.

Each soup pot got a bouquet garni—a pouch of fresh seasonings, because it's better than shaking loose spices into a pot. (Why? After infusing the stock with flavor, the pouch can be removed easily, before the herbs get bitter or tasteless. Added bonus: The stock will look purer.)

The group ended up with luscious soups: creamy shrimp-leek, chunky minestrone, velvety wild mushroom and a rich beef consomme. The latter held quenelles, little beef dumplings that taste much more like a pate than a burger.

That is because the seasoned meat mixture goes through a *tamis*, a finely and tightly woven sieve used in French bakeries, before it is shaped into teaspoon-sized ovals that are plunked into boiling water. Getting a pound of meat through the tamis with a hand-held scraper takes forever (an hour or longer, even if you have the knack), and the repetitive motion was enough for chef apprentice Jeff Porter (a former investment broker) of Saukville to break a sweat.

We all gave it a try, too, and made very little headway.

"You're way too scared," Marcel said softly, as a student hesitated. "It's just cooking."

"Just cooking," to him, is about time, patience, skill and passion. This six-hour class—in a spacious Sheboygan kitchen-bath store (smaller groups assemble at **Biró Restaurant and Wine Bar**)—did not become a seven-ring culinary circus, even as students with varying degrees of kitchen experience tackled increasingly obscure cooking tasks.

Marcel is a striking, modest man who was quiet in his confidence, dry in his humor. To avoid crying while cutting onions, for example, "have someone else peel . . . or breathe through your mouth."

If an extra-virgin olive oil comes from a combination of countries, we learn it's the leftovers mixed together. That's probably a bad thing, says Marcel, who compares it to serving dinner guests a punch of five red wines.

His advice continued, not as a lecture but as a garnish to almost every recipe step: Clean mushrooms by lightly brushing them with flour, not by dousing them with water. When a soup stock begins to simmer, quit stirring it, so the impurities can rise to the top.

This was the seventh Biró class for Bill Moren of Port Washington. So far, his worst experience has been flipping a wet crepe out of a pan and onto an oven burner. The teacher smiles slightly, because he remembers. "Get me ice, please" was his response at the time, and then the show went on.

Two class assistants watch over students' work, cleaning cutting boards, coaching the work with knives, preventing chaos as instructions get more complicated. They also are the master chef's apprentices, enrolled in an 18-month program that is patterned after European training.

This recipe for Bouquet Garni is from the cookbook *Biró: European-Inspired Cuisine* (Gibbs Smith, 2005) by Marcel and Shannon Kring Biró. No need to get rid of herb stems. Add the tied bouquet to a stockpot, then discard with other stock solids.

Bouquet Garni

2 outer leek leaves
6 sprigs parsley
5 sprigs thyme
12 black peppercorns
1 Turkish bay leaf

Lay out one leek leaf. Place the parsley, thyme, peppercorns and bay leaf on top of it, and lay the remaining leaf on top of all to form a cigar-shaped bundle. Tie the bundle securely with kitchen twine.

For a rosemary variation: Add 5 sprigs rosemary to the bundle. Tarragon variation: Add 5 sprigs tarragon to the bundle.

"We all will do each recipe together," Marcel says, at the start of the class, "so we all will know it from A to Z."

•

Biró Restaurant & Wine Bar, 817 New York Ave., Sheboygan
Ó restaurant, 920 Michigan Ave., Sheboygan
Biró Culinary School, 1019 Erie Ave., Sheboygan
www.birointernationale.com, 920-451-6940

Fast Facts

"The Kitchens of Biró" is a reality TV series that documents the recipes and culinary operations of Biró Internationale, for better or worse. Champagne has exploded, master chef Marcel Biró occasionally is dished criticism—and his enterprises are becoming known from Oregon to Texas to Vermont.

More than 90 of the 356 public television stations in the U.S., U.S. Virgin Islands, Puerto Rico, American Samoa and Guam carried the first season of episodes in 2005, with a reach to 83 million households.

The show is produced by **DWP Incorporated** (a Milwaukee company that also produces "Discover Wisconsin" and "Into the Outdoors") and it won a regional Emmy in 2005 for non-news program editing.

The *Biró: European-Inspired Cuisine* cookbook (Gibbs Smith, 2005) by the master chef and his wife, includes recipes that have been featured on the PBS series. It is for the sophisticated cook who wants to learn European culinary techniques, plus those who simply enjoy spending time in the kitchen.

Marcel pays particular attention to the regions where he has worked: Alsace in France, southern Germany, Tuscany in Italy and Andalusia in Spain. There are wine pairings for each of the 125-plus recipes, even the Austrian sachertorte.

As a company, Biró Internationale is growing. The goal is to open 25 restaurants nationwide in seven years, but the home base—for now—will continue to be Sheboygan, as will its two restaurants (**Ó** and the more upscale **Biró Restaurant and Wine Bar**), culinary apprenticeships and cooking classes for the public.

"I see a parallel between Marcel's upbringing in East Germany and the culinary history of the USA," writes California organic wine vintner Rob Sinskey, whose wines were matched with Biró's menu at New York's Beard House in June 2006.

"Behind the Iron Curtain, the lack of culinary choice was imposed on the people by their government. In the USA, the lack of culinary choice was self-imposed as people opted for the convenience and low price of industrial agriculture, corporate grocery stores and chain restaurants.

"In East Germany, the revolutionaries tore down the wall. The wall may not be as visible in the USA, but needs to be torn down nonetheless."

The vintner calls Marcel Biró a "quiet revolutionary" who has begun to do just that, as he has "replicated the European model of the village restaurant" and "has built a culinary community" in Wisconsin that appreciates Old World excellence.

•

Blue Harbor Resort turned an industrial eyesore into prime lodging.

SOUTHEAST

Sheboygan: Lakefront Revival

In eastern Wisconsin, the city of Sheboygan had long lived with its lakefront eyesore, an industrial storage area for coal and salt that was otherwise prime real estate. Today the $54 million **Blue Harbor Resort**—with its 182 suites, 64 condo units and 40,000-square-foot indoor waterpark—is a beacon unlike any other tourist attraction in the city's history.

The resort opened in spring 2004, about a decade after a cluster of cafe/boutique/lodging enterprises replaced ramshackle fishing huts on adjacent lakefront property. This is the city's **South Pier District** and **Harbor Centre Marina**.

"It wasn't something that either the developer, or the city, would tackle on its own," **Joe Walsh** of **Great Wolf Resorts** says of the Blue Harbor project. He described the lakefront cleanup and resort construction as a win-win partnership with the city of Sheboygan.

The city, Joe says, found "a destination attraction, an anchor" for suitable downtown development. Sheboygan has invested $12 million in Blue Harbor construction, plus $10 million in streets, parking, sewer and utility services.

Rooms at Blue Harbor are family-friendly and spacious.

Wisconsin Commercial Real Estate Women has since given the Blue Harbor its top award, calling it "the project which best embodies all of the criteria—job creation, economic development, increased property values, creative use or reuse of space, and overcoming high-risk obstacles."

Great Wolf Resorts, Joe concludes, has enhanced its reputation for creating "unique experiences and cherished family traditions" on the shores of Lake Michigan, an area not previously known for its beachfront resorts.

"What we have is a family day at the beach that is not like other parts of the Midwest," he argues. "Creating quality experiences are fundamental to sustainable tourism."

•

Blue Harbor Resort
725 Blue Harbor Drive, Sheboygan
www.blueharborresort.com, 866-701-2583

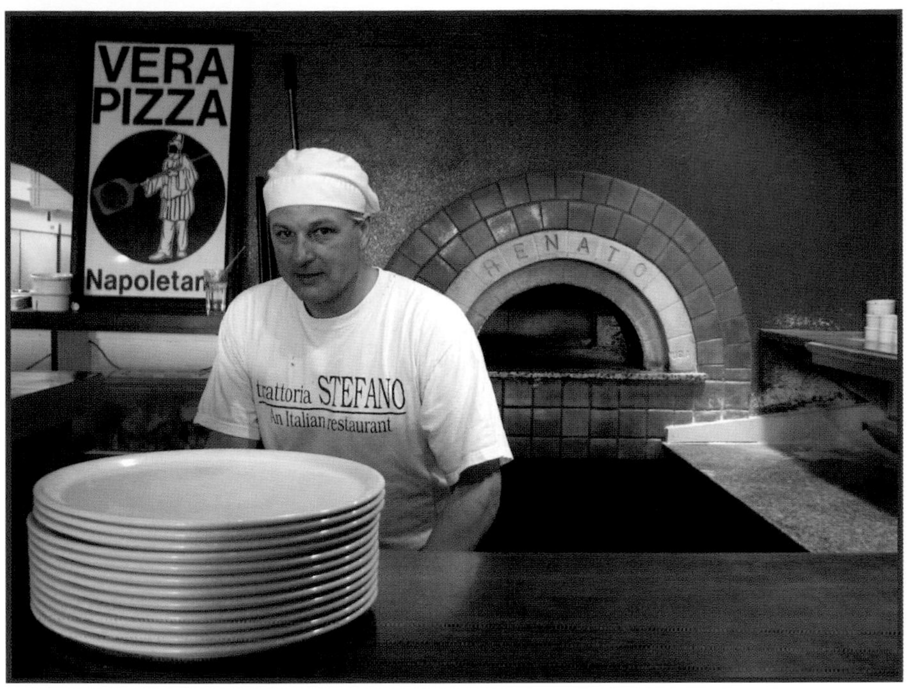

Staff at Il Ritrovo in Sheboygan know authentic pizza secrets.

Pizza Elite

Who else is putting Sheboygan on culinary maps? **Stefano Viglietti**, a self-taught chef who visits Italy annually, has two restaurants that should satisfy lovers of authentic Italian food. **Trattoria Stefano**, 522 S. Eighth St., began serving an authentic taste of Tuscany in 1994.

Six years later, the chef opened **Il Ritrovo**, 515 S. Eighth St., a more casual dining spot, specializing in Neapolitan style pizzas. It is one of 11 restaurants nationwide that have earned membership in an Italian organization (Verace Pizza Napoletana Association) that protects the way this kind of pizza is made. The elite distinction is about ingredients used as well as how they are prepared. Tomatoes, for example, are not made into a sauce.

For more: **920-803-7516.**

An Italian deli and shop of imported housewares is connected to Il Ritrovo. For reservations at the less casual Trattoria Stefano, it's **920-452-8455.**

World-class golfing at Whistling Straits in Sheboygan, along Lake Michigan's shoreline.

Sheboygan County: From Farms to Fame

Sheboygan County is the seventh best place to golf in the world, proclaimed *Golf Digest* magazine in 2000. That's right: *The world*. It ranked right after Southwest Ireland, right before Phoenix/Scottsdale. Pebble Beach in Monterey, California, and Pinehurst, North Carolina, are the only U.S. places that rated higher than Sheboygan.

I'm not a golfer, but I've seen Pebble Beach.

And having grown up on a Sheboygan County farm, I know the locals tend to care more about a good brat and hardroll than who's jetting in to play hole 18 at Blackwolf Run. The county fair is our social event of the year. We work the food and beer stands. We have a knitting club that has made caps for newborns since the 1950s; around 20 members have made close to 1,000 in a year.

As a contrast, the county's municipal airport is attracting more and more expensive private planes, reports **Alice Hubbard** of the **Kohler Company**. The Kohler conglomeration includes four prized golf courses and **The American Club**, the Midwest's only five-diamond resort.

The average county resident's exposure to these properties is an occasional wedding reception or Ducks Unlimited banquet. Or working a brat stand during a PGA event.

``Sometimes local people probably don't realize the impact we've had on the resort industry worldwide," Alice acknowledges.

But the local nonchalance and refusal to be overly impressed by money or celebrity status is part of the area's charm. It's probably one of the reasons why Sheboygan is growing up to be a gem in the eyes of outsiders.

Challenging. Scenic. Cutting edge. That's why the golf courses get high marks.

Private. Safe. Friendly. Honest. Those amenities aren't to be downplayed, either, particularly as the world grows more cluttered, anonymous and suspicious.

Alice says her company works hard to protect the privacy and identity of famous visitors from around the world. No big surprise. In Sheboygan County, we tend to have a ``that's none of your business" attitude toward private affairs. Ours and yours.

Comment cards from guests, she adds, routinely express appreciation for the ``friendly, nice people on staff."

Makes sense. Overall, there is a strong work ethic, respect for authority and pride in doing simple things well.

``We have some very affluent customers who take very good care of our staff," Alice says.

Whistling Straits' almost 200 caddies (95 work full-time) make it the largest crew in the United States. Each averages $100 per day, ``and it's not unusual for a caddy to be tipped a $100 bill."

Yes, this is golfing for the elite—green fees (at the start of this decade) were around $150, at the low end. Kohler employees—from the corporate exec to the hourly laborer—get a discount after 5 p.m. and on Sunday afternoons. That can be 35 to 40 percent off, Alice says, and an employee can bring guests to golf.

The Irish Course, part two of Whistling Straits, was the last of Kohler's courses to open, in the summer of 2000. A Sheboygan Falls farmer has since developed **The Bull**, a Jack Nicklaus course on land two miles from **Blackwolf Run**.

*Golf Diges*t notes that there were just 5,000 U.S. golf courses 50 years ago, two-thirds private. Now there are more than 16,000 U.S. courses, more than two-thirds public.

•

Sheboygan County Chamber of Commerce
712 Riverfront Drive, Sheboygan
www.sheboygan.org, 800-457-9497

Shady Lane Restaurant, near Plymouth, offers a taste of simpler living, with farm fields as scenery.

The 360-acre classroom is a place to ponder all forms of life.

WATERTOWN: IT'S HIS NATURE

A couple of miles off of I-94—near Highway 26—the sounds of geese, pheasants and sandhill cranes harmonize, compete and perform solo. Tracks in the mud reveal evidence of wild turkey, coyote, deer, raccoon.

Doug Gaulke began coming here to learn, when he was 10 years old. The place is still his classroom, only now he's two decades older and a teacher as well as a student.

Tracks and Trees Learning Center is 360 acres where Doug since 1999 has taught children and adults to slow down and see the lessons of nature. It is not simply a matter of identifying the 50 or 60 plant species of this ecosystem; it is understanding how the relationship of one life form with another will affect a bigger picture.

"I want people to interact with nature, instead of watching it," Doug says. "We try to get people immersed by getting them to use all their senses."

Foraging, wildlife tracking and wilderness survival skills are among the workshops he and **Kari Chaussee**, youth programs coordinator, conduct here and on 40 remote acres near Black River Falls—a different ecosystem because it's in the Jackson County Forest.

Students have ranged from third-graders on school field trips to adults in a monthly nature studies club. There are wolf tracking weekends for adults, seasonal camps for children.

Doug Gaulke devotes his life to nature.

Doug grew up on the west side of Milwaukee, and it is his parents who bought this property as a getaway from workday stress. They'd come here on weekends.

A farmer tills about one-half of the acreage. Doug, wife Lisa, daughter Sydney and son Sam live in a farmhouse on the property. A pole shed has been converted into an indoor nature classroom. Doug has an undergraduate degree in geography and a master's in environmental education. The latter came from Prescott College in Arizona; faculty let him design his own studies in Wisconsin.

"I wanted to do more than just read about nature," he says. "We usually don't learn how to observe in school. We just read about what other people have done."

Park and forest work with the state Department of Natural Resources didn't involve enough hands-on experience, Doug says, so that's why he decided to build Tracks and Trees Learning Center.

Doug has found that adults and children get excited about the same things. "Adults are just big kids when they get out in the woods," he says. "They want to get dirty, to see tracks, to sit around a campfire."

He examines his portion of Earth four to six days a week, "to learn or watch something. When that no longer happens, I'll probably quit teaching."

Many of his adult students "seem shocked that they can still feel what it's like to be a part of nature" and are "surprised that this can enrich their lives."

What do students learn at Tracks and Trees? Classes are about how to make fire without matches, how to make soap from bacon grease, how to tell a buck footprint from a doe's. Hikers in spring will search for wild edible plants. Families can learn basic wilderness survival measures, from how to track animals to how to build a shelter.

Some workshops reconnect people with the land. Others are about American Indian heritage. Lakota language basics are taught. So are the Seven Sacred Principles of living, a part of Gilbert Walking Bull's teachings at the class site near Black River Falls.

•

Tracks and Trees Learning Center
PO Box 411, Watertown
www.tracksandtrees.com, 920-988-7061

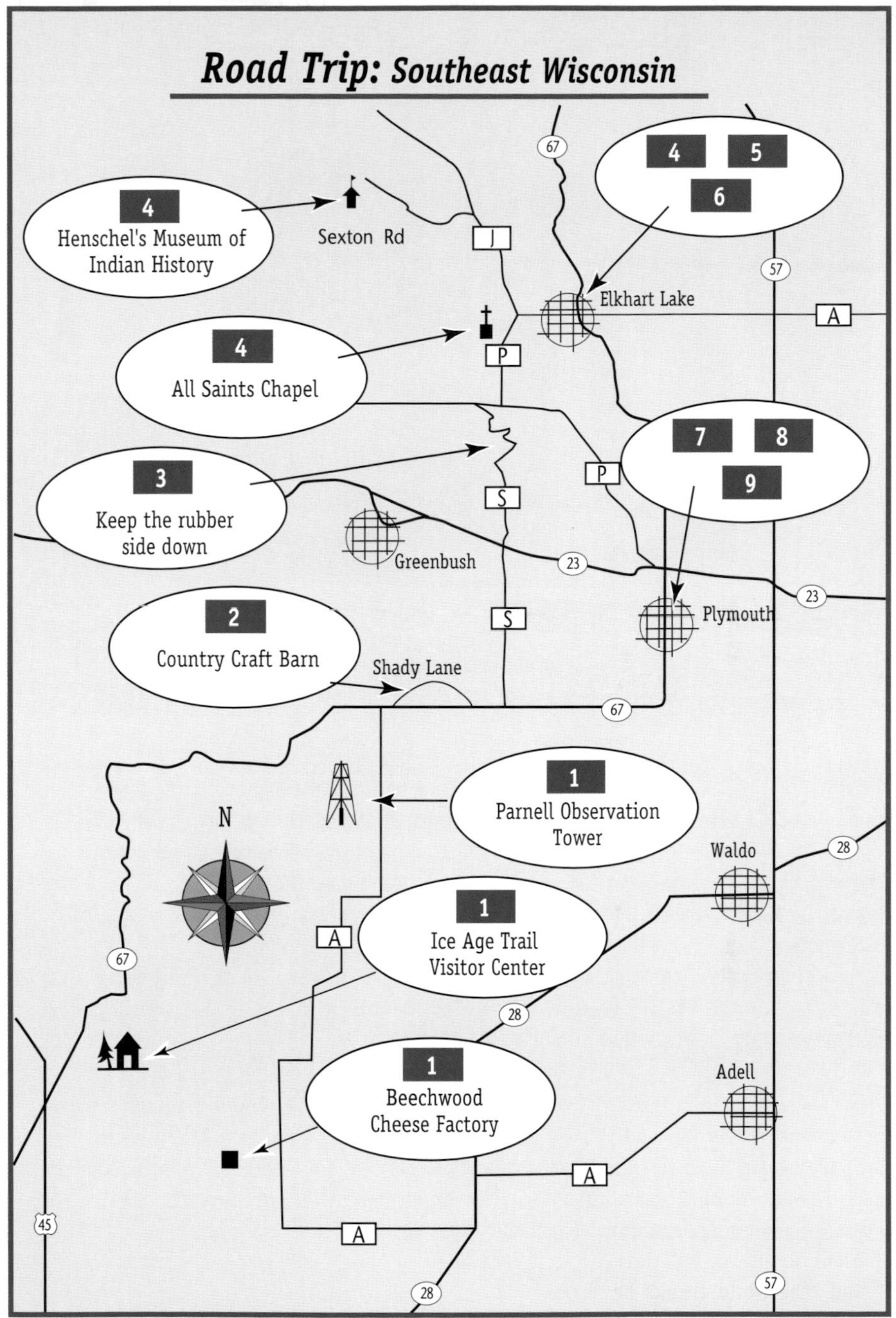
Road Trip: Southeast Wisconsin
4
Henschel's Museum of Indian History
Sexton Rd
J
67
4
5
6
57
Elkhart Lake
A
4
All Saints Chapel
P
7
8
9
3
Keep the rubber side down
P
S
Greenbush
23
23
S
Plymouth
2
Country Craft Barn
Shady Lane
67
1
Parnell Observation Tower
N
Waldo
28
1
Ice Age Trail Visitor Center
A
67
28
1
Beechwood Cheese Factory
Adell
A
45
A
28
57

SOUTHEAST

52 Stafford sometimes has traditional Irish music.

SOUTHEAST ROAD TRIP • DAY 1

1. GOOD MORNING. Start the day with a bag of fresh cheese curds from **Beechwood Cheese Factory**, N1598 West County A, Adell (one of the county's five remaining cheese factories) and head north 8 miles on A to **Parnell Observation Tower.** Pay the nominal user fee, get out and climb above the treetops. You're in the gut of the **Kettle Moraine State Forest**, and on a clear day, you'll see a couple of dozen miles.

This northern unit of the Kettles has a low profile but a wealth of hiking trails. A hub is the **Ice Age Visitor Center**, N1598 West County A, near Dundee and Highway 67. See **www.dnr.state.wi.us** or call **920-533-8322.**

2. LUNCH BREAK. During summer or fall: Drive to lush farmland for a good meal and pastoral views. Off of Highway 67, between Greenbush and Plymouth, is the **Country Crafts Barn**, W7402 Shady Lane. The crafts of 140 artisans are sold, and the cheery **Shady Lane Restaurant** is open for lunch and afternoon desserts. See **www.countrycraftsbarn.com** or call **920-893-8095.**

3. Afternoon Drive.
Take County S, all 2.4 miles of it. It's a good name for this **Wisconsin Rustic Road**, some of which has a gravel surface. Known for its curves and steep hills, the surrounding terrain is the work of glacial movement. The road is off of Highway 23, east of Greenbush, and heads into Glenbeulah.

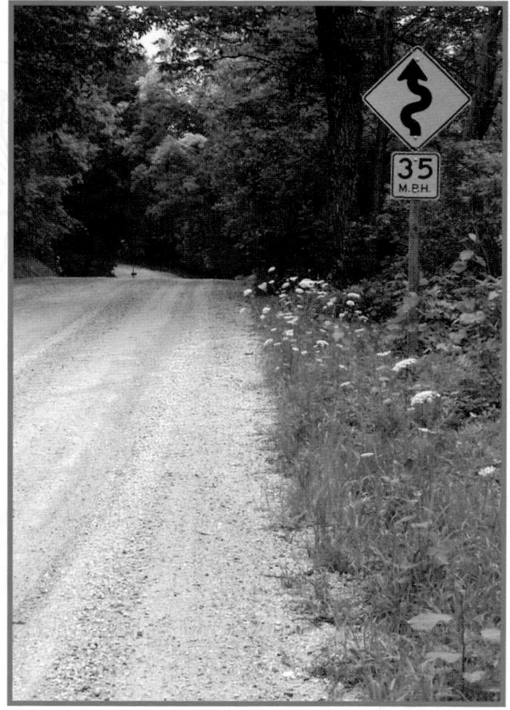

County S—a short but stunning Wisconsin Rustic Road.

4. Leg Stretch.
Look for **County P** outside Glenbeulah and head north (left) to **All Saints Chapel**, west of Elkhart Lake, which looks like it belongs in the country. It is tiny, with a generous use of fieldstone both inside and out. Foliage almost obscures the roadside view in this farming area.

Summer Sunday services have been held at All Saints since 1951. Although Episcopalian, it also is rented by other denominations and tended by volunteers. Grace Walsingham Episcopal Church, Sheboygan, oversees usage. **www.grace-walsingham.com, 920-452-9659.**

Stay the course on P, which turns into County J, and turn left on Sexton Road, northwest of Elkhart Lake. Look for signs to **Henschel's Museum of Indian History**. An extensive number of artifacts from several tribes are part of this obscure attraction, which is owned by farmer **Gary Henschel** and is the site of archeological digs. Call **920-876-3193**.

Time to retrace your tracks, head east (left) on County A and swing into Elkhart Lake. Visit **Two Fish Gallery**, 244 E. Rhine St., for a gander at the outdoor sculpture garden and indoor assortment of gallery work. Call **920-876-3192**.

5. Get Wired.
Itching to use your laptop? Wireless access is free at the **Brown Baer**, a tavern-pub with vegetarian fare as well as microbrews. Call **920-876-3319**.

6. Dinner.
For a more extensive meal made with local sustainably raised ingredients, the choice is **Back Porch Bistro**, 283 Victorian Village Drive, where the lakefront view is up close and personal. Come summer weekends, there are musical productions in the

Brooke Steinhardt's service is friendly at Chester's.

adjacent theater, a wholesome type of "Kids From Wisconsin" fare.

For a nightcap that is more quaint, ethnic and—on road racing weekends—raucous, mosey over to **Siebkins Tavern**, 284 S. Lake St., part of a 1916 and fourth generation family resort that is full of charm and nostalgia. An acceptable lake-view choice is the bar at **Lola's** restaurant, at **The Osthoff** resort.

Assuming that you're still alert, find A and take it to Highway 67, then head south (right) to Plymouth and check into a charming room at **52 Stafford**, an Irish inn downtown. The business name is the address. Order a Guinness or Harp at the pub, where traditional Irish music is performed on Wednesday nights.

See **www.harpandeagle.com** or call **800-421-4667**.

DAY 2

7. GOOD MORNING. A leisurely breakfast comes with your room. Visit **Plymouth Historical Museum** (open two days a week.) Explore downtown antique and other resale shops.

8. LUNCH BREAK. **Chester's Drive-in**, 1504 Eastern Ave. Let the carhops bring you a tray with Chester's Special: a hamburger, fries and root beer. Sound ordinary? Hah! These burgers, on the finest hardrolls around, are the best in the world. Call **920-892-7722.**

9. LAST HURRAH: Salute **Antoinette** on your way out of town. The bigger-than-life cow, near the corner of Mill and Milwaukee streets, had her teats welded on a few years ago because people kept stealing them. Quite the scandal.

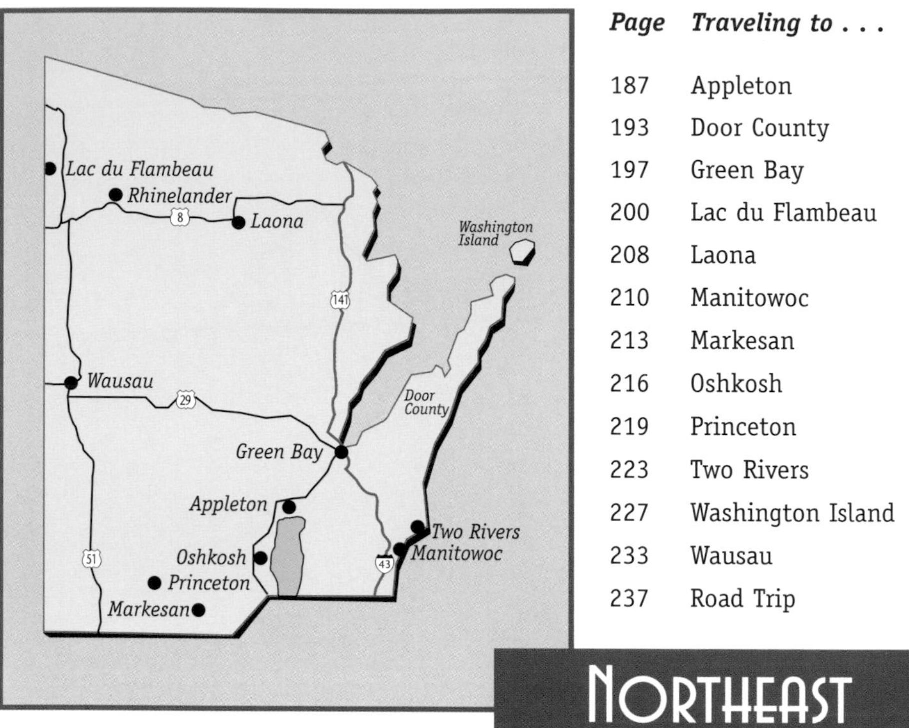

NORTHEAST

Observation: Wisconsin's emphasis on heritage reflects pride in our past.

We preserve the American Indian way of life and collect the artifacts of sports heroes. We celebrate the aura of a world-famous magician and visit decades-old family-run candy shops. We marvel at the work of our most legendary architect. And we enjoy the natural world that soothes our souls and senses.

(page 185) Washington Island Farm Museum gardens.

Wisconsin's first poet laureate.

APPLETON: PURE POETRY

Two by two, the small group of Wisconsin women is helped into traditional Japanese kimonos. It is not a quick process: Even with the fussing of two or more attendants per person, the dressing takes each of them almost a half-hour.

There is a lot of smoothing, tucking and tightening of fabric, a lot of cooing and concentration, smiling and dramatic sighing in admiration. Most of the U.S. visitors are grinning and puzzled—amused and amazed at how long the presentation takes—and they take home brilliant photos of themselves in unlikely attire.

The exception was **Ellen Kort**, who sheds one tear, then another, as she takes her turn inside the heavy and colorful fabric that is used to adorn Japanese brides. It wasn't until three weeks later, when back home in Appleton, that she begins to understand her reaction.

"Their hands, and their exquisite attention, were like my mother's when she buttoned the back of my wedding gown," she explains. "That's a connection I didn't make until I put the words on paper."

Wisconsin's first poet laureate, Ellen uses the story to explain how poetry can help the writer better understand her past, herself and her world.

The woman who wants Wisconsin to be recognized as a literary state says her job as poet laureate was "to take poetry to as many places and to as many people of all ages as possible. I feel I was able to do that—I have a sense of satisfaction that more people have become aware of the power of poetry. I did as much as humanly possible."

When she was appointed, Ellen says, only 13 states did not have a poet laureate. Terms of service, types of duties and pay levels vary wildly. A poet laureate can be appointed for a year, a lifetime, a governor's term of office. In Wisconsin, there is no state-paid salary or reimbursement of expenses.

Ellen says the four-year title has taken her thousands of miles around and outside of the state. The job was "a huge time commitment" that she felt privileged to make. "In a lot of ways, I already was doing this work," she notes. "So my work expanded."

For years before her 2000 appointment, Ellen read poetry and led poetry writing workshops in unconventional settings: Prisons. Elementary schools. Senior citizen centers. AIDS support groups. Cancer survivor programs. Domestic abuse shelters.

"You have to be an outgoing person," she says. "Poets sometimes just get used to sitting in their own space. There is a sense of solitude in our work; you tend to do it alone."

A **Wisconsin Academy of Sciences, Arts and Letters** fellow, Ellen is the author of 11 books, including seven of poetry. "Words and ideas that come from the common, speak to the common and compel all to reach for previously unknown heights" is the way Dr. John Mielke, an Appleton physician, described her in his Wisconsin Academy nomination.

As a teacher, Ellen is fond of asking her students to create and discover themselves by spilling words on paper, then deciding which ones to keep. Poetry, she says, is giving them permission to take off the masks worn as a matter of status or survival.

"One of the things I liked best was the sense of ownership that some people took of this position," Ellen says, of the poet laureate role. "Libraries, especially, were delighted to have a poet laureate. So were schools, and it wasn't just a state job, it was being glad to have 'our' poet laureate visit."

She continues the mentoring, even though the state title was handed over to **Denise Sweet** of the University of Wisconsin-Green Bay.

"There is such a strong need for it, especially in the schools," Ellen says, of poetry. "We have to reach children earlier, and teachers are overwhelmed with work. 'I'm not a poet,' some have told me. 'I need to teach from a book.' So we can be helpful here."

She will participate in a conference about women and poverty, work with a group of physicians, work with a hospice organization.

"These are the things that will show the power of poetry," Ellen says. "There is value in putting words and emotions onto paper."

•

Fast Facts

Ellen Kort's poetry is etched into the architecture in Wisconsin. Among its homes: Appleton's **Fox River Mall**, the **Green Bay Botanical Garden** and Milwaukee's **Midwest Express Center**.

•

The **Wisconsin Fellowship of Poets** is a statewide organization for poets that first met in 1950. Go to **www.wfop.org** for poetry readings, workshops and open mike nights throughout the state. The group also aims to host poetry conferences in April and November.

•

The **Midwest Booksellers Association** lists more than 80 locally owned and operated Wisconsin bookstores at **www.midwestbooksellers.org**.

•

Poetry at a temporary standstill in northern Wisconsin.

Visitors practice magic routinely at the Outagamie Museum.

Appleton: Smoke, Mirrors, Magic Acts

I'm not the first to be tempted to make comparisons between **Joseph McCarthy** and **Houdini.** Both men succeeded, for a while, as masters of illusion—the U.S. senator in his aggressive and abrasive quest to tag 205 Americans as Communists in the 1950s, and Harry Houdini in his elaborate trickster mode that seemed to defy laws of logic, physics and survival, 50 years earlier.

Two magicians, not one, both with ties to Appleton, according to **Terry Bergen**, executive director of the **Outagamie Museum.** She digs deeper.

"They created myths about themselves," she says. The politician "pretended to be an anti-Communist," she alleges, and "was never motivated by more than his own self-promotion."

She describes herself as a leftist, then adds, "I'm not going to apologize for Joe McCarthy, but he was just one man. It was the House Un-American Activities Committee that did most of the blackballing" of Americans categorized as Reds.

And Houdini? "He wanted to be seen as an American, and a superman," she says, noting that—contrary to promotional materials—he was born in Hungary, not Appleton, where he lived merely four years. Then his father, a rabbi, lost his job and moved the family to Milwaukee, then New York.

Harry Houdini—master of illusion.

"He was a brilliant publicist," Terry says, of Houdini. Kind of a pioneer for what we have today: Slick promoters who stage events routinely, shocking us to attention.

Stroll through Terry's museum, where the second floor is devoted to Houdini's antics. It is a hands-on presentation that is meant to amuse and educate children as well as adults, and about 10 to 15 percent of the museum's Houdini collection is typically out for public viewing.

And where is the notorious U.S. senator? Nowhere, for now. An exhibit, called "Joseph McCarthy: A Modern Tragedy," was never meant to be a permanent display, but generated plenty of controversy.

"We know we did it right because we didn't please anybody," Terry says. Liberals thought it soft-pedaled McCarthyism. Some of the locals considered it too harsh, not concentrating enough on other aspects of the man.

"So many people who had known Joe, politics aside, aren't ashamed of him—they saw him as a good man, and didn't want him observed just as a politician."

The museum, in the former Appleton Masonic Temple, is a sturdy stone building that cost $100,000 to build in 1924. Joseph McCarthy was one of the members.

A heavy drinker ("no one was more fun," locals told Terry), he died of hepatitis in 1957.

Much info from the former museum exhibit is online. Hunt for "virtual exhibits" on the Outagamie Museum home page.

Terry says the museum has plans for an exhibit of McCarthy artifacts. "It will be about how to interpret an artifact and learn history from it," she says.

Items will include the larger-than-life bronze bust of the senator, which sat in the Outagamie County Courthouse until 2001, when it was moved to the museum because of political protests.

Despite his brief Appleton residency, Terry predicts that Houdini always will have a presence in the museum because "he has universal appeal" and "the world thinks he

DETOUR

If the Houdini exhibit inspires you to make magic on your own, head to the **Abracadabra Magic and Costume Shop**, 508 W. College Ave. Owner/magician **Rondini** performs as well as sells magic items. He also conducts a Wizards School twice a year for would-be magicians who are 8-13 years old.

Consult **www.abramagic.com, 920-830-8754.**

Rondini is respectful of Houdini but not a fan of the Appleton museum, in part because of its Metamorphosis exhibit.

Magicians gather for the nonprofit **Houdini Days Magic Festival** in October; there are magic shows as well as workshops to inspire children to learn magical arts. See **www.houdinidays.com.**

came from Appleton." (Aside: There is a museum devoted to Houdini in Scranton, Pa. See **www.houdini.org**.)

Hers is a job that has required tough skin. Besides dealing with "Joseph McCarthy: A Modern Tragedy" controversies, Terry was buried with feedback from magicians when the museum showed how Houdini pulled off Metamorphosis, an illusion in which he was placed in a sack, then switched places with an assistant, from inside a locked trunk.

"It's an outdated method today," she says, but magicians in the United Kingdom and Germany were especially vocal about how the museum spilled the beans about a trade secret. David Copperfield contacted Terry personally, too, which led to a "Today" show debate.

That happened during Terry's first year of work as executive director, a feet-in-the-fire experience that doesn't seem to daunt her. "There will always be a conflict between the collector and the historian," she says, describing the explosion of emotion as "the most controversial exhibit reaction for the least basis."

Interest in McCarthy and Appleton was refueled by the 2005 release of "Good Night, and Good Luck," a movie about journalist Edward R. Murrow's anti-McCarthyism crusade.

Her last observations, on Houdini: "We needed a guy like him during his time. The nation was unsettled, and here was someone who could escape" improbable circumstances. And, McCarthy: "There were Communists" during his time. "People were just wrong about who they were."

•

Outagamie Museum, 330 E. College Ave., Appleton
www.foxvalleyhistory.org, 920-733-8445

•

Door County Maritime Museum is the home of history about ore carriers, fishing tugs and luxury yachts.

DOOR COUNTY: MARITIME MUSEUM X 3

Sturgeon Bay, the county seat of Door County, has a population of merely 9,700, but it has a national, and international, reputation for shipbuilding. One of three **Door County Maritime Museum** sites can be toured here. The **Sturgeon Bay** museum concentrates on the area's shipyard history, which has included ore carriers to luxury yacht production. It is a pretty setting for the annual classic and wooden boat show during the first weekend of August, plus outdoor concerts on some summer Sunday nights.

The **Cana Island Lighthouse** in pretty **Bailey's Harbor** on the Lake Michigan shore is open to visitors through late October. The working lighthouse's interior cannot be toured, but you can take a look at the oil house and the lighthouse keeper's house.

The third property is a museum at **Gills Rock**, at the peninsula's tip. *Hope*, a fishing tug that was built in 1930, is open to visitors; its last fishing trip was in 1992. Marine engines, ice fishing and navigation are among the museum exhibit themes.

The annual **Door County Lighthouse Walk** is the third weekend in May.

For more: **www.dcmm.org, 920-743-5958.**

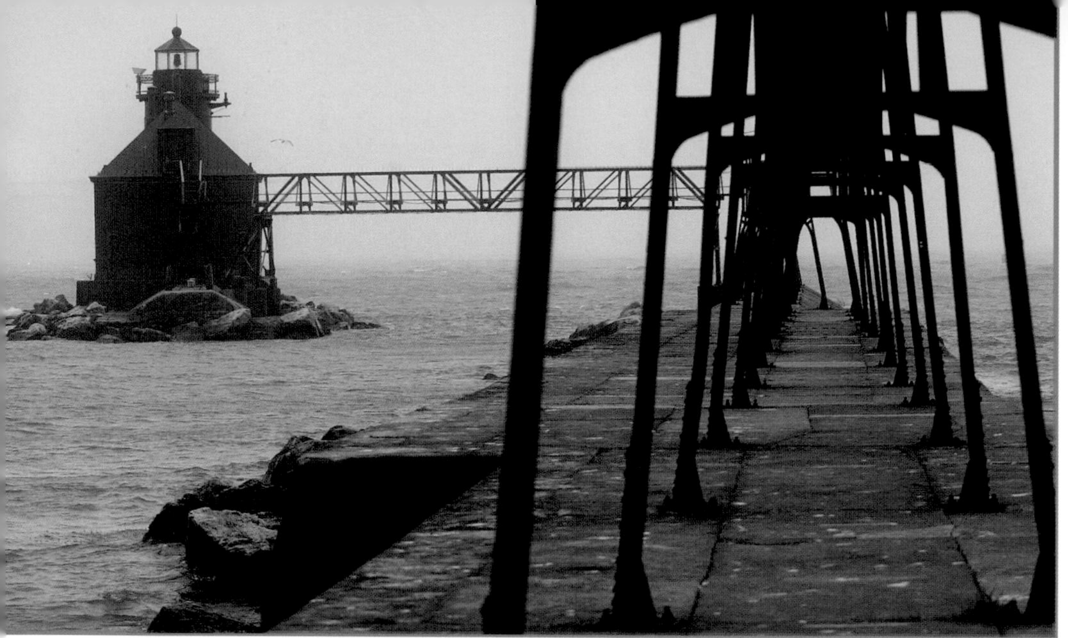

Sturgeon Bay Ship Canal North Pierhead light.

Fast Facts

What makes Door County popular, and who visits? These tidbits come from the Door County Chamber of Commerce:

The Door County Peninsula shoreline exceeds 300 miles, and Door County has more shoreline, lighthouses and state parks than any other county in the Midwest.

The county's year-round population is about 29,000, but it attracts more than 2.1 million visitors per year. About two-thirds of the tourists visit from May to the end of October.

Although Door County has been under tremendous development pressure, nearly 90 percent of its land mass remains undeveloped.

•

DETOURS

Door County, known for its exquisite natural surroundings, is an inspiration to many fine artists. But its soul is an inspiration to performers in the theater arts as well.

In 2006, the nation's oldest professional resident summer theater opened an all-weather pavilion on the shores of Green Bay. For **Peninsula Players Theatre**, between Egg Harbor and Fish Creek, this was its first new home since opening in 1935.

Side openings make this an open-air theater, during good weather. The audience comes to take a lakeshore walk and watch the sunset, as well as absorb the work of professional actors. A bonfire becomes the meeting place during intermission.

www.peninsulaplayers.com, 920-868-3287.

•

What other seasonal theater settings exist in Door County?

American Folklore Theatre presents original plays and musicals at **Peninsula State Park**, Fish Creek, in an outdoor amphitheater. It's an inexpensive theater for families camping at the park, and open to everyone.

www.folkloretheatre.com, 920-854-6117.

•

The gardens of **Bjorklunden**, an educational retreat near Baileys Harbor, is home to **Door Shakespeare**.

www.doorshakespeare.com, 920-839-1500.

•

Washington Island presents two plays per summer by **Island Players** at the **Trueblood Performing Arts Center**.

www.washingtonisland.com, 920-847-2215.

•

Third Avenue Playhouse, Sturgeon Bay, houses year-round classes and performances in theater, music and dance—and shows by **Isadoora Theatre Company**. It is a community performance center.

www.thirdavenueplayhouse.com, 920-743-1760.

•

To keep current with it all, consult **www.doorcountyarts.com.**

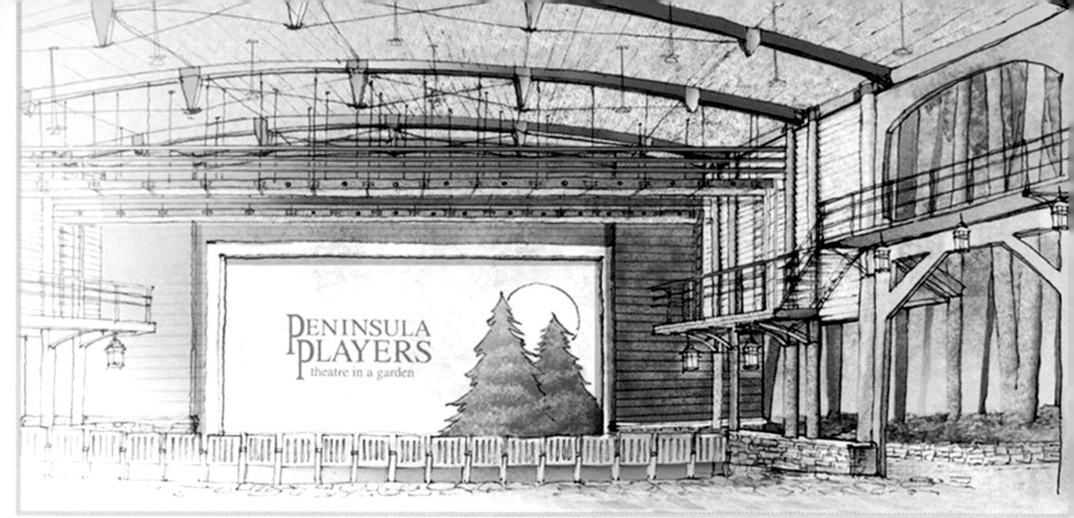

Peninsula Players is one of America's oldest professional summer theaters.

Whitefish is the fish of choice during the classic Door County fish boil, a tradition that goes back to Scandinavian settlers and lumberjacks. Although more than a dozen local restaurants present fish boils, here's how to do it for a group of eight at home, courtesy of **Dan Peterson** of **The Viking Grill**, Ellison Bay (whose fish boils began in 1961).

At Home Fish Boil

16 chunks of whitefish (2-inch slices)
16 small red potatoes (ends cut off)
16 small white onions (peeled)
1/2 pound salt
2 gallons water

Add 1/4 pound of salt to water and bring to a boil. Add potatoes and boil for 16 minutes. Add onions and boil 4 minutes more. Add fish and another 1/4 pound salt, boil for 10 minutes and drain into a colander. Serve with melted butter, lemon and coleslaw.

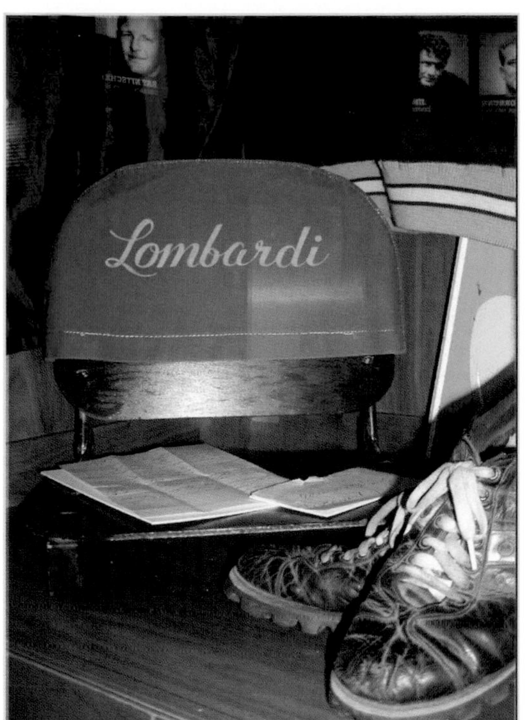

Vince Lombardi's field shoes—saved for posterity.

GREEN BAY: SOLES FROM A FAN

A $7,500 pair of shoes caught the eye of **Tom Murphy**, and he got them—for free. That kind of thing is pretty special, but not unprecedented, in his line of work. Murphy is chief archivist for the **Green Bay Packers Hall of Fame**, and the shoes were donated by **Judy Russell** of Oshkosh. They used to belong to Judy's uncle, **Norbert "Mac" McHugh**, a Packer groundskeeper and gateman who worked there long enough to see coaches from **Curly Lambeau** to **Mike Holmgren**.

Turn over the shoes, and you'll find a "V" on the back of one, an "L" on the other. These field shoes used to be **Vince Lombardi's**, and that is what makes them of high value. Now they are part of Lombardi's locker, which is among the Hall of Fame's 77 exhibits. About 99 percent of the more than $2 million worth of acquired items have been donated, Tom estimates, and about 75 percent of them are on display at any given time.

He gets several calls a week from Packers fans, regarding items they have inherited or otherwise may want to donate. When something sounds of interest, Tom will solicit several opinions and then judge the value—monetary as well as historical significance.

One of the people he has relied on is **Red Cochran**, who was an assistant coach under Lombardi. Who calls? All kinds of people, including somebody who said he had padding that was around a goalpost during the legendary Ice Bowl championship of 1967. That wasn't deemed to be of great value.

There is better potential from the call fielded from a new widower, whose wife had been a huge Packers fan. She used a wheelchair that was a customized tribute to the team, perhaps a good and unusual fit for an exhibit devoted to fan memorabilia.

Although they're not as valuable as a one-of-a-kind championship trophy, Tom calls the Lombardi shoes "a real prize" because they are the only pair known to still exist.

The invincible Vince Lombardi.

It took Judy Russell a while to decide that the shoes should go to Green Bay instead of Canton, Ohio, home of the Pro Football Hall of Fame. "More Packer fans would be able to see them in Green Bay," she finally decided.

Judy is a meticulous and razor-sharp retired journalist; we both worked at the Oshkosh Northwestern in the 1970s. Her memorabilia and knowledge of Packers trivia are vast. She has pieces of the Ice Bowl goalposts, bobbleheads of the players in the 1950s, game programs that go back to the 1920s. She also has the ticket stubs for every game that she has attended. The first was with her uncle on Nov. 23, 1952.

"It was my first game and **Tony Canadeo's** last," she says, noting that years later she was able to meet and chat with the star halfback.

What did she add to her Packers collection recently? A pewter, limited edition and autographed statue of **Brett Favre**, created by Colorado artist Michael Ricker.

Archivist Tom calls Judy a serious fan—one who will slowly read her way through the Hall of Fame displays. She was, in fact, one of the 10 finalists in the Packers' 1998 search for the team's biggest fan.

As a teen, Judy says, she buried a penny in the north end zone of Lambeau Field, "for good luck." She recalls riding a train to see Packers-Bears games when they were played at Wrigley Field, and heading to games against the Vikings at the new Metropolitan Stadium in Bloomington, Minn. (now the site of Mall of America).

Her favorite player? Bobby Dillon in the 1950s, she says, noting that he still holds the team record (52) for interceptions. Put it all together, and it seems fitting that a piece of Judy's history as a Packers fan is now part of her beloved team's home. It's also a nice reminder of what fan loyalty means.

What would the Packers' archivist consider a rare find these days? "It's difficult to find vintage equipment and uniforms used prior to the 1960s," Tom says. Team-autographed footballs, particularly from the 1960s, also will turn his head—but they need to contain the players' original signatures. Some people who think they have the real thing really don't.

"About four out of five (autographed footballs) from that time are stamped signatures," Tom says, which drops the value from "the thousands" to "a couple of hundred" dollars. To talk with him about making a tax-deductible donation to the Packers Hall of Fame, call the Hall of Fame.

•

Green Bay Packers Hall of Fame
1265 Lombardi Ave., Green Bay
www.packers.com, 920-569-7512

Fast Facts

Another rich piece of Green Bay history is **Bay Beach Amusement Park**, the only place we know in Wisconsin where kids can take a ride for a quarter. It's good entertainment for the little ones (although some of the 16 rides aren't for children under the age of 2 years). They sit in lady bugs, race cars, helicopters and jeeps. Pay 50 cents to ride the merry-go-round, Ferris wheel and a half-dozen other high-speed options.

Around 1910, swimsuits were rented for a dime at this park's beach, bringing in as much as $450 per day. President Franklin Roosevelt spoke here in 1934. A dance hall became the place to be seen in the 1930s and 1940s. Pony rides began in 1931, and they still are offered.

Located at 1313 Bay Beach Road, rides and concessions are open seasonally, May through September. Consult **www.ci.green-bay.wi.us, 920-448-3365.**

•

Dillman's Bay Resort has survived through four generations.

Lac du Flambeau: Enduring Resort

On my desk is a *Wall Street Journal* story about six-star hotels. Think personal butlers, private swimming pools and four-digit nightly rates for suites that likely are larger than your childhood home.

On my mind is John Hildebrand's *A Northern Front*, a book about the tension between people and their environment. We gravitate to the wilderness because of its purity but leave scars when we claim it as our own for a weekend, a summer or a lifetime.

On my bulletin board is an "Escape to Wisconsin" bumper sticker, a remnant from the state's most effective tourism campaign. I'd say "successful," but sometimes I wonder about how that word should be defined in the long run.

This world, country and state contain much to pamper us without adding in all the conveniences of modern living. The clarity of a spring-fed lake, the fire of a campsite after sunset, the stunning brilliance of wildflowers on roadsides—each becomes a bigger and rarer gem as life at home grows more crowded, commercial and complicated.

Within the haven that is Wisconsin are multimillion-dollar expansions at several resorts that will make them more state-of-the-art, more competitive in the tourism marketplace, more seductive to the overstressed people who seek a place to relax.

A resort near Lake Geneva began a gutting and expansion that will exceed $100 million. It came on the heels of a $40 million overhaul of a nearby competitor. Then came word that a Wisconsin Dells resort will pursue an almost $200 million expansion, called the largest in the history of area. The magnitude dwarfs all kinds of projects by competitors, in a city long known for its lust for outdoing itself.

These are economic strategies that will measure success in dollars and cents—not just for one business, but multiple communities. That is how **Denny** and **Sue Robertson** need to measure progress, too, but it has taken creative thinking as well to preserve what has lured travelers to their **Dillman's Bay Resort** for four generations.

Their business is on the shores of White Sand Lake, on the **Lac du Flambeau Indian reservation.** In the 1950s, Sue says, it was one of 210 resorts in the area. "Today, if there are 10, I'd be surprised."

Like any other business—grocers to diners to farms—it is tougher for the little guy to survive.

Travelers may say they don't come to the Northwoods because of a hair dryer, cable TV or central air—yet their expectations in lodging don't necessarily change because of the scenery. Can you get a feel for rustic living without roughing it? Sure. Does that mean you'll appreciate it? Perhaps.

"The resort has always been about more than the beds and check-ins," says Sue, whose parents and grandparents also owned the resort. "The draw for me has been the water, getting red eyes—as a child—from all that swimming, meeting people from Chicago who would come for one or two weeks at a time."

Her grandfather, **Gust Peterson**, set a world record when he caught a 52-pound and 52-inch muskie on **White Sand Lake** in 1936. Three years later, the mounted fish was destroyed in a fire that also took the resort's main lodge.

After another fire in 1992, the Robertsons spent $800,000 to rebuild.

It was not an automatic decision, but another generation wanted to get involved and the couple figured their creative arts program, which began in 1978, had a solid reputation. But they didn't stop there.

"We were afraid our niche was becoming our identity," Denny says. "We felt a need to diversify" to avoid being pigeonholed. "If you are just one thing, you run the risk of having interest wane."

So now there are specialty packages—for fishermen, golfers, wedding weekends, women's getaways, Elderhostel classes. The resort is dog-friendly. Use of bicycles and a canoe are a part of the room rate, which can be as little as $100 in summer.

There are units big enough to house family reunions. Some have gas fireplaces and Jacuzzis. Others have twin beds and soap but no shampoo, a coffeemaker but no coffee.

Although the Robertsons own one-half of the resort, 15 other parties own the rest. So the investment and risk are shared.

The place is not small. It can handle 225 guests comfortably, but in spring and fall may have as few as 20. Being open during winter is not routine.

Factor in a change in travel habits: Fewer people want to stay put for a full week, or rent the same cabin year after year. They are fickle about food: "At first people wanted three meals here, then two. Now some want to just eat in their unit or go to a restaurant" in nearby Minocqua.

So the resort owners—in partnership with daughter Stephanie and her husband, Todd Skotterud—call in a caterer when more than 15 sign up for a meal.

Sue notes that her parents first operated the place as a camp for boys in 1935. That lasted one year because they grossed only $500 and realized it would be more conducive to woo fishermen.

"It's about listening to what customers want," she concludes, "and then trying to adapt."

•

Dillman's Bay Resort, 3305 Sand Lake Lodge Lane, Lac du Flambeau
www.dillmans.com, 715-588-3143

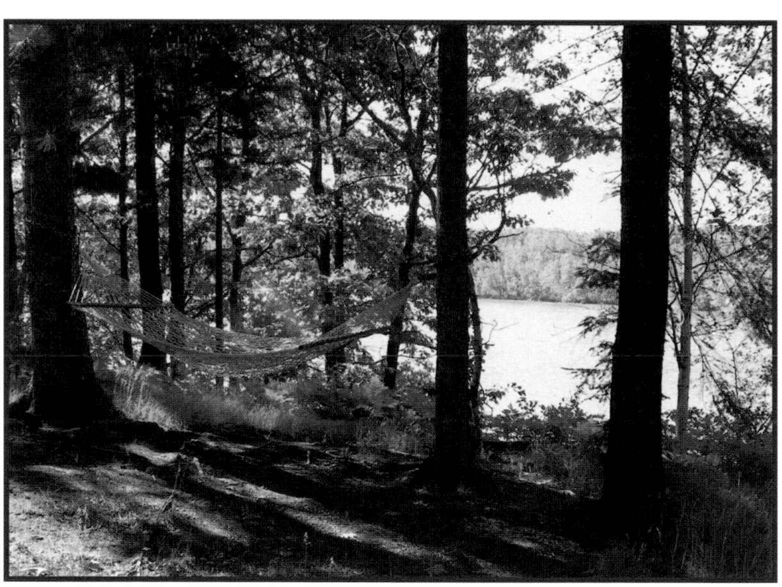

Simple pleasures: shade, a hammock and a pretty view.

LAC DU FLAMBEAU: TRIBAL TOURISM

Nick Hockings gladly holds on to the past.

The past matters to **Nick Hockings**, and he gladly relives it daily, especially during the summer.

Waswagoning—on the shore of a pristine lake in the heart of Lac du Flambeau country—is one way for Hockings to keep his Ojibwe tribe's cultural traditions alive, and its historical record accurate. It also is evidence of the depth that American Indian tourism can have in Wisconsin, given the right determination and resources.

Waswagoning is an authentic 17th century American Indian village, developed by Hockings in 1994, shortly after traditional spring tribal spearfishing drew the ire of protesters and sparked violence. The court system eventually sided with the tribe.

Lac du Flambeau means "Lake of the Torches," Waswagoning means "The Place Where They Spearfish by Torchlight," and guides at the historic village will explain the mindset of their ancestors as well as techniques that are a part of tribal traditions.

Nick and others from the **Ojibwe's Lac du Flambeau Band** trapped and skinned the animals whose hides drape and warm the wigwams at Waswagoning. They have stripped birch bark to make waterproof baskets and canoes, built a smokehouse out of basswood, dug fire pits and cleared walking paths.

They know how a spinning stick can turn dried grass into fire, how wild rice is harvested, why deer tallow is eaten in winter. Life rhythms, then and to some extent now, change with the four seasons.

This attraction is about attitude as well as the skills that were needed to survive.

The Ojibwe has seven clans, Nick explains, each with its own role to make sure the community's needs are covered. So the gentle deer clan provides a sense of home as well as actual housing. The bear clan protects the others, acting as police, legal guardians, medicinal herb/plant experts.

Nick's commitment, as a part of the bird clan, is to be a keeper of the traditions

Baskets are woven by hand, just as the Lac du Flambeau did centuries ago.

and a spiritual guide. That makes Waswagoning a good match for him; he has spent his adult life explaining and demonstrating American Indian culture in other forums too.

Ed Hall of the U.S. Bureau of Indian Affairs says the Smithsonian National Museum of the American Indian has "helped bring the significance of Native American cultures to the forefront," but the average tourist has yet to distinguish one tribe from another.

He observes that more Wisconsin tribal members are participating in all levels of the tourism industry, but as tourism offerings become more sophisticated and wide-ranging, development holds more inner struggles.

"What are you willing to exchange dollars for, and what will you not" turn into an attraction, he asks. Sacred sites and rituals, tribes tend to agree, are not appropriate to capitalize on commercially.

In Wisconsin, the foundation for strong cultural tourism has been set, according to Gayle Junnila of Minnesota's state tourism office. In Minnesota, she says she is waiting for tribes "to tell us what they want to do here."

"We are sensitive to the difference between gaming and cultural heritage," she says, but no attraction can be promoted until it is solidly established.

"You have to have a viable product—you have to have activities, events, attractions that are open on specific dates. People need to know these things will be there when they arrive during a vacation."

Ed wants American Indians to acknowledge and interpret the negative aspects of history as well as cultural traditions. "They are a part of our story too," he contends.

For the Lac du Flambeau, the abandoned government boarding school that was closed decades ago remains untouched. It is a silent symbol of conflict; students were punished for speaking their native Ojibwe language, forced to discard their native dress and wear school uniforms, and disciplined because of their heritage.

The Lac du Flambeau population of 2,000 quadruples in summer. Although the biggest business easily is **Lake of the Torches Resort Casino**, the community does not want the impact of tourism to be limited to the thrill of gambling.

Waswagoning is not the only local attraction that is about history and heritage. At the **George W. Brown Jr. Ojibwe Museum and Cultural Center**, elaborate dioramas and other exhibits document Lac du Flambeau history and lifestyle.

There also are craft and nature workshops for the public, conducted by tribal members, as well as powwows, typically weekly in summer.

"How has gambling affected our culture?" Nick Hockings asks, rhetorically. "We've always gambled. It's always been a part of our lives."

American Indians for centuries have competed, entertained and settled arguments by way of a game, while wagering canoes to arrows. There is a big difference between that and warfare, Nick says, but "the demonizing still exists" because American Indians tend to be complacent or at a loss about how to stand up for themselves.

More than $10 million in 2005 was spent on the Lac du Flambeau downtown. Most noticeable to tourists will be street lights that resemble torches, streets stamped with animal prints, cobblestone walkways and the addition of 11 retail shops.

Among the band's high-profile local artists are **Greg "Biskakone" Johnson**, whose Ojibwe bead work is in demand as far away as France and Japan, and **David Peterson**, one of the few birch basket makers who uses traditional bark harvesting and weaving methods.

For more: **www.lacduflambeau.org, 877-588-3346**

•

Waswagoning, Hwy. 47 and County H, Lac du Flambeau
www.waswagoning.org, 715-588-3560

•

George W. Brown Jr. Ojibwe Museum, downtown Lac du Flambeau
www.ojibwe.com, 715-588-3333

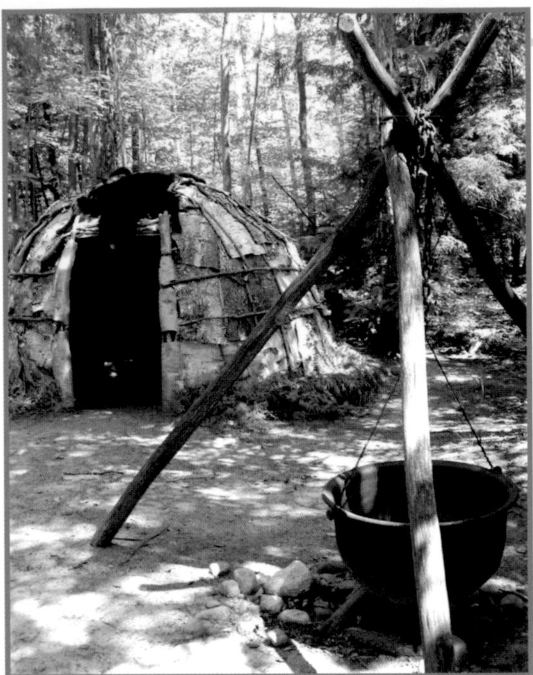
Bark-covered huts were once commonplace.

DETOURS

Polkas, threshing, fiddles and Polish sausage probably aren't the first things that come to mind when the topic is American Indian tourism. But state tourism officials have rewarded the **Menominee** and **Stockbridge-Munsee** reservations for their willingness to think along those lines.

The two tribes and nearby communities of Gresham and Shawano used a $40,000 Joint Effort Marketing grant to work as partners and cross-promote each others' events. Five "**Experience Northwoods Traditions**" weekends are a tribute to the diversity and uniqueness of local culture—and an effort to attract tourists for more than gambling.

"We're looking at being more than a casino," says **Cassie Molkentin** of **Stockbridge-Munsee**, a band of the Mohicans. "We want to share and educate tourists about our background."

There are 18 miles between the **Mohican North Star Casino** and the **Menominee Nation Casino**, and the two tribes have begun to think more like partners than competitors. Small to medium-sized casinos such as these are being overlooked because of the larger Ho-Chunk, Potawatomi and Oneida gaming facilities in Wisconsin, says **Jim Reiter**, general manager of the Menominee Nation Casino.

So cross-promotion means making prospective casino customers aware of the **Pine Hills Golf Course** at Stockbridge-Munsee, the only course in the state that is operated by American Indians. That tribe, in turn, lets its customers know that the Menominee have a hotel at their **Keshena** casino.

"Our goal is to get more people into our area," Cassie says. "We already know that our customers go to both casinos." Neighboring town business owners, she adds, have been frustrated because casino traffic isn't stopping.

"Experience Northwoods Traditions" provides ways for travelers to get acquainted with the reservations as well as Gresham and Shawano. The JEM grant requires participation from at least four tourism entities, which provide matching funds for the fall project.

"We knew of each other before, but we didn't work together," says Jim, who adds that participants have learned "we're not each other's enemy—we're all in this together" because of the challenges of rural tourism.

A part of the work ahead is to toot their own horn about accomplishments, be it the Menominee's donations of $280,000 in 2004 for local community projects or its successes in forest preservation.

"People actually come from Europe to look at our woods and hear about our rotations, our work to keep it all going," Jim says.

Wisconsin's biggest powwow occurs when tribes converge at Indian Summer Festival, in Milwaukee every September.

The joint fall celebrations, each on a different September or October weekend, include Farm Heritage Day, Gresham; European Heritage Tribute, North Star Casino, Gresham; Apple Traditions, Shawano; Woodland and Logging Heritage, Menominee Indian reservation; and Mohican Cultural Day, Wea Tauk Village, on the Stockbridge-Munsee reservation.

Jim says the **Menominee Logging Museum**, a seasonal attraction, was "a gift to our tribe from a collector who knew of our forest preservation work." There are 20,000 artifacts and seven buildings to tour.

For more about the events: **www.northwoodstraditions.com**.

•

For a copy of the "Native Wisconsin" tourism guide to the state's American Indian communities, consult the **Great Lakes Inter-Tribal Council Inc.** at **www.glitc.org** or **715-588-3324**.

The state's best known stop for railroad buffs is the National Railroad Museum in Green Bay, but smaller towns also have sites worth visiting.

LAONA: TRAINS & SOUP

Tiny Laona, an unincorporated community in Forest County, is an old lumber town that carefully preserved a part of its heritage. **Camp Five Museum** is on the National Register of Historic Places, and the museum complex is 640 acres that contain 10 former lumber camp buildings.

It is where lumberjacks lived until about 1940, when the invention of chain saws and trucks replaced the need for trains to move huge logs out of this part of **Nicolet National Forest**. **Don Kircher**, a retired high school teacher who has managed Camp Five as a tourist site since 1969, says he hires about 40 Laona area residents (high schoolers to retirees) to operate the museum in summer.

Part of this seasonal attraction is a 20-minute ride on a 1916 steam train that used to haul logs. The ride is 2 1/2 miles and scenic—past a lake, a river and into the heart of that gorgeous forest.

"It's been a good experience," Don says of his work, which he was drafted to do because he was a teacher and thus had his summers free. Admission fees, he says, cover just a part of the cost of Camp Five operation and upkeep. Money from the estate of Gordon and Mary Connor (who used to run this and other lumber camps), plus other donations, keep the attraction open.

"Everything has to be custom-made," Don says of the old train, to explain the need for money. Boy Scouts come here to earn merit badges in natural resources, or archaeology, he says, explaining one aspect of Camp Five's value. Regarding archaeology: What is found in the former camp dump on occasion becomes part of the museum's exhibits.

Three hours is the average time that a family spends at Camp Five. There are walking trails and nature tours on the property.

Laona also has a great recipe for soup that has served its residents well for many years. The annual **Community Soup** began in 1919 on Silver Lake beach. Families showed up with whatever was growing in their garden, and they added it or meat to a soup pot.

People visited while the soup simmered, and then everybody would share a meal.

Now the ritual is more organized and more people are fed at the event, on the first Sunday of August. The Lions Club assigns an ingredient to each family in the town, they bring it to the beach, and the soup eventually is ladled out to a couple of thousand people. (About 1,400 live in the town; visitors are welcome to eat for free.)

"We put it all into large kettles, and you bring your own bowl to eat it," explains Don.

Laona is near the intersection of Highways 32 and 8, about 40 miles east of Rhinelander, or less than two hours northwest of Green Bay.

•

Camp Five Museum, 5480 Connor Farm Road, Laona
www.camp5museum.org, 800-774-3414

•

A 1915 railroad chapel car can be toured on the American Baptist Assembly grounds near Green Lake. **Car #7**, known as **Grace**, was constructed for $21,000 and had worship services held in it until 1946. It has been renovated and no longer travels, but it is open for tours and, occasionally, small group meetings or worship.

For more: **www.glcc.org, 800-558-8898.**

Chapel Car Grace, built in 1915, still is available for worship near Green Lake.

The city's biggest tourist draw is the nation's biggest cooking store.

MANITOWOC: REALLY COOKING

He has a pleasant and disarming way of hawking his merchandise. Today, it is porcelain dinnerware—22,000 pieces that are being sold for a pittance because of someone else's warehouse fire.

"Look at this—$3.99," **Pete Burback** says, lifting one attractive platter after another from a 3-foot-tall box. "What a deal. It's killing me."

He laughs, a tad manically and then moves to a different storage crate. "There's more—see? Can you believe this?"

Within a half-hour, Pete will have talked up the porcelain with a dozen customers, greeted his kids' doctor with a hug, fetched a 10-foot ladder and hooted about his newest challenge: finding bone marrow spoons, to fill a customer's request.

The owner of **Cooks Corner**, in downtown Manitowoc, seems to be having the time of his life. He describes his business as the nation's largest kitchen store and the city's biggest tourist draw, attracting 170,000 visitors per year.

"We get busloads," Pete says. Who decided this place is the nation's largest? There is a shrug, then this: "Nobody's called me to say 'you're full of it.' "

With that comes another laugh. The Manitowoc store has been 20,000 square feet since 1998. For four years before that, it took up 3,000 square feet in the 1849 Schuette Brothers department store building, as a place to buy parts and seconds for Mirro, West Bend and NESCO cookware.

Today there are more than 15,000 kitchen products for sale, 49-cent orange peelers to $799 kitchen work centers. If you want something and can't find it, ask.

"We get mountains of requests," Pete says, and—for now—he does all the product buying.

"Our store is a destination, versus a specialty shopping stop. For me, it's just fun —we're trying to be the best."

Much of the inventory is online, too, so employees typically wheel carts around the retail area in early morning, to fill orders that need to be mailed. Order more than $99 in merchandise, and the shipping is free.

It has been a challenging venture for Pete and **Cathy Burback**, his wife since 1985. They know what it's like to dip into their own savings to meet the payroll.

"I think I'm in the right place, at the right time," Pete says. His competition, to some extent, is Williams-Sonoma, Crate and Barrel, Sur La Table, Bed Bath & Beyond—but Pete will argue that these cater to a more upscale clientele.

He works hard to make Cooks Corner look and feel less intimidating, with deep-discount warehouse shopping as well as more conventional retail space.

Example: There is a 157-foot wall of just kitchen gadgets.

"Everybody eats and cooks, or at least will have to use a pot or dish at some point. Anybody can find something of use here."

There is also a 12,000-square-foot Cooks Corner as an anchor at **Trasino Centre** in **Appleton**. It includes a demonstration kitchen as well as retail/warehouse sales space.

Pete wants Cooks Corner to be known as a kitchen resource, the place to go for advice about food preparation, even if it means sending a customer to a competitor.

The array of kitchen gadgets is dizzying.

Employees tend to have a solid background in cooking, or at least a genuine interest in it that can be supplemented by "comprehensive product training."

Cooks Corner has more than a dozen from-scratch fudge choices. That includes TDF (To Die For), which has layers of Lindt chocolate, vanilla, caramel, chocolate fudge and pecans—topped with a caramel drizzle. The fudge name came from an in-store contest: Customers sampled the fudge and then submitted appropriate names for it. Cooks Corner sells other gourmet foods, too. Product sampling is commonplace.

•

Cooks Corner, 836 S. Eighth St., Manitowoc
and **1920 N. Casaloma Dr., Appleton**
www.cookscorner.com, 800-236-2433

Books decorate this castle.

MARKESAN: A CROP OF BOOKS

Some people with a passion will make sure you hear all about it. They are self-proclaimed experts who are slick and aggressive about soliciting attention for their collection, cause, crusade, candidate.

Others proceed more quietly, but with just as much verve. The fire seems more a matter of love or personal mission than for public accolade or profit.

About seven miles south of Green Lake, past a field where wild turkeys strut and peck at snow-covered vegetation, is the **Castle Arkdale**. In the middle of nowhere, it is a former manure storage tank that now holds thousands of used books. There are century-old books, banned books, five-for-a-buck kids' book, rare books, first-edition books.

"People can be overwhelmed a bit," longtime farmer **Lloyd Dickmann** acknowledges as he begins a property tour in a machine shed bursting with more stacks, boxes and displays of books. All told, there are about 500,000 titles on this farm.

This is the passion of **Leonore Dickmann**, a retired University of Wisconsin-Oshkosh education professor. She wasn't around when we visited, but Lloyd knows his wife's story well.

Some Castle Arkdale treasures are collectors' items.

For more than a decade, Leonore stored and sold books from a nearby one-room schoolhouse. She called it Happy Tales Bookshop, and it had no heat or indoor bathroom. Many of the books came from auctions, flea markets and rummage sales—"we'd take everything for one price," Lloyd says.

Such book-buying trips have taken them all over the country.

After an electrical fire destroyed the family farm's barn in 2000, the machine shed was built and all the books were moved in. When that got too full, Lloyd emptied and power washed an adjacent, 400,000-gallon manure storage bin, added knotty pine walls and a castle-like entrance. It opened in 2003.

Why a castle? The thought "had to come from my subconscious," Leonore writes, noting that books about King Arthur kept turning up during the 15 years she has been in the book business. She focused on castles and King Arthur for a while, through research and in the books she bought, so there was a literary presence to match the castle motif.

That type of rigor is not unusual; she also has shown a penchant for researching ghosts "or whatever topic somebody wants," Lloyd says.

Castle Arkdale merchandise is organized in all kinds of ways: author-signed books, famous animals in literature, books about books, books about American geniuses, books that influenced world thought.

Prices are penciled inside each cover. Some lie on tables that are covered with homemade quilts, with comfortable chairs for lounging nearby.

The result is an amazing space for diehard book lovers and scavengers. It is a massive bookstore that is unadvertised and is typically open only one day a week. "We may put out a little sign when we're open," Lloyd says, but it was nowhere to be seen when I visited.

The Dickmanns are getting more selective about the books they buy or accept as donations. There is not room, for example, for more Reader's Digest condensed books. "Everybody saved them," Lloyd notes. "There are so many out there."

Magazines generally are of little interest unless they are from the 1930s or older. The biggest sales volume is from children's books. The biggest money per book comes from the rare titles, like a 1942 first edition of Steinbeck's *The Moon Is Down*, which sold for $75 recently.

Lloyd, a good-natured guy, is a farmer who works about 300 acres and grew up in Fond du Lac County. He shares his wife's enthusiasm for Castle Arkdale.

How much does Leonore love books? "She always has 10 to 15 (titles) going at a time," Lloyd says. Sometimes she'll read them out loud, so they can be on the same page together.

Leonore was not the average college professor, having earned Johnson and Danforth foundation awards plus UW-Oshkosh's Outstanding Educator Award in 1972. She continues to work as a consultant in creativity and literature.

Her "Seven Sides of Symmetry" curriculum work in the 1970s, described as "a model for education in the future," was presented to the United Nations for discussion.

•

Castle Arkdale
W1778 County K, Markesan
920-398-3375

You need a sharp eye and a chocolate lover's nose to find Hughes' Home Maid Chocolates.

Oshkosh: Chasing Chocolates

The boxes are plain, lightweight and stamped simply in red or black. The contents are luscious, fresh and full of chocolate—a jumble of textures and flavors. There are no neat rows, no candy identification chart—and no need to pay more than $9.50 for a pound, providing you can show up to pay up.

Since 1940, chocolate lovers have headed to the south side of Oshkosh, a couple of blocks west of Lake Winnebago, to order **Hughes' Home Maid Chocolates**. It is as special for its setting as it is for the dozen kinds of candy produced.

The business, which does not advertise, looks like any other bungalow on Doty Street. It is in a residential neighborhood, in the house where **Tom Hughes**' grandparents lived and learned how to make chocolates that others would buy.

Tom, born in 1959, is running the place at full tilt. The candy is made and sold in the basement. Box upon box is filled, stacked and stored upstairs until a customer takes it out the door.

I visited as a large, heated copper kettle of toffee was being spread onto a greased marble tabletop. Then the goo was rolled and cut into small squares, which were broken apart as they cooled and drenched in light or dark chocolate.

"We can't smell it, because we're always around it," Tom says, grinning.

The rhythm is smooth and fast, the atmosphere Zen-like and congenial. The work gets done as customers take a peek from the checkout counter.

It is an endearing and cramped space, with bright, stark walls in a white cave where employees deftly dance around each other's steps in order to prevent calamity.

Inga Rathkamp of Pewaukee and Harriet Joy Quinn of Milwaukee make an annual pilgrimage to this house for Christmas shopping, checkbooks in hand. (Credit card payments aren't an option.) They have done this for several years.

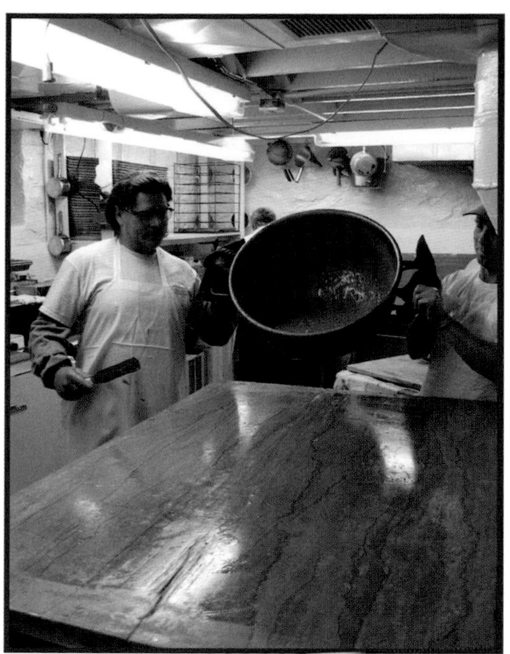

Tom Hughes uses his grandparents' recipes.

How much is sold? "A lot," Tom says, asserting that the floor-to-ceiling stacks of boxes that fill more than one room will vanish by the time Santa hitches up the reindeer.

Choices include oysters, which have a vanilla or chocolate center, are dipped in chocolate and rolled in crushed peanuts. Snow on the mountain is layered pecans and caramel in milk chocolate, plus a vanilla cream topping. Pudding, by Hughes' definition, is a double chocolate candy.

There also are the more traditional vanilla, maple and coconut creams; peppermint and wintergreen mints; caramels, nut clusters, nougats and toffee.

"It's pretty much the same recipes as my grandparents had," Tom says.

Coming to 1823 Doty St. to shop in person is the way most people do it. Don't try to phone in an order unless it's for at least 50 pounds of candy. "Then we'll set it aside for you," a phone clerk says.

That will happen, especially at Christmas time, but the customer still needs to pick up the order. There are no shipments or deliveries, unless they are placed through **877-762-4563** or **www.mailmechocolates.com**, a chocolate reseller that operates independently from Hughes' Home Maid Chocolates. That move hikes the price to $18.50 per pound, plus about $7-17 for delivery.

Candy making by 11 full-time Hughes employees, six seasonal workers and a couple of part-timers goes on from mid September to mid May. The shop closes from Memorial Day weekend until after the Fourth of July.

"Nobody wants to buy chocolate when it's 90 degrees out," Tom says.

Oh, yeah? Just try us.

•

Hughes' Home Maid Chocolates
1823 Doty St., Oshkosh
920-231-7232

DETOURS

More Chocolate!

Meltaways are a specialty of Seroogy's.

It would be a crime to ignore three other longstanding and high-quality candy makers in the Fox Valley.

Seroogy's, De Pere, specializes in meltaways (mint, peanut butter, almond, chocolate or chocolate crisp) and cashew clusters. The business, run by brothers Jim and Joe, began in 1899. The recipes haven't changed.

For more: **800-776-0377, www.seroogys.com.**

•

Oaks Chocolates, Oshkosh, has Seroogy's beat by nine years in longevity. There are three locations (including a shop at the factory outlet mall on Highway 41). In December, 'tis the season for handmade candy canes: peppermint, wintergreen, cinnamon, cherry, anise, lemon and clove. Also check out the Melty Bar candy bars.

For more: **920-231-3660, 920-231-2323 or 920-230-4548.**

•

Wilmar Chocolates, Appleton, has been around a mere 49 years, but its candy makers have won more than a dozen Wisconsin State Fair awards for almond bark to Wisconsin butter toffee. Want to try them all? Boxed assortments include the Award Collection.

For more: **920-733-6182, www.wilmarchocolates.com.**

•

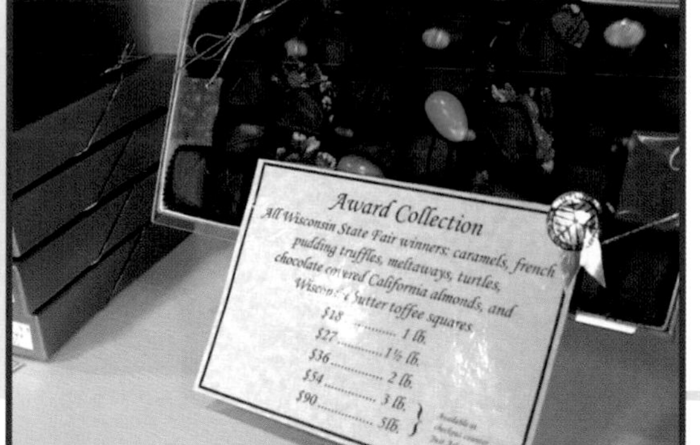

Wilmar Chocolates include Wisconsin State Fair champs.

NORTHEAST

John Castino says Mimi's, an Italian restaurant, was once a furniture store that also sold caskets.

PRINCETON: OFF SEASON, ON TARGET

It is mid-January, but winter has taken its time to reappear, at least in southwestern Wisconsin. After our holiday landscape melted into a dank and leafless gray-brown, it didn't take long to wish for sunshine, a fluffy blanket of white and somewhere interesting to go.

For much of the state, winter is our quiet time. Fewer tourists, less value? Nah. It can mean just the opposite. More elbow room, less need to hurry and scurry.

Some people frame this as our off-season, but it's hard to get comfortable with what that suggests. The phrase is about as attractive as "off key" or "off kilter."

This time of year can be so much more attractive than that, a time for renewal and reconnection—between people or with nature. Even in Green Lake County, best known for its lovely golf courses and longstanding summer resorts.

Princeton, population 1,500, presents the state's largest weekly and outdoor flea market from late April to October. The paces changes in winter, but the town is far from dormant.

Water Street has a quietly impressive stretch of shops that is about more than antique hunting. This is thanks, in part, to Princeton native **Tracy Porter**, the artist/designer (**www.tracyporter.com**) whose home and personal furnishings—featured at Target stores—have earned accolades from Oprah as well as *Elle* and *Good Housekeeping* magazines.

Tracy and her family have a studio in Ripon and live near Princeton. Her story, success and presence have lured other entrepreneurs to Princeton as well. They fill wonderfully creaky old buildings with art, furniture, gifts and home accessories. Consider **daiseye**, which advertises earth-friendly and one-of-a-kind treasures, many made with reclaimed materials—wood to tin.

There are other one-word business names, too: **Elvin, Dish, Embellished, Henry's, Pastimes** and **georgies** (which sells Tracy Porter items).

StarDancer is the place to get pierced or tattooed. **Wee Cycle** is all about stuff for kids, and parents-to-be.

The tough breakfast choices may include Peach Pecan French Toast, Banana Crepes or Cherry Waffles at **Once in the Blue Moon**, but not in January or February. The proprietors are on vacation, knowing that hungry people are in good hands at nearby **Mimi's** (whose staff takes its vacation in March and a part of April).

John Castino opened Mimi's inside of a former furniture store, which had an upstairs casket showroom, in July 2000. The menu is full of northern Italian cuisine, and the place is named after his grandmother, whose fetching portraits are on the walls.

"She was Irish and never cooked," he says, with a grin.

John was drawn, from Chicago, to Princeton's more sensible property prices. He was charmed by the tin ceiling that "looks like a wedding cake," the hardwood floors, the slower pace of existence.

This is where authors do readings and "garden people" gather in summer. There is a basket of reading glasses at the bar, in case you leave yours at home, and a view of the Fox River, where you can see sturgeon spawn in April.

"We are a new twist on old small-town America," John says, noting the lack of chain stores. Since the mid-1990s, retailers from San Diego, Boston and Minneapolis are among those who have opened shops.

For a night of pampering, head east 10 miles, to the **Heidel House Resort** in **Green Lake**, which has been a comfortable, amenity-filled getaway for 60 years. General Manager **Scott Krause** was selected 2005 Innkeeper of the Year by his peers, the Wisconsin Innkeepers Association.

Panoramic lake views, an indoor pool and sauna make this a good winter stay, and room rates are much lower than in summer.

The fine dining at **Grey Rock Restaurant** is among the best in the state. Portions are hearty; the menu includes steaks, chops, rack of lamb, duck and fish that is stuffed, seared or coated with nuts.

For Sunday brunch, in the more casual **Sun Room**: a half-dozen kinds of Bloody

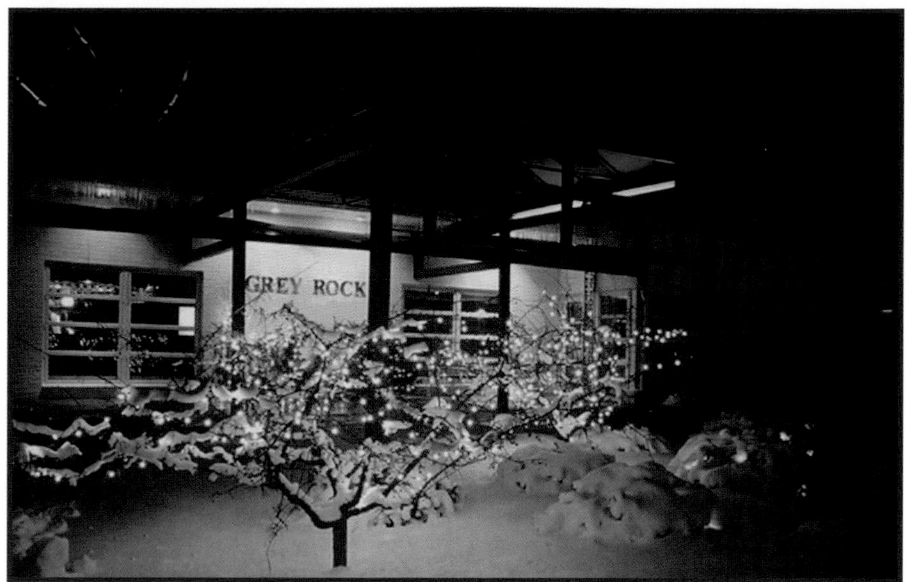

Heidel House's Grey Rock Restaurant offers fine dining year-round.

Marys—with gin, with Cajun spices, with seafood, and so on. Nice lineup of food, too, like sour cherry bread, homemade granola, blueberry blintzes.

To feel less guilty about grazing and lazing around, pack the cross country skis or hike trails at the resort and neighboring **Tuscumbia,** the oldest golf course in Wisconsin. Do it at dusk, and wildlife likely will be spying on you.

Green Lake, the town, tends to turn in early during winter, but one exception is the **Thrasher Opera House**, which sometimes has live entertainment on Saturday nights. Bowling and golfing on ice are two of the quirky diversions during **Winterfest**, held in February.

Four miles west of Princeton, you'll find **Mecan River Outfitters & Lodge**, a family-run business with 10 miles of cross country skiing trails, easy to moderately difficult. It is a pristine setting, with an inexpensive trail fee, and we arrived during a gentle snowfall.

The log cabin lodge is cozy and convenient, a good place for one of you to relax while the other refines skills on the hills.

There is a bar, a 35-foot fieldstone fireplace, football on TV on Sundays and a casual restaurant. Five rooms are for rent, each woodsy in theme and roomy in size. Most have two beds apiece, so it's an especially good place for families or hunting/fishing/hiking/biking friends to crash. Too plush for you? Other lodging options are camping space and rustic/secluded cabins.

Accommodations at Mecan River Outfitters are particularly cozy for friends, families.

Jewels to junk—the odd mix of commodities that make flea markets an adventure—are what shoppers find in Princeton's shady **City Park** on Saturdays from spring to fall. It's farm produce to antique collectibles, free admission and parking. There are typically 180 weekly vendors who are open for business at 6 a.m.

•

Princeton Area Chamber of Commerce, 708 W. Water St., Princeton
www.princetonwi.com, 920-295-3877.

•

Green Lake Area Chamber of Commerce, 550 Mill St., Green Lake
www.visitgreenlake.com, 800-253-7354.

•

Heidel House Resort, 643 Illinois Ave., Green Lake
www.heidelhouse.com, 800-444-2812.

•

Mecan River Outfitters & Lodge, W720 Hwy. 23, Princeton
www.mecanriveroutfitters.com, 920-295-3439.

•

In an ordinary neighborhood is an extraordinary house to rent.

TWO RIVERS: WRIGHT RENTAL

I would have liked to stay for the night, or at least until dark, but I had access to the next best thing: two women whose words and passion could help describe the architectural gem on Adams Street in Two Rivers.

Jean Schelhorn of Ohio and Frances Crockett of North Carolina are longtime friends who paid $295 per night to stay in an ordinary working class Wisconsin neighborhood in fall 2005. When I met them, they were doing the laundry and talked about raking leaves.

This was a house that they wanted to take care of, they explained. It was not enough to simply pay to stay.

"You FEEL the outside while you're inside," Jean says, and she is not talking about temperature. "When you're sitting here at night, that's when you'll notice the little things," her friend adds. Jean raps on a door, noting it is simply plywood, and points out a light switch that was installed horizontally. She persuades me to lie on the biggest bed, so I can see the view from it.

Frances talks up the kitchen, not because of amenities, but because of how a skylight brightens the room. "It feels like a tower," she says.

Come nightfall, you'll only be able to read a book at a desk or in the master bedroom. The soft amber lighting makes the space seem sacred.

This is an unusual house with many moods, and it seems destined to become Two Rivers' biggest tourist attraction. Every window is a picture frame, every corner full of history and style. The **Bernard Schwartz House** is the newest of three **Frank Lloyd Wright** houses in the nation that can be rented for as little as two nights. (The other two

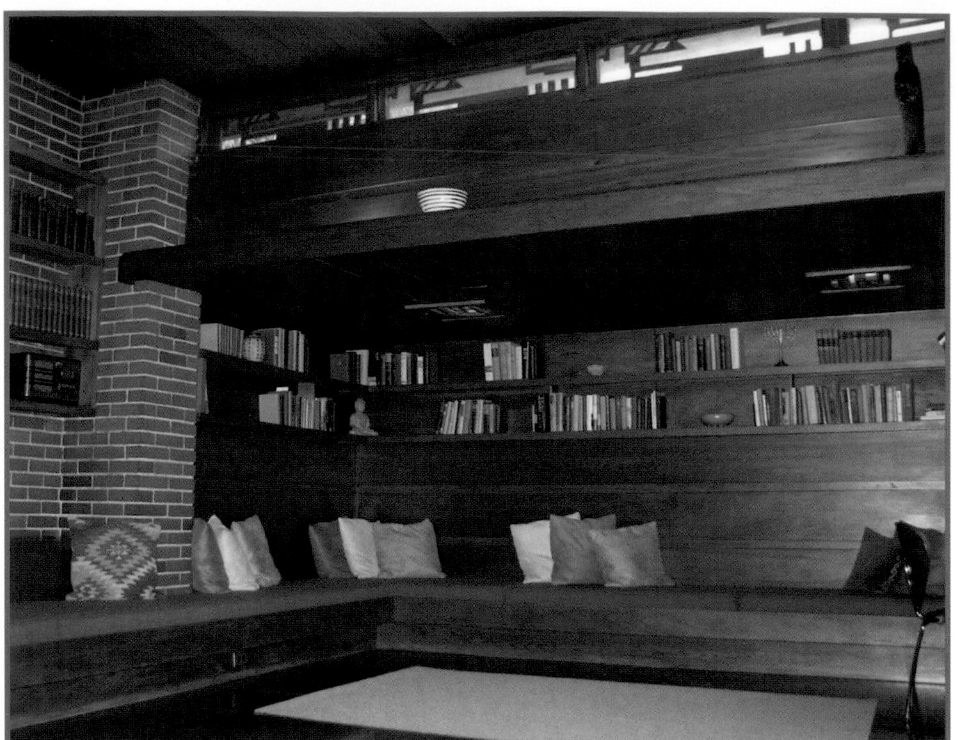

Colors, lights, design and furniture are all marks of Wright.

are the **Seth Peterson Cottage**, near Baraboo, and the Louis Penfield House, in Ohio.)

Wright designed hundreds of houses, of which about three dozen are open for public tours. The Schwartz House is the dream house that *Life* magazine in 1938 commissioned Wright to create for a typical family that earned $5,000-6,000 per year (about $55,000-65,000 today).

Schwartz, a manufacturer of dairy filters, liked what he saw in Life and had Wright build it (minus an outdoor swimming pool) the next year. At 3,000 square feet, with four bedrooms, three baths and fireplaces, the Usonian style house overlooks the pretty East Twin River.

Lisa Proechel and **Michael Ditmer** of Minnesota bought the house for almost $300,000 in 2003, spending about $200,000 in two years for maintenance and repairs. More will be invested to bring the building back to its original design.

"Our intention is to give people a once-in-a-lifetime opportunity to live in a Frank Lloyd Wright house," the couple says online. "We don't want the Schwartz House to be a museum but a house to be lived in and experienced in a relaxed and deliberate pace."

A skylight helps the kitchen feel like a tower.

Visibility increased after *Wall Street Journal* writer Terry Teachout stayed at the two Wisconsin Wright properties. "The Peterson Cottage feels like a work of art," he observed, "the Schwartz House like a comfortable home that just happens to be heart-stoppingly beautiful."

Environmentally, the owners describe the house "as green as you can get," with radiant floor heating (and "no forced air system to spread mold, dust and other indoor pollutants") and no paint/chemicals on floors, walls or ceilings.

"It's very much in his vernacular—forward thinking and unconventional," says **Robert Jagemann**. He is chairman/CEO of **Bamco Architects, Manitowoc**, which has been involved with the Schwartz House restoration.

Robert says this house may have the oldest continuously operating, in-floor heating system in the country. Its carport was one of the first three built in the U.S.

Among the children raised here was Steven Schwartz, who has stopped for a surprise visit. A guest journal describes his fond memories of the house. Visitors get an education in other ways, too; there is a library of books and videos about Wright.

Do the owners have their eye on any other Wright property that is for sale? Yes, Michael says: "I'd like to have four or five of these places and have them all be vacation rentals."

A student of architecture, Michael says he's been a Wright admirer since he was a teen who visited the architect's **Taliesin** workshop and residence near **Spring Green**.

Guided tours of the Schwartz House are by appointment.

•

Bernard Schwartz House
3425 Adams Street, Two Rivers
www.theschwartzhouse.com, 651-222-5322

DETOURS

The only other Wright house in Wisconsin that is being rented to vacationers—the 1958 **Seth Peterson Cottage**—was one of the last jobs commissioned to Wright.

The secluded site has generous views of Mirror Lake and wooded terrain. It sleeps four (one of two beds folds out from corner bench seating) but is big enough to entertain about three dozen people. A large, stone fireplace is the most stunning interior feature.

Minimum stay is two nights. To make a reservation, call **800-822-7768** or go to **www.sethpeterson.org**. Guided tours of the cottage are offered monthly.

•

The Louis Penfield House, near Cleveland, Ohio can sleep five people and also has a two-night minimum. Ceilings here are taller that most other Usonian designs, because the first owner was 6-foot-8. The structure is not open for tours. To learn more, go to www.penfieldhouse.com or call 440-942-9996.

In all cases, a damage deposit is collected before any of the three Wright houses are rented. Prospective guests in Two Rivers also can expect to have a conversation with an owner, about why they want to stay at the property.

The Seth Peterson Cottage is an intimate space that overlooks Mirror Lake, near Baraboo.

Washington Island follows a different pace than Door Peninsula.

WASHINGTON ISLAND: SEASONAL SURPRISES

As autumn nears, let's plan an island vacation, one that doesn't require airfare. The laid-back pace and varied moods of Washington Island, an exquisite parcel of land at the tip of Door County, tend to get ignored when summer ends.

Let that be your gain. Locals say the weather tends to stay warmer longer in this part of Wisconsin, thanks to the kind effects of Lake Michigan.

Get ashore via private plane (there is a small airport) or a half-hour ride from the Northport Pier on the **Washington Island Ferry**, which operates all year. Reservations aren't taken. Don't arrive late. But do take some kind of vehicle, or consider biking—the terrain is even and pretty, a mix of forests and meadows, wheat and cornfields, with sandhill cranes and deer lingering throughout.

One beach is sandy, another full of smooth and flat white stones (remove one and it's a $250 fine). Elsewhere on the island, another ferry takes people—but not their vehicles—from Jackson Harbor to Rock Island State Park, where there is a beach, 10 miles of

Fiber arts are sold, taught at Sievers.

hiking trails, exhibits in stone buildings and space to camp. This ferry service operates from Memorial Day to Columbus Day.

Business signage is minimal on Washington Island, and road signs are small. So reserve a place to stay before arriving, and ask for directions. There are a couple of dozen lodging choices, scattered around the island, but you need to have a clue about where to go.

The range includes B&B farm stays and simple motel rooms to dynamic waterfront views and gourmet restaurant fare. **Sunset Resort**, a fourth-generation family business established in 1902, includes a beach on Green Bay and a cheery, nostalgic lodge that serves a Scandinavian breakfast.

There are charming public attractions, most of which close by late October. For example:

Washington Island Farm Museum has antique machinery, household and harvest tools, farm buildings and a pioneer cabin from the late 1800s. There are penned farm animals and gardens, too. Honey, dried flowers and other items can be purchased on the honors system; just drop your payment in the collection box.

Stavkirke, a stave church whose architecture resembles a sturdy Viking ship, is a rugged reminder of the area's Norwegian heritage. It is in a quiet, woodsy area and owned by Trinity Evangelical Lutheran Church.

Sievers School of Fiber Arts presents classes in weaving, basketry, knitting and other skills. The business was first known for its fine looms and spinning wheels, products that prompted customers to ask for the wide array of classes now offered in three rustic, airy and inspiring studios.

No patience for that type of hobby? You'll most likely still appreciate the consignment shop that sells a wide assortment of students' work, from beaded jewelry to bed quilts. It, too, is open seasonally.

One local claim to fame that visitors can help uphold all year has to do with **Nelsen's Hall**, a Danish pub built in 1899 and the oldest legally and continuously

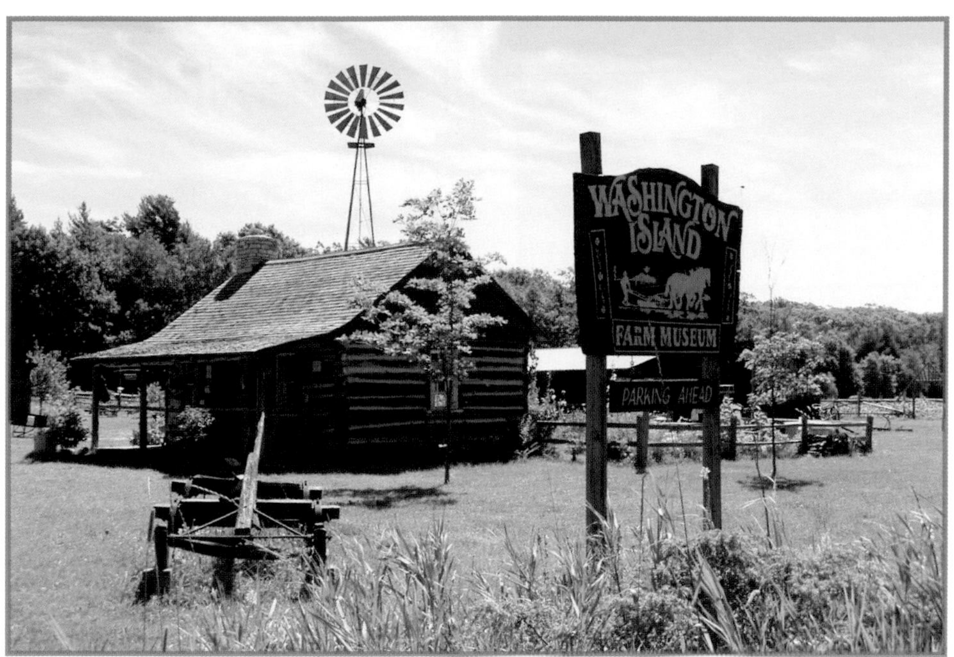

Artifacts of farm life are preserved in a picturesque, authentic setting.

operating saloon in Wisconsin.

During Prohibition years, proprietor **Tom Nelsen** got a pharmacist's license to dispense a stomach tonic to local residents. "Even though Angostura Bitters is 90 proof, Tom was allowed to serve his tonic, so his saloon remained open," a pub history states.

So drink a shot of bitters there, and it will get you membership into the Nelsen's Hall Bitters Club. Some locals say it'll also settle your stomach, for a while.

More than 10,000 people join the club each year, the owners say, and that helps give Nelsen's a place in the *Guinness Book of World Records*, because more bitters (per capita) are drunk there than anyplace else.

•

Washington Island Chamber of Commerce
PO Box 222
Washington Island 54246
www.washingtonislandchamber.com, 920-847-2179

NORTHEAST

Suzanne and Marge team up to prepare delectable-looking and tasty cuisine.

Get Cooking

Honey. Salt. Lemon. Bread. We are sipping cinnamon-orange iced tea and learning "Four Band-Aids for Cooking," as declared by **Suzanne Breckenridge**. When you mess up in the kitchen, there's a good chance that one of these items can help save your meal and reputation.

The tidbits to be gleaned during this summer afternoon gathering will even be more plentiful than the range of colors and ingredients that cloak the Asian Nicoise salad being prepared by Suzanne and **Marge Snyder**, co-authors of *Wisconsin Herb Cookbook*.

Welcome to the **Washington Hotel Culinary School** on Door County's Washington Island. These Madison women are the guest instructors today, and their "Cooking With Herbs" demonstration will produce a four-course meal that the intimate group—from England, Philadelphia, St. Louis, Escanaba, Madison—consumes as we are alternately entertained and educated.

There is an easy banter between the students and teachers. There are samples of fresh herbs, jokes about basil being an aphrodisiac, lessons about how to make our own spice combos, warnings that oregano leaves turn bitter when the plant is three or more years old.

We head outdoors, to the lush and decorative herb garden in the hotel's front yard. A bit later, hotel proprietor and chef **Leah Caplan** will be back to snip lemon balm, as an impromptu addition to our curried cream of red pepper soup. She arranges private and customized cooking classes as well as these public demonstrations.

"We'll get gourmet cooking groups," the Culinary Institute of America grad says, "or three or four couples—friends who want to get away for a weekend. We have a good wine list and a good fireplace" for winter retreats.

What makes the cooking class experience different here? A part of it is the setting: The island, six miles by five miles, has only 700 year-round residents and is accessible only by ferry or private plane.

Culinary class costs depend upon the subject matter, duration and whether accommodations are included.

The hotel, a former home for captains of Great Lakes ships, has been around more than a century. Awaken in one of the eight bedrooms here, and it is more than quiet. It can be silent: no people, no traffic, not even birds chirping. That's what I found.

A part of the culinary experience is about priorities and standards: The chef believes in using local ingredients in creative ways, and her restaurant menu changes with the seasons. "*Local* means it can get from farm to table in the same day," she explains.

Signature dishes include whitefish, a commonplace fish that shows up in unconventional ways. There's smoked whitefish dip, smoked whitefish pizza (with spinach, sour cream and bits of boiled egg) and whitefish Escabeche (a South American dish).

The hotel has one of the few brick ovens in the state, and that also plays a defining role in the hotel's menu, mission and vision.

"The whole menu revolves around the brick oven," Leah says. "It retains heat in a way that a conventional oven doesn't." It also makes for a glorious crust, be it bread or a pizza.

The hotel contracts with local farmers to grow wheat, and the first fall harvest was 6,000 pounds. That goes through the hotel's small stone mill, producing chemically free flour for restaurant use and retail sale, bread mixes (there are three varieties) and fresh loaves that are sold in the hotel gift shop and delivered regularly in Madison.

•

The Washington Hotel, 368 Rangeline Road, Washington Island
www.thewashingtonhotel.com, 920-847-2169

Fast Facts

A part of The Washington Hotel moved to Madison in 2005. The **Washington Hotel Coffee Room** is the cozy Lake Room of **Lakeside Fibers**, 402 W. Lakeside St. A wall of windows shows off one of the best lake views of the city. Local, sustainable and organically produced bakery, bread, soup and sandwich choices are top quality. A small gift shop, tucked amongst the skeins of yarn, is stocked with items made and sold at the hotel. Beverage choices range from free-trade coffee to smoothies made with Door County fruit.

•

Beer produced by brewmaster **Kirby Nelson,** of **Capital Brewery**, **Middleton,** includes Island Wheat beer, which is made from wheat grown on Washington Island.

•

Stavkirke on Washington Island, built the Norwegian way.

Birds in many forms abound in Wausau.

WAUSAU: BIRDS IN FLIGHT

"A bird does not sing because it has an answer. It sings because it has a song."

I like that quote. It's either a Chinese proverb or the observation of college football coach Lou Holtz, depending upon the point of reference.

No matter. We'd all likely fare better with fewer answers and more awareness, but it's getting tougher. When life was simpler, seeing a robin was one way to know that spring had arrived in Wisconsin, just as hearing a flock of geese signaled the need for a fall trip to Horicon Marsh.

Now goofy weather patterns have made a lot of things in life less certain, and that makes me even more relieved about Wausau's love affair with birds. It is real and true, a deep and unusual devotion.

The **Leigh Yawkey Woodson Art Museum** contains some of the world's most compelling bird art. It is a way to appreciate the character as well as the plumage of these remarkable creatures.

They are shy and proud, vulnerable and serene, shaky survivors and ruthless predators. There is a graceful, ballet-like dance of cranes in a bronze sculpture by Elliot Offner of Massachusetts. The intense eyes of a snowy owl haunt a watercolor by Leigh Voight of South Africa.

On and on it goes—a tribute to one piece of life. The moods of these birds are endless, shown through oils, sculpture, Victorian needlework, Russian icons. There are compelling photographs, technical illustrations from the 1700s, porcelain figurines, waterfowl decoys.

Each fall, artists worldwide contribute to the juried **"Birds in Art"** exhibit, a competition that typically increases the Wausau art museum's permanent collection by a

On the museum grounds is a 1.5-acre sculpture garden.

piece or two. (The permanent collection totals 3,500 objects, and counting. About three-fourths have a bird or nature theme.)

"Birds in Art" was the idea of legendary wildlife artist **Owen Gromme**, who died in 1991.

The National Wildlife Federation contends bird watching is the second most popular form of family recreation, behind gardening. It is a hobby that requires only eyesight, and one that spans generations because of what birds represent.

"We see parts of ourselves in birds," theorizes **Marcia Theel**, the Wausau art museum's spokeswoman. "I think we have a secret longing to fly, for the freedom that comes with flights.

Migration, she adds, represents "our draw, our connection to a place in the world. We want to go home, to seek out what is good for us."

There were less than a dozen birding festivals nationwide in the early 1990s. Now there are hundreds that celebrate those with the ability to soar—check out the **American Birding Association** at **www.americanbirding.org** and *Bird Watchers' Digest* at **www.birdwatchersdigest.com**.

Some people say there are more birders than golfers, which adds to the incredible splash that Wausau has made since the Woodson Art Museum opened in 1976.

It's a particularly inspiring place to be in spring, as new life cracks open in nests, dirt, forests and barns. In 1995, an outdoor sculpture garden was added—it is a delight in rain as well as sunshine.

•

Leigh Yawkey Woodson Art Museum
700 N. 12th Ave., Wausau
www.lywam.org, 715-845-7010

Wildife rehabilitator Patrick Comfert holds a screech owl.

Winging It

Here is what will make a difference: temperature, wind gusts, precipitation, snow accumulation, availability of open water. Here is what you might find: long-tailed ducks from Lake Michigan, snowy or boreal owls from Canada, turkey vultures that should be in Central America, lots of angry crows.

Angry crows? "If crows sound like they're really, really mad, they probably have a screech owl nearby," explains **Karen Etter Hale**, executive secretary of the **Madison Audubon Society**. If they're noisy, but sound only "medium angry," they could be chattering about a red-tailed hawk.

What good is this advice? It could be extremely pertinent if you're participating in the **Christmas Bird Count**, an annual event that helps document bird behavior, migration and population by species. The count began in 1900, and it is done between Dec. 14 and Jan. 5. Each designated area has one calendar day to complete the work.

Madison birders used to report seeing more screech owls than any other place in North America. The tally after the 1994 Christmas Bird Count was 143, but by 2002 the total had plummeted to 17.

That's not necessarily evidence of the bird's massive departure, Karen says, but instead suggests a lack of effort to find them—or knowledge about how to find them.

When bird lovers are deliberate about their search for screech owls (one of the smallest types of owls, averaging 8 to 9 inches in length), they will begin their work before dawn, armed with a tape of the bird's calls, or knowing how to mimic the call on their own.

As a nocturnal creature, this bird doesn't make itself visible during the day and tends to keep itself quiet at night, unless it's responding to a call in its own language.

Professional ornithologists participate in the annual Christmas Bird Count, but so do newcomers to birding. The inexperienced are matched with veterans; teams are assigned to specific routes in a designated geographical area.

The volunteers keep track of what they see and hear, both type of bird and unusual behavior. There are written reports, and some people also take pictures. It's great if they can do this from dawn to dusk, but shorter time commitments also are acceptable.

Of the roughly 100 Christmas Bird Counts in Wisconsin, Karen says the Madison area has one of the highest levels of participation. So she encourages people there to consider venturing away from their home for the day.

She is a Waterloo resident who in the mid-1980s decided to join the Christmas Bird Count at Horicon National Wildlife Refuge, near Waupun.

"I was one of only three or four people counting in the entire marsh," she recalls. It has more than 21,000 acres. That meant a lot of driving in the area, not walking, so it was particularly helpful to know the location of open water outlets.

"You're making your best guess," Karen says, and much of the success of a Christmas Bird Count is out of human control.

If open lakes are abundant, great blue herons will likely be found. The lack of adequate food sources for snowy, northern hawk and boreal owls has caused these birds to move to the Midwest.

An increase in blue jay and crow sightings in 2003 suggests neither species had yet suffered traumatically because of the West Nile virus. There were a lot of robins and bluebirds in 1998, when the weather was noticeably warmer than usual.

All in all, it's a great party—if the birds decide to show up. In 1991, totals dropped by as much as 75 percent because the weather was frigid and winds hit 40 mph.

The National Audubon Society says more than 50,000 people nationwide participate in a Christmas Bird Count. The effort is called "citizen science in action."

•

Christmas Bird Count, National Audubon Society
www.audubon.org, 800-542-2748

•

There are more than one dozen National Audubon Society chapters in Wisconsin.

The **Wisconsin Department of Tourism** has split the state into five parts and has begun to produce birding guides that are specific to each geographical area. The first installment—*Lake Superior/Northwoods Edition* of the *Birding Guide*—takes a look at the 18 northernmost counties. To get a free copy: **www.travelwisconsin.com, 800-432-8747.**

A painted turtle basks in the sun on a lazy summer day.

Rhinelander Road Trip • Day 1

1. Summer School. Lifelong students will especially enjoy this part of Wisconsin during the **School of the Arts at Rhinelander**, a five-day University of Wisconsin Continuing Studies program in July, with fun and low-pressure classes in visual, performing and computer arts. **www.dcs.wisc.edu, 608-265-8041.** Sessions are at James William Junior High School, 915 Acacia Lane.

2. Happy Hour. Free hors d'oeuvres come out late Monday through Thursday afternoons at **Rhinelander Café and Pub**, 33 N. Brown St., the city's oldest restaurant. Stick around for supper, where the choices include Greek entrees, like rack of lamb and lemon-chicken. **715-362-2918.**

3. Jazzy Digs. A plethora of cottages, resorts and condos exist because of the tourist trade. For more than a place to sleep, friends recommend **Holiday Acres Resort**, 4060 S. Shore Dr. (Highway 8-business route, left on Ohlson Lane). It is on Lake Thompson, a fourth-generation family business that has existed since 1926. Cottages are winterized; jazz is the music of choice (there is an annual Jazz Fantasy Camp, plus other annual jazz events). **www.holidayacres.com, 715-369-1500.**

4. Fast Breakfast or Lunch. **Joe's Pasty Shop**, 123 Randall Ave. (backtrack to Highway 8-business route, right onto Randall), has been in operation since 1946. There are a dozen meat pie choices, including egg-sausage, plus a Pasty of the Month (it's corned beef and cabbage in March). Sold frozen, too, in case you want to take 'em back home or to the cottage. **www.ilovepasties.com, 715-369-1224.**

5. Past Lives. On display at **Pioneer Park** (Highway 8-business route) is a replica logging camp, early logging equipment, an 1892 restored Soo Line depot and railroad artifacts, Admission free; donations appreciated. **715-369-5004.**

6. Bring a Canoe . . . and simply look for water. It ain't hard to find. **www.rhinelanderchamber.com, 800-236-4386.**

7. Dramatic Dinner. **Pinewood Country Club**, 4660 Lakewood Road, Harshaw (Highway K west for 11 miles, to Lakewood Road, then right three miles), has an 18-hole golf course and also presents well-known musicals and plays in a dinner-theater setting throughout the year. **www.pinewoodcc.com, 888-674-6396.**

Day 2

8. More of the Same. The point is to relax, absorb and get acquainted with your natural surroundings. Remember, it's not about a search for new amusements in a different place every day, unless you're chasing a hodag (the legendary and infamous mascot of Rhinelander). If you insist on variety, consider the nearby **Three Lakes** area, whose 20 lakes take up 7,626 acres and are home to 16 kinds of fish. It is 20 miles northeast of Rhinelander, off of Highways 45-32, in Nicolet National Forest. **www.threelakes.com, 800-972-6103.**

Photo Credits

Photographs by Mary Bergin unless noted otherwise.

iii — *Edgewood College Photo*
1 — *Ashland Daily Press*
4 — *Thomas Meyer, WI DNR*
12-13 — *Big Top Chautauqua*
18, 20 — *Leinenkugel Brewing Co.*
ii, xiii, 17, 21, 57, 58, 61, 62, 64, 66, 84, 87, 91, 92, 103, 135, 136, 187, 208, 209
Henry A. Koshollek/The Capital Times
22 — *Hayward Lakes CVB*
27 — *Frank Feiker, WI Historical Society*
28, 79 — *David Sandell/The Capital Times*
29 — *Paul Vanderbilt, WI Historical Society*
30 — *Angus McVicar, WI Historical Society*
34,35 — *Potawatomi Bingo Casino*
68 — *Roth Kase USA*
73 — *Ellen Peebe*
75 — *Bill Spence*
vii, 81, 109, 176
Mike DeVries/The Capital Times
84 — *Maria Snyder/Adventure Andy's Travel Co.*
86 — *VocationVacations*
94 — *Mineral Point Chamber of Commerce*
99 — *John Newhouse, Mt. Horeb Area Museum*
101, 102 — *Potosi Brewery Foundation*
107 — *Jura Silverman/Fall Art Tour*
108 — *Bob Russell/Fall Art Tour*
118, 121 — *Wisconsin Dells Visitor & Convention Bureau*
123, 124 — *Wisconsin Quilt History Project*
126, 128 — *Road America*
145 — *Kohler Arts/Industry Program*
153 — *St. Josaphat's Basilica*
159, 237 — *Frank X. Sandner*
160 — *Inn at Pine Terrace*
164 — *Bergin Family*
167 — *Racine Art Museum/Christopher Barrett Hedrich Blessing, Chicago*
168 — *Racine Art Museum/Michael Tropea, Chicago*
173, 174 — *Great Wolf Resorts*
179, 180, 194
Michelle Stocker/The Capital Times
191 — *Outagamie Museum*
193 — *Len Villano*
196 — *Peninsula Players*
207 — *VISIT Milwaukee*
221 — *Heidel House*
226 — *Don Sanford Photography*
234 — *Rich Rygh/The Capital Times*

The following stories are copyrighted by *The Capital Times*, Madison, Wisconsin:

12 Bayfield: "Under the Big Top Chautauqua"
21 Couderay: "Tracking 'Moose'"
38 Phillips: "Set in Concrete"
46 Warrens: "Urban Processing"
57 Baraboo: "Saving Cranes"
61 Browntown: "Simplified Living"
64 Dodgeville: "Artisanal Cheese"
68 Monroe: "Say 'Queso'"
71 Green County: "Cuilinary Tourism"
77 Madison: "Food Fetishes"
79 "Always in a Food Mood"
81 "A Woman's Touch"
83 "A Room of One's Own"
89 "Bowling for Art"
91 Mineral Point: "Shake Rag's Rebirth"
95 "A Passion to Preserve—Pendarvis"
98 Mt. Horeb: "Tomorrow's History"
104 Sauk County: "A Sense of Place"
114 Valton: "The Painted Forest"
135 Greendale: "Making It From Scratch"
145 Kohler: "The Art Factory"
148 Milwaukee:
"Hispanic Pride"
155 "Third Ward Reborn"
167 Racine: "RAM: Museum as Sculpture"
169 Sheboygan: "Culinary Bliss"
176 Sheboygan County: "From Farms to Fame"
179 Watertown: "It's His Nature"
187 Appleton: "Pure Poetry: Ellen Kort"
235 "Winging It"